Iraq:
Providing Hope

Iraq:
Providing Hope

Eric Holmes

Timberwolf Press
http://www.TimberwolfPress.com

Iraq: Providing Hope

Timberwolf Press Inc.
202 N Allen Drive Suite A
Allen, TX 75013

Please visit our website:
http://www.timberwolfpress.com

ISBN 1-58752-252

Printed in the United States of America
10 9 8 7 6 5 4 3

CONTENTS

Preface   vii

Contributors & Acknowledgements   x

Chapter One - The Deployment   1

Chapter Two - The Hardships   18

Chapter Three - The Green Zone   44

Chapter Four - The Stories   93

Chapter Five - The Iraqi Americans   133

Chapter Six - The Events   151

Chapter Seven - The Folks at Home   217

Chapter Eight - The Results   237

Chapter Nine - The Homecoming   283

End Notes   293

"We have a great opportunity to extend a just peace by replacing poverty, repression and resentment around the world with hope for a better day."

– George W. Bush*

Preface

This book is a collection of stories, stories from the men and women involved in freeing Iraq from the oppressive Saddam Hussein. It is the stories of those who fought, those who are standing in harm's way, those who are rebuilding the country and those who support them. It is their story, and it is told here because otherwise it is not being told.

I've talked to dozens of people and every single one, without exception, says the same thing, "Tell our story. America doesn't know what we've been doing; they don't know how bad it was here, they don't know all the good we've accomplished." The people, military and civilian alike, are risking their lives, living under austere conditions and doing it because they see the purpose. They see the good of humanity they are serving.

In the 1960s and 1970s, Iraq was the most progressive, open, liberal and growing society in the Middle East. Since Saddam Hussein took over, the world went down hill for the Iraqis. Saddam Hussein patterned himself after Joseph Stalin, the man who murdered tens of millions. Saddam Hussein created a police state; his party controlled the government, the military, and all aspects of life. Saddam Hussein used spy cells and informants to intimidate any dissidence. Saddam Hussein used ruthless, merciless torture treatments on anyone he suspected of being disloyal and their families also.

* *Commencement address at United States Military Academy, June 1, 2002 as reported by Bob Woodward, Plan of Attack, (New York: Simon & Schuster, 2004) p. 132.*

In his Iraq, there were no rights, no freedoms, no truth. In today's modern society, it is difficult to imagine that life could actually be so oppressed even as the United Nations labeled him as the greatest human rights violator since World War II.

Saddam Hussein's first official act after seizing control and proclaiming himself president was to have half of the ruling party officials shoot the other half. This was just the beginning. His tortures were hideous. He attacked two of his neighbors and threatened others; he used nerve gas for the first time in history since 1918, he butchered his own people, and he starved his people while he lavished himself in billions of dollars of extravagance.

It is no accident that this is called Operation Iraqi Freedom (OIF). This is about freeing the people of Iraq from their dictator and saving them from being victims of his heinous crimes. This is what the people of OIF want America to know. They are in the process of providing the greatest humanitarian assistance of this generation. Twenty-five million people are now freed from the oppressive regime of a sick, demented, ruthless dictator whose murder count is estimated at one million.

The most amazing thing is most of us never knew or could comprehend how much danger these Iraqis have lived under. We are so accustomed to our freedoms that it is difficult to fathom what life was like for these people living in constant fear.

Secret informers were everywhere, ready to report anyone. People were taken from homes without any notification to relatives; sometimes parents were taken and children were left without even a note to say what happened. People were beaten, raped, starved, electrocuted, burned, and maybe finally executed. Families would wonder for years about the fate of missing relatives. If one tried to run away, the remaining family would be tortured. Parents would be forced to watch their children beaten and raped.

Many Americans don't know any of this. Americans want peace, they see the dead and wounded Americans with a sadness in their hearts. They see America as marching off to war. They see America as aggressively attacking an innocent country. What they don't see is that these people are sacrificing their lives in a great act of love and kindness. What they don't see is the liberation. This is why this story needs to be told.

Iraq was not a country; it was a feeding ground for a selfish villain. To go in and free this people is a great act of humanity. A damsel is locked in a tower; a knight fights a dragon and then frees her. He is a hero. A criminal robs a bank and holds the tellers a gunpoint; the police storm and rescue the people. The police are heroes. A man leads a nation in a long, bloody war to free slaves. He is a hero. Twenty-five million are held hostage by a madman; people rush in and free the people. They are heroes.

Sometimes police are killed in the line of duty; sometimes the criminals are shot in the process. We grieve the loss of life. We wish that there were no evil. Still there is and still the evildoers need to be stopped.

Our tendency is to not believe; it is to hide our eyes and pretend that no one could be so evil. For years, this is what we did. The Americans now in Iraq see the mass graves, see the videotapes of the tortures and see scars on the people. They see the infrastructure withered due to two decades of neglect. They see the people who are thankful that now they have a chance to build a life free from tyranny.

Right now, America and thirty other nations are involved in liberating a nation from a madman. They are re-building a country so it can have the basic necessities of life like clean water, processed sewage, modern healthcare, education and a legal structure dedicated to the rule of law and respect for human rights. A whole generation was raised under Saddam Hussein and knew nothing but fear. Now they have hope. They have hope that they can live a life of freedom where they can strive to better themselves, come and go as they please, and live in safety. They have hope for a better tomorrow. In the name of humanity, people have sacrificed and died to provide hope. Hope for equality, hope for safer life, hope for eventual world peace – that's the least we can do – provide hope.

This is why it is fitting to honor those who have sacrificed to provide hope for the Iraqis. These are the stories of the people who are making this a reality. The dictator and most of his highest-ranking supporters are captured, an interim government is in place and free elections and a new constitution are just around the corner.

This book is their story. It is the story of those who endured and suffered to ensure freedom for us and provide hope for Iraq. It is dangerous and deadly. It has caused personal hardships. The results have been tremendous. We are thankful.

Contributors

(in order of appearance)

Gordon Cimoli * Allison Rowe * John Galt * Paul Colbert * Fred Wellman * Jeff Qunell * Matt Brady * Jim Gilson * Kristen Lewis * Matt Gapinski * J. Mark Maddox * Scott Travis * Patrick * Ben Wallen * Anonymous (1) * Heather Grodin-Putman * Bob Ohls * Carlos C. Huerta * Michael Hanes * Chris Gehler * Kelly Thrasher * Kim Darby * Anonymous (2) * Fayrouz Hancock * Omar Masry * Kamran Gardi * Salwa Ali Al-Oumaishi * Anonymous (3) * Anonymous (4) * Michael Hanes * Dom Caraccilo * Anne Trenolene * Mike Sheridan * Michael Parkhouse * Rick Clay * Alex Fyfe * David Weston * Zeyad * Joel Hagy * David Couvillion * Bonnie Carroll * Jennifer S. * David Gifford * Michael Sapp * Vi Holland * Barbara Ivey * Tim * Bob Adams * Rick Hinshaw * Tommy Carson * Dan Sudnick * Steve Smith * Joaquin Croslin * Mike Jason * Geoffrey Burgess

Further Acknowledgments

Tom Aiello * Jerry Allen * Jason Allen * Tom Ayers * Mark Bell * Aaron Bennett * Ineke Boelter * Lance Borden * Shirley Bridges * Kile Brown * Max Brumenfeld * Robin Burk * Curt Burner * Lyle Caddell * Dennis Cahill * Paul Christianson * Irina Clements * Jeff Crilley * Joaquin Croslin * Joe DeAntona * John Delaplaine * Tom Doherty * Jonny Drake * Susan Eckert * Tom Endres * Darren Feher * Rita Flaherty * Greg Fontenot * Addie Marie Forchette * Johnny Fornes * Tad Gerlinger * Glenn Gordon * Fred Graboyes * Matt Graessle * Dustin Greene * Chris Grose * Mark Guner * Jim Hake * Katharine Hanley * Janet Jay * Mike Kershaw * Mike Konczal * Kristen Lewis * Jim Liwski * Donna McAleer * Venessa McDermott * Kenny McDonald * Kent Miller * Jennifer Morgan * Jeremy Nathan * Don Nickolson * Jeff Norman * Jon Nussbaum * Shawn Olds * Bruce Ollstein * Maria Or * Bob Pikna * Bill Porter * Jack Price * Bob Pritchard * Jeremy Putman * Steve Redmond * Sean Roberts * Mark Rothemich * Steve Rubright * Dan Rucker * Ed Ruggero * Matt Sistrunk * Randy Smith * Nancy Stevens * Steve Stover * Harry Tunnell * Kimberly Walter * Claudia Webb * Kurt Westerman * Rick White * Tom Wilkerson * Rob Woodmansee * Travis Zimmer

Chapter One
The Deployment

We all hear the news about this or that division leaving for Iraq. Ten thousand from Fort such-and-such or another battle group moving into the Persian Gulf. What we miss is a sense that these are real people, all with very personal stories of leaving family behind, having to deal with keeping life going while away for so long. Besides the active duty soldiers, thousands of reservists have been called and sent over. Many of these have the added dilemma of losing customers if they own a business, taking a drop in pay, and falling behind in their civilian job skills. There are 100,000 individual stories; only a handful are presented here.

Chief Warrant Officer-Three Gordon Cimoli is a UH-60 Blackhawk helicopter pilot stationed in Germany where he lives with his wife, Stefanie, and their three children. He has been in the Army for 15 years and this will be his second time in combat.

[Gordon Cimoli]

I woke up Saturday [February 8, 2003] with a sense of relief that we finally had some days off where I would be able to relax and spend time with my family. Over the past month we have all been extremely busy with preparations for the deployment and the hours we now spend at work grow exceedingly long. Before I go to work, I kiss my sleeping kids and by the time I come home from work they are sleeping again. None of us have really seen our families this month and I fear this is just a preview of what is to come.

The phone rang. Stef answered it, then came up stairs to tell me that I had to leave tonight instead of Tuesday. Great. I still hadn't packed yet and still didn't have any time off to spend with Stef.

We spent the rest of the day running around trying to make sure that we had everything taken care of and by 5pm I still wasn't packed. I had to show up to work at midnight.

Stef took Benjamin and Anabelle with her to the PX while Emily and I packed my bags. She helped me decide some things I should take and some things I should leave. I had to talk to her about leaving. I am glad we had some time for us to be alone for a change. The past weeks left me little time to spend with anyone other than the guys at work so this was a welcomed change. As we packed, I saw Emily sneaking notes into my bags with little messages like, "I miss you, Daddy."

Everything was rushed because of the quick notification. We tucked the kids in bed and finished last-minute household tasks until 11pm. I loaded my bags in the van then helped Stef rustle the kids out of bed. At 11:24pm, the kids and bags were all loaded so we drove to the hangar.

When we arrived, it was a mad house. There were cars and family members everywhere. I parked the van near the hangar and had Stef and the kids stand by while I unloaded my bags.

Sunday, February 9th, 2003

We are still at the hangar and it is just after midnight. I was issued my pistol, magazines, a box with communications equipment and my night vision goggles and heads-up display. We all have a lot of stuff to carry. Add to that my backpack to carry on (it has my laptop and a blanket in it), my load-bearing vest, helmet, flak vest, protective mask etc. and you can imagine how cramped we would be on this trip.

We had a formation to get accountability and were then allowed to spend time with our families. We went to the van to spend our last few moments together.

Emily and Stefanie were visibly very sad. Benjamin and Anabelle don't fully understand the impact of my leaving so they are acting normal. As I am saying goodbye to Stefanie I can see Emily crying in the back of the van. She is trying to hold the tears back but through the glare of the streetlights I can see her eyes glistening from tears. I went to the back of the van and sat with her and gave her hugs and kisses for a while and tried to make her laugh. It breaks my heart to see her so sad and know there is nothing I can do to stop it.

At 2:15am, I give them my final kisses and they drive away into the dark, cold night. I watch as the taillights disappear into the distance.

I go back inside the hangar and gather all my equipment and load the baggage into the busses that will take us to our point of departure. The buses are all packed tight with people and all the extra equipment they have to carry. There is no room for comfort. We are traveling with all that we will have to live with for as long as we are gone. There are 2 to 3 bags each.

We drive into the morning for 3-1/2 hours. We arrive at a personnel holding/processing area, unload the bags, then reload them into a flat bed trailer. We then move inside to be processed for manifest.

We move into a building and lay down on a cot for about 30 minutes before being called to leave. We are all tired from being up all night. We saw a private crying. Our unit is together so it's not like any of us are leaving alone but still hard to see Emily so sad. We talked about our experiences and went to sleep.

We load back in the buses and are driven to the airbase to load our plane. We move into a USO building and wait for a few hours before getting back on the buses again. The USO has snacks, drinks, games, post cards, paper, and envelopes. They are volunteers and are very nice to us. I wrote a letter to Stef and to Mom then rested until noon. We load another bus and are driven to the plane. We are flying a Civilian 757 from ATA.

We stand around for an hour while everything is loaded. There is not enough room in the hold below deck so some of the bags are put into the seats in the cabin. We can only sit in rows 24 and forward because of the baggage in the other seats. Again, we are packed and have to sit with all of our gear. It seems even more uncomfortable than the bus. The Stewards are rude and telling us that we are being slow – this statement almost incites a riot as all the soldiers are already pissed off at the whole situation. One of them said, "Don't take any crap from these soldiers, if they give us any crap they will not fly on this flight." I overheard this and assured him that none of us wanted to be on this flight so go ahead and kick us off of it.

3

We finished loading at 2pm. We are packed like sardines and it is a 6–7 hour flight to Kuwait. Kuwait is 2 hours ahead of us so we will not arrive until at least 11pm. No real sleep since the night of the 7th and this is the evening of the 8th now. I have a window seat on the left wing. It is a sunny day and pleasant outside. I can see some small hills around the airbase and there is a constant flow of aircraft landing and taking off.

I'm in a drone state staring out the window, then I wake up. We passed the Swiss Alps! That was pretty cool to see. The mountains rose up out of the clouds and seemed to reach up and touch us as we flew over. After a snack I fell asleep for awhile and woke again. It was dark outside. We passed over the Nile River in Egypt and could see the Luxor all lit up—similar to what you see at the hotel of the same name in Vegas except that this was the actual monument.

More time passed and then the pilot came over the intercom: "We are going to ask you to close all the window shades and we are going to turn off all the cabin lights for our approach into Kuwait." It was 10:28pm Kuwaiti time. The cabin became very dark. This was the first indication that this was for real. We still had another 30 minutes to go before we would land, but this snapped people into realizing that we were heading into the real thing.

We grabbed our bags and were put into another bus. We were at Kuwait International Airport. We all moved into a large Bedouin tent where we were briefed on basic information. We all then moved into another tent to rest for an hour until we were called to come unload the bags and reload them onto some trucks for their trip across the desert to our new home.

Monday, February 10th,

We have essentially been in transit since the 8th and it was now 1am on the 10th. We were all tired.

The night was cool but not like Germany. There were a lot of aircraft arriving and departing and all of their lights were off. It is all pretty surreal.

At 4am we finished playing with the bags and were allowed to sleep. I curled up on the wooden floor of the tent between two others. We shared my poncho liner to stay warm and fell asleep for a few hours.

At 6am we were all woken abruptly and told, "You need to get on the bus now!" We gathered our gear and headed outside, into the bright morning and loaded onto another bus. This bus was driven by a Kuwaiti civilian and ours was just one in a line of many. We loaded the bus at 6:45am and at 8am we were still sitting there, packed like sardines again. We were told that it will take many hours and we will be driving through open desert.

The bus was bouncing around over sand dune and we finally arrived at the gate to Udairi. Our new home. We all got out and looked around at our new home. Very desolate, a lot of tents and trucks and flat for as far as you can see. It is very bright with the sun glaring off the white sand.

We found cots and moved into our new tent. The tent is supposed to sleep 60 people but we put 35 in it – just our Company. We walked back to where the buses dropped us off and moved our bags into our new house.

-Gordon Cimoli

Allison Rowe is a single Second Lieutenant on her first duty assignment at Ft. Campbell. She is a recent Graduate of the United States Military Academy and is a Military Intelligence Officer. This is the first taste of being on her own, both in the Army and in life.

[Allison Rowe]

By the end of December 2002 most everyone at Fort Campbell, KY had some idea that there was a great chance of the entire division deploying to Iraq once the New Year came around. The only question was how long it would be before we got the official word to leave. For about a month and a half before getting the 'call' the 311th Military Intelligence Battalion planned, trained, and prepared so we could deploy within a moment's notice. I wasn't really certain as what to expect or even what the desert would have in store for me. All of my focus was on preparing my platoon for the unknown.

January was bitterly cold month. There was snow on the ground and the air was frigid. Those cold weather boots we were given during initial issue didn't feel so weatherproof after hours of standing at the railhead. Hours and hours were spent at the CROF or the Campbell Rail Operations Facility on post. One of the main events during a deployment is insuring that all of your unit's vehicles make it on to the rail cars so they can be shipped to the port. But even before that could happen, each of my platoon's vehicles – there were 7 or 8 of them – had to be mechanically inspected and pass an emissions test (so to speak) prior to being authorized to mount the rail cars.

Before deploying there really wasn't much time to think about what Iraq had in store for us. The majority of the time was spent attending meetings, signing for new equipment, loading vehicles on railcars, and packing bags to get ready to leave. Practically every piece of the equipment my platoon deployed with was brand new, including a few of the vehicles.

A couple of weeks before the deployment, it seemed as though every day was spent in meetings. Here is a brief description of what the majority of those couple of weeks were like. By 0518hrs I was out and off to one of the commander's one billion 0600 hrs meetings. All of these meetings were really starting to wear people out especially since we were having a 1700hrs meeting every day, too. I mean really, how much is going to change between 1700 and 0600 the next morning EVERY DAY?!? People really should be given time to spend with their families or getting their affairs in order.

From this experience I was able to see that yes, it is important to gather a company's key leaders to ensure that everything is right on track especially right before a deployment. However, having the time to spend with family is important also and that cannot be forgotten by our leaders. Also, for us single soldiers, people tend to forget that we have to get our affairs in order all by ourselves. We don't have spouses or teen-age children to assist with our pre-deployment prepping; everything has to be done by us and us alone. So, time spent on excessive and redundant meetings is valuable time and rest lost.

My birthday was on February 25th and Nicole took me out to dinner to celebrate. Joe and Jeremy were there as well. We went to the Outback there in Clarksville.

Nicole knows I enjoy keeping journals so she got me this one and said it was for all of my desert adventures! Thanks, Nicole.

The fact that we were deploying didn't hit me until the night before I reported to the company to get on the plane to fly out. Two weeks before leaving I felt like I was going a 1000 miles a minute. I lived in a townhouse in Clarksville, TN, and I had to close everything out before I departed to include my cable and telephone services and make arrangements to close out my rent. I was glad that my parents were able to come down from Virginia and do all the final closeouts for me, otherwise I would have been in a world of hurt!

Paying a year's worth of rent on an empty townhouse, for example, was not something I was looking forward to doing.

I think I woke up about 2:30 am the day I departed the United States heading for Kuwait. I reorganized and packed a few more items into my oversized bags and actually had to force some of the stuff in there. All the extra stuff that wouldn't fit, I left in a laundry basket for my parents to take home to VA with them and to use it as a "please send me" basket. Periodically over the course of the deployment, I'd ask them to send more underwear or more deodorant and they would take those items from the basket of goodies that I had already purchased and get them in the mail for me. I also left some last minute notes and directions for my parents to do the final closeout. It was a strange feeling leaving the place I had known as home for the past year or so. I felt very lonely and remember feeling sad even.

That morning I locked up the house and drove off to my local storage unit where I left a few more of my personal belongings. On the way there I used my cell phone to make my final State-side calls for the next year. I called my sister Lauren who was at the time in her senior year at West Point. I called my sister Kirsten who was a plebe at West Point. I think I woke both of them up from their sleep. At least I know I woke Lauren up and perhaps I never got a hold of Kirsten to say goodbye, but asked Lauren to tell her for me. Finally, I called my parents and told them that I loved them too and said goodbye to my brother Dennis who was also at home. With that, I opened my storage unit, removed the battery from my cell phone and stored it away where I wouldn't see it for the next 12 months.

2 March 2003

So the plane ride over here to Camp Wolf, Kuwait was pretty nice. Sat in Business class seating and had about 4-1/2 feet of leg room. It was really nice.

After spending several hours in at Camp Wolf, I ran into several friends from West Point.

We took a long bus ride to the middle of nowhere to camp NJ. The bus had no heat. There were 8 of us on the bus, including the driver, and all of the bags (MOLE, A bags, duffle and carry on). I slept on top of 2 tough boxes the whole entire ride. Obviously, the heater wasn't working.

-Allison Rowe

John Galt is a pseudonym for a retired Army officer. He wished to join the effort and offer his assistance however he could. Being a military brat and a Gulf War veteran he felt right at home volunteering to join as a civilian to help his country.

[John Galt]

Days To Weeks To Seasons

In January 2003, I received a phone call about possibly going to work rebuilding Iraq. No specific time or date or even a specific job. A man I greatly respect and admire asked me to serve the Nation, again. I said yes! Having spent a lot of time in the Middle East as both a kid and adult, I am excited. I really enjoyed all my times in the Middle East. Getting to Baghdad, however, proved to be an exercise in patience.

Forty of us were selected. These civilian positions would help relieve the U.S. Military of non-military duties and let the military focus on hunting terrorists. The qualifications were unique: security clearance, military and business experience, with Middle East experience as a plus.

After the war, we were ready to deploy within 10 days. We canceled our vacations, sometimes our jobs and put our lives on hold.

We were ready and waiting.

Days turned into weeks. Apparently, contractors battled in D.C. over who was to provide the personnel to staff part of the Coalition Provisional Authority (CPA) while the summer played out. Troops continued to do their duty in Iraq.

Sunday, November 02, 2003

Waiting at Home

I continue to wait and wait and wait to get to Baghdad. As currently scheduled, I might make Kuwait 10 days after I left home. Who knows how much longer it'll take to get to Baghdad. Ah, the wonders of bureaucracy!

Meanwhile, the news at home is hard to ignore, even though I know it's not complete and focuses on the bad, not the good.

There are hundreds of thousands of people in Iraq working to rebuild the country. Not just U.S. forces, but forces and civilians from around the globe. While each life lost is precious, let's not forget that the majority of the people there are alive and working day and night to accomplish a daunting task. We must not let them down.

Meanwhile, I'll continue to try to take the negative reports with a grain of salt, hoping all the while that I'll soon arrive safely in Baghdad.

Monday, November 03, 2003

In-processing

Heading toward Baghdad starts with a whimper of bureaucratic layers and delays. After months of waiting to be called for immediate duty in Baghdad, I must first "in-process." Why "in-process?" Our government and the public demand that we be specially trained and qualified in order to go "in harm's way." We just can't pack up and head to Baghdad. I understand, but it seems a waste of time and money to train me after having spent more than 20 years in the military. And before I can even get to training, I have to stop in Houston to fill out employment papers – about ten minutes work crammed into five hours.

The next day it's on to Fort Bliss in El Paso, Texas, to link up with a wide assortment of people, our only common denominator being heading to the Iraqi Theatre of Operations. (Note how quickly we start adopting the military lingo. It makes everyone feel like we're part of the Mission!)

For the next three days our group endured safety orientation, medical screening, dental screening, Red Cross briefing, first aid, chaplain, cultural aspects familiarization, unexploded munitions, nuclear, biological & chemical (NBC) training, gas mask training, equipment issue, and legal briefing. Why? Think of the PR mess when one civilian gets hurt or sick and the public learns the military didn't prepare them for what to expect. Or someone dies without a will. Some in the public would be outraged and blame it all on the callousness of the United States Government, not on the incompetence of the individual or happenstance. So, it's a necessary detail to help us avoid silly issues once we truly deploy.

We also received our CACs (Common Access Card) as Department of Defense (DoD) contractors. The CAC card became our first – but not our last – badge needed for Iraq. The CAC card has a picture – which, as usual, looks no better than a driver's license picture. With a bar code, a chip and a swipe strip, our key information is retained. We can code, chip and swipe our way throughout those DoD places where we must go. One CAC card fits all.

Tuesday, November 04, 2003

Herding Cats

Many in our group complained we were treated like children. Okay. There were about 250 of us, virtually all with college degrees and considerable work experience, and we all had to be processed (together) though a lot of government forms, training and medical issues. However, even with simple guidance, we all screwed up one time or another. Sometimes multiple ways!

For example, the Record of Emergency Data form, DD93, required us to list our children. But you couldn't list a "son" as a "son" because a "son" is actually an "03." Almost everyone with a son got ahead of the instructor and wrote down "son," not 03. Whoops! Gotta start over again. Pass out about 75 forms and begin at the beginning.

In order to achieve 100% effectiveness rather than 100% efficiency, the result is about as good as herding cats. No one can deploy to Iraq without meeting each and every one of the minimum requirements. No one! Anyone who has been in the military understands the process to get 100% effectiveness – it compromises the heck out of 100% efficiency. Those who don't understand unfortunately become the squeaky wheels and do little more than slow down an already interminably long process.

I was a unique one. I flunked my DNA test! Saw a note on the bulletin board that I needed to "re-do" my DNA. Huh??? My error was that I used a pen to record my birth date, instead of a pencil. (Did that mean my intelligence DNA was deficient?) I re-did the form with a pencil.

But it could have been worse. The lack of privacy throughout the process resulted in everyone reading the note on the bulletin board informing a certain woman that she had to "re-do" her Pap smear. Nice touch.

Ah, the joys of herding cats.

Thursday, November 06, 2003

801 Yankee

"Hurry up and wait" took on a new meaning as we stayed another three days at Fort Bliss, Texas. During in-processing, Fort Bliss was bearable. But waiting and waiting without any transportation or entertainment was excruciatingly boring. We repacked. We watched TV. We ate. We called to tell relatives we were okay – and we waited. We played cards. We ate. And we talked.

Who are these 250 people? Why are these people going?

One, because it's the right thing to do. Believe me, the desire to do the right thing, even overseas, is alive and well in the United States of America. Too bad our leadership – in both parties – does not know how to call out the best in their fellow citizens.

Two, for the adventure. There are still a lot of independent, entrepreneurial, "mountain man" Americans. Many of us cannot continue to work at the routine and the redundant. Many of these people view the large majority of the public as being trapped by banality and triviality – worrying about which talentless actors are dating which talentless actresses, or about driving the latest cars, or thinking emulating ridiculously skinny models means anything to the rest of the world.

Three, there are those who are clueless about the serious consequences of Iraq duty. They are in for a sudden shock.

After many long, boring days of waiting, we finally depart on 801 Yankee, a civilian 747. There were only about 200 of the original group left, others having gone home or having other travel arrangements.

There was no roll call that morning, but we were all present. A sense of sobriety seemed to have taken over the group. The dogs searched out equipment and we went through the routine screening. People were checked by a magnetic wand while they held their arms out with pistols or rifles in their hands! Something's amiss with that visual.

For the farewell, members of the 380th battalion lined the way. I suspect the sergeants and privates were there because they wanted to be there, not by order. The "Brass" of Fort Bliss was at the bottom of the stairs to the plane to wish us a farewell.

I shook hands with and said thanks to the Battalion Commander and Command Sergeant Major of the 380th CRC Battalion.

A flight attendant gave the safety briefing. Like, please put your guns under your seats with the barrel pointed toward the skin of the aircraft. And, if there's depressurization and the masks fall down, "put it on first before putting it on the children." Given there were no children, the flight attendant laughed and said we could skip that part.

The plane took off. The pilot said she'd try to tip the wing to let everyone see the send off. She did. I couldn't see the faces, but I'd bet the commanders and the NCO's and privates of 380th were still standing watch.

801 Yankee was on its way from America to the East.

Final Leg to Baghdad

We stayed in Kuwait for a few days – for more processing. Another safety brief. Another equipment issue. Another badge exclusively for use in Kuwait. And another sticker on the ole CAC badge as evidence that we had Kuwaiti visas.

The last leg of the trip was aboard a US Air Force (USAF) C130 transport departing from the base near Kuwait City. There would only be 20 of us on this leg, and they lined us up next to the aircraft to give us instructions.

We're taking a quick hop to Mosul in the north to drop off a few of our number, and then we head down to Baghdad in the center of the country. In case of hostile fire, they'll do a Graveyard Spiral where the C130 drops about 2,500 feet a minute from way up high to way down low. Hold on to your stomachs.

And don't forget to sit on your flack vest. The bad guys are below and you're straight above. Sitting on the flak vest was recommended just as a precaution. I sat on my flak vest.

As we waited alongside the C130, the rapidly heating, black tarmac was full of air traffic – cargo jets arriving and special equipment being processed.

The lead USAF bird was waiting for cargo to be loaded in the forward cargo bay. A large platform carried by a cargo vehicle accompanied by several top USAF NCOs came from the far hanger and slowly proceeded to the lead USAF bird. The vehicle came to a gentle stop. The platform was slowly raised to the forward cargo hatch. Six caskets draped with American flags were loaded onto that plane to begin their final journey home.

In our hearts, we knew our work was about to begin in earnest. And watching the solemn work for the last journey of those who gave their all, I silently promised it would not be in vain.

Saturday, November 08, 2003

Galt Arrives!

Two weeks after leaving home, I arrived in Baghdad. My initial description is it's like the wild, wild, west. Lots of opportunity for those willing to put their noses to the grindstone.

Tuesday, November 11, 2003

The Rockets' Red Glare

I arrived in Baghdad about 5:00 p.m. on Saturday. Fortunately, we didn't have to do the Graveyard Spiral and I am very glad. That drop is faster than a military parachute jump and I could do without that kind of fun.

We landed at "BIAP." (Rookies call it Baghdad International Airport.) Military aircraft constantly coming and going. We grabbed our equipment, trying to look nonchalant, as soldiers lined up to take our places in the C130. They're heading home. Some for leave, some for compassionate reasons, and a few for reassignment. They look happy. And we're happy for them.

On the drive from BIAP to the Coalition Provisional Authority (CPA) HQ, parts of Baghdad flew by, until we hit the standard big city traffic jam. My first impression is mixed: Is it 1965 or 1983 or 1986 or 1990 in the Middle East? The sun-bleached buildings, the winding roads and the exhausted people look so much the same as they did on my multiple other trips to, and stays in, the Middle East.

The CPA HQ in the palace is a like a beehive – swarming with activity. But we're too tired to take much notice just yet. We drag our equipment into a tent just outside the palace, grab something to eat, then head for bed to end a very long day.

Then it rains. The old timers have not seen rain since they have been in country. We all watch the welcome small splatter of rain.

I tell them we've brought them luck. They say we've brought them rain.

At 2:00 a.m. I had to get up. Comfort call, you know. ;-) That's when I realized it's 325 steps from my cot to the comfort place. Co-ed no less (just lock the door).

And it's still raining.

In the distance, there's a firefight. Incoming rockets seem to start it and small arms fire is traded between the CPA forces and the bad guys. Red tracers, bullets with a special compound making them visible at night; sporadically fill the eastern night sky. For every red tracer, there are at least three or four real bullets in between. The combination of the rain and tracers make me traverse those 325 return steps faster than I imagined I could.

Wonder what tomorrow holds in store?

-John Galt

Paul Colbert and his wife Mandi were stationed in Germany when his unit was sent over. Paul is a CH-47 Chinook helicopter pilot.

[Paul Colbert]

Denzel Washington's character in the movie *Fallen*, states that there are moments in everyone's life that they realize a particular event on a particular day will separate their life into two segments. For the rest of their life, they will look at their life as two individual pieces, one before that event and one after that event. My life changed on the 9th of February, 2002.

I was a different man then compared to the man I am now. Although I am not among the youngest soldiers involved in this conflict, I have matured far beyond my twenty-six years because of the things I have done and the things I have seen. With this synopsis, I hope to not only convey my thoughts and actions during Operation Iraqi Freedom, but also to remember for myself the things I have experienced and how far I have come as a man, a soldier, a husband, a brother, a Christian, and a veteran. I would hope, though vainly, that no other human from now until the end of time would ever know war again.

War is an evil beast, feeding on the hearts and souls of those involved, and in this day of modern technology and devout media, those watching the events from thousands of miles away. I would hope that my children and their children could possibly read this story, my story, not as a triumphant one, but – simply put – a tale. Many other soldiers, sailors, airmen, marines, agents, and unknowns lost their lives in this conflict, and with the ever-present Grace and Hand of God, I will be able to finish this story in the same manner as I am starting it – alive and well.

Tears and shuddering brought grown men down to the size of small children, and wives left holding children and toys watched from the sidelines as their beau mounted a wheeled chariot and rode away into the inky night, some maybe never to return. It was a sobering experience, and I went through it three times. I, luckily left on a Monday afternoon, which, after discussing and agreement, found Mandi at work and me at the hangar. I will never forget that day, mainly due to the fact that I had never cried or felt such a deep pain in my heart, not as she drove away and I waved to her like Papa used to do to me, but as I walked into an empty house, alone, with only a duffel bag and my helmet back to accompany me.

I tried to grab the wall, but it offered no support, and I felt completely, totally alone. I crouched down on the carpet in the middle of the house and I cried. I cried so hard I began to shudder and my lungs hurt because I was screaming. I wouldn't know the smell of my wife's hair, nor the touch of her hand for another 9 months. That kind of dread is nothing I would wish even on the worst of enemies, because no matter how much love is in your heart, and no matter how many tangible and intangible things you might have of her, it's not the same. You can't reach out just to stroke her face, nor can you hug or kiss her, sleep late with her, wake up early just to watch her sleep, or even have a simple meal with her. She might be in your heart, but it's simply not the same. I don't know, and have come very far in realizing this, what I would do without Mandi, but at that particular moment, I never even knew what I was getting myself into, or, worse, if I would be able to get myself out at all.

We took the two-hour trip to RAFB via bus and spent the next many hours on Purple Ramp (the part of the airfield they put all the deploying units in) until we boarded a Delta Boeing 777 the next morning (almost 19 hours after we left) heading for Kuwait. The plane was unbelievably cramped and weapons and helmets and flak vests and every sort of field gear were in the aisles and under the seats in a maxed-out plane. The actual flight wasn't bad and I slept like a baby, which was some of the first sleep I had been able to take in almost two days. I sat next to CW2 Matt Page on the way down and remember sending Mandi a text message telling her I was there. We traveled on bus from the plane, after swiping our ID cards for FITW (Federal Income Tax Withdrawal) and in-processing. We went to Camp Wolf, just outside the airfield and plopped down on the floor of a tent with no cots and virtually no space. This was at about 11 at night. We eventually got notified that we had buses to take us to Camp Arifjan, about 20 miles southeast of the airfield. We got to Airfjan at about 4 in the morning.

-Paul Colbert

Fred Wellman is a Major in the Army with a big optimistic heart and sense of humor. He once resigned from the Active Army only to be called up as a reservist after 9/11. Since then he has stayed in. He leaves behind his wife and four children.

[Fred Wellman]

It was an interesting period for me that started when we arrived on February 28th [2003]. We landed at Kuwait International at about 0800 and were hustled on to buses for the little in-processing camp on the airfield.

It was pretty hectic as they tried to jam almost 15 minutes of briefings into an 8-hour period! This was pretty stressful so we all took naps. Finally, that afternoon we boarded buses to head to Camp Udairi in northern Kuwait. I was smart enough to jump off the bus at the last moment to seek relief at the latrine in anticipation of the predicted hour and a half trip.

Well, four hours later we were still driving up the dirt road leading across the desert. This ended up being very educational as we witnessed the Pakistani drivers' version of the Indianapolis 500. This involves taking 20 person buses that are supposed to be in a neat little convoy and seeing if you can beat each other to the exact same freaking location. It was entertaining as hell to see a bus three inches from your window swerving to miss a HUMMV coming the opposite direction.

I am sure I would have enjoyed the adventure more if I had not been so dutiful in starting my hydration program. I had been drinking substantial amounts of bottled water to ensure I would not dehydrate at the wrong moment. Unfortunately, I really needed to do some "dehydrating" about half way to our destination.

This quickly grew to a serious pain. I thought I could use the bottle I conveniently had in my hand except for the fact that I had a young female lieutenant sitting right behind me on the bus. I am from Missouri and am a little shy about standing up on a moving bus and attempting to do the maneuvering to ensure proper transfer of my bodily fluids into a bottle with a 22-year-old woman sitting two feet away. Call me uptight but it is who I am.

So, needless to say I was hurting like I have never hurt by the time we got to the gate of our camp at 2300. Well, we had to wait for them to get clearance and I really had to go so I got the driver to open the door and ran to the dark side of the bus. As I frantically wrestled with the various buttons impeding my relief I noticed the sound of a rain shower approaching. I looked at the sky and saw stars and when I looked down the row of buses I realized that the shower I heard was about 300 desperate soldiers like myself christening the outer berm of our new camp. Seems I was not the only one properly hydrating that day... to include about twenty females. It was quite the scene, which was complete with lightning from people taking pictures of the world's largest urination.

Which brings me to another one of my theories about soldiers in combat. I have decided that the average American soldier is really just an extremely heavily armed tourist. Everywhere we go we are taking pictures or posing in front of something. I can imagine them crossing the bridges into Baghdad and the lead guy going, "Hey wait a second, before we kill all these guys and capture this strategic bridge... can you take a picture of me in front of this tank for my wife?"

-Fred Wellman

Chapter Two
The Hardships

In The Face of Danger

The most obvious hardship of eliminating Saddam Hussein and re-building Iraq is the reality of being shot, rocketed, mortared, bombed, or hit by a mine. The Hussein loyalists fought for several weeks and since then insurgents, terrorists, anarchists, or whatever they are called, have continuously attacked U. S. and allied soldiers, the new Iraqi defense forces, and civilians.

A very moving tale from some wounded soldiers was compiled by Nina Berman in a photo essay found on the Wounded Warrior Project web page. This brings to home the reality of the true danger that our troops are under. A very small sample of the pain, danger and anxiety of combat are presented in the following stories.

[Gordon Cimoli]

Saturday, November 22, 2003

I think today counted as another one of those once in a lifetime days...

My morning began with waking up at 6am...I dressed, shaved and then met up with the other air crews at 6:30. Today's mission was to fly the Personal Security Detachment (PSD) for General Abizaid (the US Central Command Commander--4 star General). We would take them to the places that the General will visit soon. It was another cool morning--57 degrees. As usual it was clear with no clouds in the sky. Just cold out! We headed out to the aircraft and began our preflight. As it turned out, the other aircraft was having some troubles. The cold weather has been playing havoc on the hydraulic seals on the aircraft. We managed to continue on and, like every other day, work through these issues and take off about 20 minutes late. We had 3 passengers who we were dropping off in Baghdad and then we would pick up the PSD in the same place.

We were flying today with two aircraft and four people each. Due to the recent Surface to Air Missile (SAM) threat, we have been flying much lower and much faster than we have over the past 6 months or so. I guess you could say our flying style has come full circle. In the beginning of the War we flew low and fast. Somewhere in the middle we gave up on flying extremely low and slowed down a bit because we now had the doors off. Later on, we began flying high...thousands of feet high so we could fly direct to our destinations and save time in the aircraft where it was extremely hot. Then came the SAM's...and suddenly everyone was convinced, once again, that flying low and fast was our best defense. So, on any given day, there we are, flying at 50 feet off the ground avoiding towns, wires, huge flocks of migrating birds all while avoiding the other aircraft and maintaining some sort of formation. The workload is much greater than when flying at a moderate altitude. You are constantly searching for hazards to your flight path and calling out possible threats as you do so.

So (as most B.S. aviator stories begin), no sh%t, there we were. It was just after 9am. Our two aircraft were approaching Baghdad from the north to land in one of the "Sea world" landing zones (LZ's). The sun was shining bright and the flight was proceeding as planned. We were even making up time due to the speeds we were flying at. I noticed a funny looking streak of smoke in the air to our 12 o'clock. It was a few miles away. The streak was very linear but then had a...screwy twist and then started out in another direction. It was about 5,000 feet in the air in the direction we were flying so it was easy to keep it in sight. I soon noticed another streak, a very thin one, come out of the other streak and then saw a small flash or glint of something metallic.

We continued inbound. At this time, we heard radio traffic on the "Sheriff" frequency. That frequency is used as a common net for convoy traffic to communicate on and to get help when needed. We were out of range of one of the radios transmitting and could only hear one side of the conversation but it certainly sounded like someone on the ground was talking about receiving fire and that they needed help. We listened in just in case they needed our help. At the same time as the Sheriff frequency got busy, we heard

Baghdad tower talking to an aircraft apparently in distress. As we listened to Baghdad tower, I looked to the smoke streak and clearly saw an aircraft with a HUGE flaming trail behind it. This aircraft was over the airport at 5,000 feet or so and was leaving a large smoke trail behind it as it flew. The fire trail was huge. It looked like the Space Shuttle re-entering the atmosphere. As we listened to tower, we were given instructions to hold outside the airspace due to an emergency in progress. We then heard the Sheriff frequency again. This time we could hear both sides of the transmission. Someone was saying that they witnessed two SAM launches and was enroute to the area.

At that point, it all came together. What we saw was not any old emergency; it was an aircraft getting attacked by at least one surface to air missile! We all realized this at the same time and our hearts sunk out of fear for our own safety and certainly fear for what would happen to the aircraft that we saw in the air trailing flames as it descended. We listened to both radios intently trying to gather any information we could. We were ready to provide assistance in the event that the aircraft did not make it to the airport. Everyone was extremely calm and cooperative. Tower cleared the airspace. An Apache was providing visual assistance to the pilot of the attacked aircraft.

After a few more minutes, 2 search and rescue aircraft from the Air Force were running and waiting to provide assistance. Everyone was there to help. Tower had coordinated all the crash and rescue services to help this aircraft. The pilot spoke with a Middle Eastern accent but was easily understood. He said that he thought his aircraft was struck by something and that it was now on fire. He requested to land at the airport and to have help there when he landed. He continued to descend but said he was having issues with the flight controls or hydraulics and would need more time to descend, turn and line up on final for the runway. We continued to hold, varying our holding pattern, and watched the aircraft as much as we could. The flame would disappear then reappear as he turned the aircraft. Everything seemed to be well under control. The pilot was still calm and at one point told the tower, "No more talking now." He continued to descend. Tower advised him that his landing gear was down but his reply indicated that it was not showing the same indication within his cockpit. He called back to tower to ask if his aircraft was still smoking and/or on fire.

Tower responded that they could not tell but the Apache, who was now hovering and facing the aircraft could clearly see and responded, "You are still on fire and still smoking from the left wingtip." The pilot confirmed that he was on fire and continued. Then there was silence. We could not see the aircraft because of how low we were, but within a few minutes, tower cleared us to continue inbound. We could see a huge billowing smoke cloud on the runway where the aircraft just landed. From what we could gather in the ensuing transmissions, there was only one person injured. We could see the aircraft on the end of the runway with many emergency vehicles around it. CPT Hester commented that it looked like a civilian DHL aircraft. We landed at our pad, dropped off the personnel and picked up the PSD. We took off, heading south. As we flew, we heard the Sheriff frequency talking about a grid for one of the launch sites. We wrote it down, put it into our GPS and found that it was only 4.1 kilometers away to our front. We announced this to the lead aircraft with a suggested immediate turn to the left. We stayed low and fast and moved out of the area.

Our first destination was Babylon. We landed there at 10am. While waiting for fuel, I pulled out my map and plotted the grid that we were given. As I pulled out my protractor and put the pencil to the map, our mouths dropped when we saw the location of the launch site. It was on our route of flight, at our first checkpoint out of sea world! We could not believe it so we plotted it again. Yep. We were correct the first time. The launch site was within the square that we draw on the map to represent our start point...directly on our course line. We recounted our steps and original time lines and quickly realized that, had we been on time this morning, we would have been passing over that point at the same time the launch occurred. We all believe that we would not have been shot at (because we are flying too low and fast to get acquired) but it would certainly have made a much more interesting story to tell for sure!

The rest of the flight was relatively. We flew to the 82nd Airborne Divisions sector and landed in an extremely tight LZ, had lunch then continued on to their airport (TQ) to get gas before heading north to Kirkuk. We headed back from Kirkuk in a race against the setting sun. We dodged flights of birds and actually hit one squarely with the center windshield. It startled me as it hit with a loud THWACK and a blood streak up the windshield but we continued on. We lost the race with the sun. We landed here on Balad to get gas one more time before finishing our trip by returning our passengers to Baghdad. The sun continued below the horizon and every minute meant it was getting darker and darker...there was no moon illumination to help out so, en route to Baghdad we put on NVG's and continued to the Sea world LZ then back home. In all, we logged 6.4 hours of flight time--5.0 Day, 4. Night, 1.0

NVG's...all in a 12 hour duty day (yes, we had an extension for flight time! haha).

On the internet I found one small blurb about the incident. All it said was a DHL commercial plane landed with its wing on fire and no one was injured. The military did not recognize that it was hit by a SAM.

-Gordon Cimoli

Jeff Qunell is a civilian engineer working for the Corps of Engineers in Seattle. He and eight others from the same district went together to assist in construction projects.

[Jeff Qunell]

There were most definitely numerous guardian angels with us on that January 29th morning (coincidentally on my 9th wedding anniversary). I was driving the second vehicle of the convoy that was ambushed on that morning. When I arrived in country with our team, I was pleased to find that the FEST-A (Forward Engineering Support Team - Advance) members are predominantly Christian. The 3 members that were on this convoy are Christians and I'm not certain about the other passengers (Gail, an AFN reporter in the lead vehicle; Burat, Shooter from Nepal in my vehicle; two soldiers in the third vehicle). God's hedge of protection was most definitely around us and we are so thankful for His grace, His mercy and His presence in our lives.

I believe we all have replayed and continue to replay the ambush scenario in our heads over and over. It's real easy to wonder about God's purpose in an incident like this. We found ourselves thinking of the small occurrences that put us in that spot of the road, in that moment of time. Prior to our departure, our team gathered and prayed thankfulness to the Lord and for safe travels. At our scheduled departure time, we were supposed to meet and have our convoy brief. We were awaiting the arrival of our third shooter. We tried tracking him down without any success. We ended up locating an alternate Gherka (sp?) shooter after 30 minutes had passed. Burat, our alternate shooter was not supposed to be on duty until noon on this day, so we had to wait for him to gear up. I picked him up from his container housing unit and as our convoy headed for the compound gate; he realized he had forgotten his ID. So, we headed back to get it.

Then the convoy left the compound. Approximately 10 minutes outside the gate, we encountered what appeared to be some sort of construction activity. The road was barricaded with barrels (55 gal drums perhaps). We saw apparent workers sweeping the road behind the barricade. Traffic was detoured to the right on some small side street that was very congested with traffic. There was a large automobile transport truck parked on the side of the road that further narrowed the street causing additional traffic congestion. This scene was very suspicious to us all as the first 2 vehicles of our convoy turned onto the detour street and were stopped by the congestion. Moments after stopping, automatic weapons fire rang out.

It was a very surreal experience for me. I honestly wasn't sure what the noise was for a moment. All I knew was that it was very loud and it was to my left. It was so loud (with my window up) that I reacted with a sort of defensive flinch. I don't recall turning my head to look to my left. I believe this is because I had realized what the noise was an instant later while viewing the bullet ridden SUV in front of me. The firing stopped and my shooter, Burat, fired a couple of rounds in the air since he was on the right side of the vehicle with no visible hostilities. I could only think of the condition of my teammates (who have become very good friends to me).

After a brief hesitation, Norm bolted left and went between the barricades and sped down the sidewalk. I followed in right behind him, plowed into one of the barricades and we tore out of the kill zone (the 3rd vehicle fell in behind me). There was no construction going on. It is evident that this was a calculated ambush. The barricaded road turned out to be a very good escape route. We had 2-way radio communication with each other and I inquired if every one was okay. Steve replied that "we have a hit, we have a hit... we're heading to D-Rear!" We were making our way towards "Division Rear," where a more equipped aid station was located. We ran into further traffic congestion a short ways away, but we forced ourselves through it by honking and flashing our lights. Still in very slow congested traffic, with apparent gunshot injuries, we spotted a military convoy returning to "D-Main." Without knowing the extent of any injuries, we opted for the quicker route by following the convoy back to our compound BAS.

When we arrived to the D-Main BAS, Norm stepped out holding his neck. I was very concerned, as I didn't expect him to be the injured one. He drove quite well during our escape. As it turns out, he drove with one hand because he thought he was holding pressure on a bleeding neck wound. Not only did he drive one-handed, but he also honked with the same hand. I asked him how he did that because he said he didn't let go of his neck during the entire route back. He couldn't remember. I understand there was an opportunity for Steve to briefly check the wound and he didn't think it looked serious. He placed a bandage on it and Norm continued to keep pressure on it. A bullet had passed through the rear window, through the driver's headrest (slightly deflected by its frame), through his flack vest collar, then through his DCU collar.

To this day, Norm continues to wear this shirt, which still has a piece of the "flack" material adhered to it. I later realized that Gail had taken a more direct hit right in her back (very close to her spine). The bullet had gone through the rear door, third row seat, through her seat and into her flack jacket (no plates). It is truly a miracle that the flood of AK47 bullets did not mortally injury anyone in the lead vehicle. You must realize that nearly all of the rounds appeared to be heading for someone. They were miraculously stopped or deflected.

One round whizzed by Steve's head in the front passenger seat. The vehicle framing that it hit (near his head) caused small bullet and/or steel fragments to injure his face. Also miraculous is that only 3 rounds hit the vehicle I was driving. Upon inspection of the lead vehicle bullet holes and their path, and realizing that I was DIRECTLY behind the lead vehicle (perhaps 5-ft of space between us), it would seem that many of the rounds should have come from our vehicle based on their location and trajectory. The fact that those rounds totally missed our vehicle is incredible. It is a true testimony that God protected us and certainly answered our prayers.

It is evident, after inspecting the vehicles, that this was a very calculated, planned ambush that was intent on killing the entire convoy. Every occupant in the lead vehicle had a bullet hole heading for their head or center mass. It is also evident that there was more than one shooter from different locations. If the bullet heading for Norm hadn't been deflected by God, there would be a very different story to tell.

Again, I am so thankful to God. My praise to Him is amplified as a result. As I continue to grow in Christ, I will always follow His will for me, in this country and at home. I hope that sharing our praise report will help bring others to Jesus. What a trip this will be if I can help save even one person. Although it has been difficult being away from my wonderful, loving wife and 2 young daughters, I know that God's plan is awesome and shall reap unthinkable blessings. His plan to have this story told by your hand can only be good.

-Jeff Qunell

[Paul Colbert]

Although cutting conversations short in the Army with your loved ones is not an uncommon thing, it's another ball of wax when you're trying to explain to your wife that you have to go "NOW!" because you've got numerous incoming mortars. Balad soon began to grow to inordinate proportions, in excess of 22,000 troops, as a result of it being dubbed a primary Air Force APOD (Airport of Debarkation) and primary logistics hub of the entire country. Because of the high volume of rotary wing and fixed wing traffic (everything from small C-12, two prop VIP transports to massive C-5s and C-17s) and the constant flow of truck convoy after truck convoy along the roads and into the gates of the base, it didn't take long for the Saddam Loyalists (Sadam Feeyhadeen) to realize that it was an important target.

We had a stretch where we were all greeting each other some time between midnight and 2 a.m. for thirteen days straight in the hangar, clothed with flak vests and Kevlar helmets. About 85% of the time, the mortars landed on the north side of the airfield where the 3rd COSCOM (COps Support COMmand) was stationed, along with the 21st CSH (Combat Surgical Hospital), so it didn't take too long for the good guys to realize that the bad guys knew exactly what they were targeting – the main logistical vein of the entire Task Force and the 21st CSH (Combat Surgical Hospital).

Although most of the mortars landed to our north, we were very close to the fuel bags, a series of about a hundred 10,000-gallon diesel-fuel bladders exposed and very prominent. Several mortars landed near our area, but only two affected 12th Brigade with any impact. The first hit when I was overnighting in Kuwait. A mortar came in over the top of the Brigade Headquarters and struck the side of the Raytheon (Civilian-contracted Aircraft Maintenance) Hangar and blew an entire Snap-on Roll-away tool chest, sending about 1,000 ratchets, wrenches, pliers, and other various tools into the side of, none other than, 89-099, the same aircraft that had numerous other holes punched in it around Objective Rams. We gave the Flight Engineer, SGT Lance Reynolds, good ribbings, mainly due to the fact that the aircraft had finished its final post-phase test flight earlier that day and was ready for acceptance the morning after it got hit. All told, it had almost 100 individual holes

25

punched in the sheet metal, and an engine, engine transmission, combining transmission, and an APU (Auxiliary Power Unit) had to be replaced because of damage. Luckily, no one was seriously hurt from the blast (one crewmember from A/5-159, "Hookers," Washington Reserves, got some shrapnel in his leg), even with its proximity to the Brigade Headquarters.

The second mortar landed about half a mile from our tents and I will never forget that sound. Mortars have a very distinct sound to them, unlike any other sound of gunfire, artillery fire, or tank rounds. Because mortars are fired at a high lob with a small charge and even with "cheese charges" (small chunks of explosive that are pushed into the blades of the mortar to propel it farther than normal), they are silent, accurate, and difficult to pinpoint. Mortar tactics are never by-the-book, especially with enemy fire. The Iraqis, we later found out, were emplacing mortar tubes deep in the ground at the appropriate angles to fire on Balad all around the base in the farm fields. Mere inches of the tubes were visible, and because the enemy covered them with grass, they were nearly impossible to locate. That particular night, the mortars landed so close to our living areas that you could hear the metallic "tink" of metal against concrete and then the explosion. We knew that they were close, and with the exception of the missions we flew at the beginning of the war, that was the only time I had felt that close to death itself. Many more mortars fell that night, none as close as the first, thank God, and we all lived to tell the tale.

-Paul Colbert

Matt Brady was a platoon leader of an OH-58D Kiowa Warrior troop, 3rd ID cavalry squadron. His unit's mission was to fly ahead of our ground counterparts and search for, engage, observe, and report the enemy to the division as it rolled behind them. They were the first Americans many Iraqis had seen and were fighting everyday until they reached Baghdad.

[Matt Brady]

I was a platoon leader of an OH-58D Kiowa Warrior troop, 3rd ID cavalry squadron, or 3-7 CAV, DIVCAV. They since been partially disbanded, but our mission was to fly ahead of our ground counterparts and search for, engage, observe, and report the enemy to the division as it rolled behind us. We were the first Americans many Iraqis had seen, and we were fighting everyday until we reached Baghdad. True heroism was demonstrated on one flight in particular by a National Guardsman from Mississippi, CW4 "Bart" Carter!! He was an augmentee to our troop, a maintenance test pilot, and my wingman for the war (although he'll tell you that I was his).

On the heaviest day of fighting in the Southern city of Al Samawah, we had been taking RPG fire from one row of huts on the west side of the city. He volunteered to Fly low and slow DIRECTLY in front of the huts to draw the enemy fire, and reveal his position to myself and the cav tanks and brads. Fortunately for Bart, the RPG gunner held his fire, but I'll never forget the courage it took to fly that maneuver for the sake of the squadron.

-Matt Brady

[Fred Wellman]

As soon as it got dark there was a pretty good firefight on the perimeter. They rolled tanks out and ended up killing four knuckleheads who attacked a very over-protected airfield...with rifles. I mean you have to be kidding me. They attacked tanks with rifles. So, four of them died and none of us got hit. I was laughing because all of the Division Headquarters guys were running out to where we were standing watching the firefight and telling us to get our body armor on and helmets like it was the end of the world. I was telling them I wasn't too concerned when a bunch of idiots with rifles attack a company of Armor and Mech Infantry. Needless to say we survived unscathed.

All night long there were huge bursts of gunfire going into the air and tracers going every direction. It seems it happens every night as celebration shooting. We were not sure if it was good guys or bad guys that night because it was Saddam's birthday. As it turns out it is hard to tell the difference between a good bullet and a bad bullet so we just put on our flak vests and hoped they were all poorly aimed bullets either way. We all sat outside on the ramp watching on the hoods of our vehicles. It looked like the Fourth of July in PTC. I was waiting for people to start oohing and ahhing.

-Fred Wellman

[Matt Brady]

Just another example of bravery came from my commander, CPT Kara Bates, class of '97. During the battle of As Samawah, she and her SWT (scout weap-

27

ons team) volunteered to cross over the Euphrates in the middle of the city and fly close to 60NM upriver, unescorted, no CSAR capability, out of radio contact, and recon a possible crossing site for the division. The Iraqis guarding the bridge were so surprised to see the aircraft, they spazzed around for a while to find their weapons before they could fire on them. After taking heavy fire, she returned to advise the squadron that the bridge was suitable for crossing, and the squadron bypassed As Samawah as the primary crossing point. Just to volunteer to go that deep into enemy territory, that vulnerable, took tremendous courage in my mind. She was the best commander I've ever seen.

-Matt Brady

Many times in the face of danger some will rise to a higher state of selflessness. Below are just a few examples of heroes from the Second Armor Cavalry Regiment.

- Corporal Michael R. Guza, noticed a burning apartment building while on a routine patrol on 20 August 20, 2003. With flames burning brightly from each window, Michael Guza entered the building numerous times to assist the occupants from the burning building. Of the nine he rescued, eight were women and one a handicapped man. Michael lowered two from the second story window. [1]
- Private First Class Joseph Morris was driving a vehicle when it struck an IED (Improvised Explosive Device) on June 27, 2003. Everyone in the 2-vehicle convoy was killed or injured except Joseph and one other soldier. PFC Morris gathered the wounded, administered first aid, and drive back to the base camp with three flat tires. He also called in the MEDVAC and alerted the Quick Reaction Force. Joseph saved six wounded soldiers, one who would have lost an arm if not for his quick actions. [2]
- On August 19, 2003 a suicide bomber blew up the United Nations building. Staff Sergeant Leander Nunies, dazed by the blast, was still able to quickly help evacuate survivors, set up a triage point and start first aid before the medics arrived and then evacuated casualties by driving ambulances to hospitals. [3]

- Sergeant Lewis Davis was one of the first soldiers arriving on the scene after the explosion. Lewis made repeated visits inside the building to evacuate the wounded and provide first aid to the critically injured. [4]

- Sergeant William von Zehle, a 52-year-old reservist of the 411th Civil Affairs Battalion, was wounded by flying glass in the blast in a nearby building. William rushed to the scene and was told two men were trapped. He worked for over three hours, reassuring the men while moving debris to release the trapped men. Finally one was freed but sadly the other died after three hours. The man who William was working hard to save turned out to be the U. N. special representative Sergio Vieira de Mello. [5]

Another example of bravery under enemy fire was exhibited by the marines and sailors of the 24th Marine Regiment. On April 10, 2004 Weapons Company was on patrol when it was ambushed. An IED exploded, sending shrapnel into the face of Corporal Billy Wallis who ignored his injuries and loss of blood and returned fire.

Other Marines dismounted and sought cover behind a house and returned fire on the terrorist four hundred meters away. One Marine took a bullet to the head and Petty Officer 2nd Class Greg Cinelli exposed himself to enemy fire to bring the injured to safety, administered first aid, evacuated the wounded to the battalion aid station, and then quickly returned to the battle.

Corporal Zachary D. Smith, under verbal instruction from a senior Marine arriving on the scene, led his four man team across five hundred meters of open farmland while receiving enemy fire. Eventually marine helicopters attacked the terrorists' position and killed fourteen. The marine who was saved by Greg Cinelli lost his eye from the bullet. [6]

Many other descriptive stories of bravery, initiative and resourcefulness are related in *On Point*, a book produced by the Center for Army Lessons Learned. Some of the heroes mentioned in this book are Sergeant First Class Paul R. Smith, Specialist Dwayne Turner, Lieutenant Colonel Christopher Hughes, First Lieutenant Jason King, Private First Class Anthony Jackson, Lieutenant Colonel Marcone, Sergeant Steven Horn, and Private Sean Watkins. [7]

Jim Gilson was a navy pilot stationed in Pensacola, Florida with his wife and three children when he applied and was accepted to go to medical school. Jim had some free time before school would start in September 2004, so he volunteered to go to Iraq.

[Jim Gilson]

Working in the CPA as the Deputy Chief of Protocol, I really did not have many chances to get in harm's way. That is until I started volunteering for extra duties. At first I was volunteering to work with the doctors in the hospital during the night shift. This made sense to me since I was about to give up my Navy flying and start medical school in Bethesda. Then one day, I was getting into a car and was leaning over to pick up something I dropped in the passenger seat when I felt a cold liquid dumped on me. I had left my door open and someone had just thrown something on me. In reality, I had no time to think because as soon as the liquid hit me I was hit with a match and covered in flames. For a second I thought about trying to decide to chase after the assailant and put out the fire or put out the fire than chase the guy. I didn't think long about this and chose to work on the fire. I ended up going to the hospital that night but as a patient instead of as a volunteer. I had second and third degree burns on my arm and leg. The assailant was not caught but was a small boy about eight years old on a moped. He drove past the check point into the Green Zone without being stopped.

Another thing I volunteered to do was ride as an escort for a meeting in Al-Hilla. On the way back was my first firefight. We were in two cars and I was in the back seat behind the driver. We were cruising really fast when I heard pop....pop, pop, pop. I couldn't tell where it was coming from. Looking back, I see some junkie Iraqi car swerving back and forth with two guys shooting AK-47s at us. Our second vehicle was taking hits and not returning fire. Our driver picked up speed. Now it was like some Hollywood action movie. I'm hanging out the window with half my body outside of the car and I'm firing back. The cars are swerving all over the road. Poles and mirrors from other cars are just missing my head. The part of town we were driving in was very poor and there was little other traffic. Still there were lots of people on the sidewalks. The drivers are really picking up speed and we are doing sixty or seventy miles per hour. Once we got airborne as we jumped the median. I'm the only one that is getting any shots off, and now the bad guys are aiming at me. Eventually I must have made some good shots as suddenly the car spun out and skidded to a stop. All three in the car died.

I wasn't looking for recognition that day. I was just happy we all got back alive that day. That was the real bottom line.

Now I'm starting medical school and having a really rough time. I was on the promotion list for 04 and now I'm an ensign again with my pay cut in half. Try living in Bethesda with a wife and two kids on ensign pay. This is tougher than my life in Iraq.

-Jim Gilson

[Paul Colbert]

Getting to Tikrit from Balad was almost a straight shot north. Most of the major towns and cities, for obvious reasons, were along the Tigris and Euphrates Rivers. The Euphrates provided the cities in the south with their riverine environment; the Tigris had its equal grasp on the cities in the center of the country. Tikrit was no different and was actually built on a cliff on the western short of the Tigris, about 30 minutes north of Balad. Unfortunately, though, all the Iraqis knew that we flew that route back and forth, day-in and day-out. Two Blackhawks, one from 12th Brigade piloted by a good friend of mine, CW2 Javier Gutierrez from B/3-158 Aviation, and another from 101st, piloted by a classmate of mine, CPT Ben Smith, would meet the fate of RPGs (Rocket Propelled Grenades) mere kilometers apart on the east side of that same river. I, myself, along with Josh O'Brien in the second aircraft, was shot at with an RPG in June doing a 4ID Resupply. We knew something had gone wrong because of the sudden presence of Apaches scouting the area almost immediately, but didn't know exactly what had happened until an intelligence report was released that same night informing us of the specific details.

-Paul Colbert

Kristen Lewis is a lieutenant in the Main Support Battalion (703d MSB) from the 3rd Infantry Division. She was in Kuwait and Iraq from January 2003 to August 2003. Kristen, who is in the Transportation Corps, was out on the road quite a bit and saw a lot of Iraq and its people. Her husband, Billy, was also part of the main push to Baghdad. He is a tanker with the 3ID.

[Kristen Lewis]

I'm sure there are plenty of more interesting ambush stories out there... but here's mine. Let me first start off by saying there was one chapter or verse from the Bible that I read several times in Kuwait prior to crossing the berm — Psalm 91. This becomes relevant at the end of this story.

I took the 0500 convoy to Baghdad International Airport (BIAP) every morning after we took control of the area. We had a Logistics Resupply Point (LRP) set up there that we pushed supplies to. One particular morning as we were getting ready to go out, I looked at our commo sergeant, SGT Baty, and said, "You know, it's really weird going out everyday and staring out my door looking for someone to pop up out of nowhere and shoot at us." Up until this point, we hadn't really experienced these attacks on convoys like we see now on the news.

We made it too BIAP with no issues. We weren't supposed to be out when night fell so we had to leave BIAP no later than 1600. It was about a 3 hr drive with a convoy, little over 2 hours without a convoy following. We drove along two major highways for half the distance and minor roads for the other half. While rounding up all the drivers to prepare to go back to our base camp I found myself talking to one of our mechanics, SGT Merchant. I told him I was nervous about going back. I'd never been nervous before. He looked at me and said he was too. It was just strange that I'd mentioned something to my commo sergeant and one of my mechanics that day. We started our way back.

Along the first highway we were shot at. First, an RPG was shot that missed us and exploded off past me, the lead vehicle. A second RPG was shot that exploded just after my last truck. Then a barrage of small arms fire came at us. I just remember looking and seeing the smoke from where the RPGs had been shot and hearing the firing come from the right and started firing my M16. I heard the NCO, SGT Edwards, on my .50cal start shooting so I jumped on the radio. By then, I heard my gun truck (another .50 cal) start shooting too along with other M16s from the TCs of the trucks in the convoy. I radioed back to SGT Merchant, my rear vehicle. He said everyone was still moving, which meant to me at least the drivers were okay. We're taught to get out of the kill zone, then stop and make sure everyone is fine.

Well, let me back up a second because this is kind of funny. When the first RPG exploded my driver hit the brakes and started to slow down. I started yelling at him (a lot of expletives) and he hit the gas. Later I asked him why he slowed down and he said he heard the explosion and saw smoke coming from the back of the vehicle and thought we popped a tire. Nice. So, SGT Merchant gave me the go that everyone was okay and that the convoy was keeping up with me, we were going about 45 - 50 MPH. At this time I was radioing over and over to our BN TOC to let them know we were taking fire. I couldn't reach anyone. Eventually my Battalion Commander answered. He was in a vehicle about thirty minutes ahead of us. About three miles farther down the route from the ambush site is the place were the two highways cross. This crossing is always crowded with Iraqi's selling fruit, magazines, and other junk. Usually we set up both .50cals to stop traffic coming from either direction. This time I just kept the convoy going full speed ahead. I was so angry at this point. I knew in my head that all the Iraqis standing in that area heard the gunfire and RPGs and I bet some of them knew what was going to happen. That's the part that got to me, that you couldn't trust anyone, not even the kids. We went about ten miles farther up the route then I stopped the convoy. I walked down the line and everyone was fine, the trucks hadn't even been hit. That's when I remembered Psalm 91. How we made it through all of that with nothing... I have no idea.

-*Kristen Lewis*

[Paul Colbert]

Rammadan started the last week of October (about the 29th or so), and the first few days were beyond uneventful. Nothing happened, anywhere. No bombings, no IEDs (Improvised Explosive Device), no raids, no attacks, no hijackings, no kidnappings, no ambushes, and no mortars. It was a very eerie calm, but, unfortunately, the calm before the storm. Two days after this lull, though, Javier Gutierrez's Blackhawk I talked about earlier got shot down in Tikrit. Three days after that, though, I had my "day on," while John Wingeart had his "day off." I had taken my day off the previous week and John worked a whole shift for me. It was good stress reliever and a great way to get all the little nit-noid things done you never had time to get to. Unfortunately for my day on, it all took a downhill slide when Capt. Greg Pound (USAF Navigator that worked in the ASOC – Air Support Operations Center) came around the corner from his cubicle with a yellow post-it, with a callsign and place – "Greyhound 25, Ar Ramadi."

At a little after 8 in the morning, Greyhound 25 and 27, two CH-47Ds from F/106, "Elvis," Iowa/Illinois National Guard, took of from FOB Ridgeway (Al Taqqadam Airfield) heading towards Baghdad's Airport with 30+ soldiers heading to Germany for leave. Our aircraft had been providing the 82nd Airborne Division with 8 Chinooks to do such moves into and out of their area of responsibility – the western part of Iraq all the way out to the Jordanian and Syrian borders. After take-off, the lead aircraft was hit by an SA-7, crashed, and instantly killed 16; three more, including the Pilot-in-command, CW3 Bruce Smith, died of their wounds. In total, 19 lost their lives, and 16 survived, miraculously.

Besides the ASOC guys who had gotten intel from a sighting from an American fixed wing aircraft through K-Mart (the controlling agency nickname for the CAOC – Coalition Air Operations Center) in a secure chat room. I was the first person in the Army to know about it. From there until the end of the day, I would hardly ever leave my desk and even had lunch and dinner brought to me by different people.

Losing an aircraft is one thing – we'd lost several up to that point. Losing and aircraft and losing lives is even another – we lost a 5th Battalion aircraft before the war started in a dust storm with four souls on board. Losing and aircraft and losing a lot of lives because the aircraft was shot down is a totally different animal. I'm writing this on New Year's Eve, and even though the shootdown happened almost two months ago, there is still a team from Ft. Rucker here in Baghdad discussing the "how's" and "why's."

Greyhound 25 changed every way we conducted business in the Chinook world. That day, FRAGO 1038 (the 2 November Daily Tasking Update) restricted any Chinook from flying without ASE (Aircraft Survivability Equipment) or during the day with passengers. That meant that 98% of the missions would have to be flown under the cover of darkness.

-Paul Colbert

Other Hardships

Besides the very real and horrifying reality of death and serious injury, the people in Iraq have had to endure a few other hardships. It's tough enough to live a year away from loved ones, on top of that your life while away is filled with relentless heat in the summer, long hours and little time off, cramped and austere living conditions, portapotties, MREs, canteen baths, camel spiders, scorpions, long wait for mail, and the knowledge that as soon as you get back home you could be shipped back in a few months.

Below are a few stories about sandstorms, threats of chemical attacks, and techniques to fight the tedium of what to do with the time off once you get it.

Sandstorms

As we live in our fertile nation where farms, forests or cement covers most of the land, it is difficult to imagine the intensity of the sand storms that can spring up in a desert. Occasionally in Texas, we'll get what the meteorologist will call a sandstorm. This is usually a yellow sky for a few hours and maybe a light dusting on cars and outdoor furniture. In a land of vast acreage of shifting sands, a sandstorm takes on a whole new meaning. There isn't much anyone can do, but bundle up and wait it out.

[Allison Rowe]
6 March 03

So... yeah each time I write I start with "so"...[smiley face] We had two really bad dust storms/sand storms today. The first one I wasn't prepared for, but the 2nd one I was!

I had just washed my clothes and hung them to dry when I walked over to the male tent to see my soldiers and SFC Burdin. Shortly thereafter I made my way back to my tent and was pretty much blinded since I didn't have goggles or my neckerchief with me. My face felt, and still feels like I had it sandblasted! Lots of small holes where the skin was once smooth.

During that storm, I had to get SFC Burdin to point out where the LLVT guys were standing on the berm, because the visibility was so bad. My clothes turned brown again...the ones I washed.

When I went to dinner I was all bundled up. That sand storm was so bad that people from PAD 6 ended up over here with us on PAD 1. The company had to do accountability following dinner because visibility was about three feet and people hadn't come "home" yet.

Oh yes, Jason McAnally laughed at me with all of my gear on, but guess whose eyes were burning after that second sand storm?!? Of course not mine since I had my goggles on! [smiley face]

-Allison Rowe

[Gordon Cimoli]

For 2 and a half days we endured (and I mean endured in the most dire sense) the worst sandstorm that this area has seen in decades (again, a quote from the papers). The sand began to blow and visibility got down to less than 25 feet for most of the following days but one night, something very eerie happened--it was 4:00pm and the sun was blocked out by the sand. So much so that the only thing you could see was red light. It looked like we were on Mars. I have pictures of this that you can see when I am able to send another CD home to Stefanie. It was amazing. After that, the wind just stopped and it was calm for about 10 minutes before the direction changed and we got beat again and this time, the sun was completely blocked so it was dark and it was still 2 hours before sunset.

-Gordon Cimoli

[Fred Wellman]

The most important was to fly each aviator and get them a dust qualification in day and Night Vision Goggle conditions to ensure they could take off and land in the incredibly dangerous conditions we faced. Every time our aircraft would land it would be enveloped in a huge cloud of dust.

It is actually not too bad for a Blackhawk because we can see through the chin bubble beneath our feet and the two crew chiefs in the back call out the landing instructions to us. Our Apache brothers had a much tougher time of it. The aircraft has only two pilots and your downward visibility is horrible. Eventually this would lead to losing three AH-64's to crashes during the invasion to take-offs and landings in their own Assembly Area.

-Fred Wellman

[Paul Colbert]

Tallil was a desolate, unforgiving place, evil as any point on the earth. She was mean and indiscriminate. Her dust was endless and her hot breath flowed as free as the oil under her earth. Literally in the middle of the desert, we arrived in Tallil the beginning of April and stayed there a little over six weeks. There wasn't a single day that the weather didn't play some kind of factor in everything we did. Many days weren't earthly. The sky was red as blood, as though you walked out of your tent and onto the face of Mars. Even though the aircraft were mere hundreds of feet away, they were awash in dirt and dust and sand almost daily. When the weather did break, though, we never really flew any important missions, which made our stay at Tallil even more unbearable. There wasn't a single day that all of our gear wasn't covered in a fine layer of dust from the blowing wind. And if the dust and weather didn't kill you, the bombs would.

-Paul Colbert

Chemical Attacks

From the very beginning U. S. forces took the threat from a chemical attack to be real. Extensive training was done by all in quickly donning the protective mask and suit with any indication of an incoming missile. Saddam Hussein used chemicals against Iran and the Kurds in northern Iraq. The constant drill of putting on the mask at all times made for some interesting stories.

[Gordon Cimoli]

Finally, a bit of humor (although it may not seem like it from your perspective): Last night we were all performing various missions and some of us were relaxing. The sun was down and it was almost fully night. There was a light breeze blowing but it was pleasant. Kenny Somkovic and I were standing outside when we saw a huge explosion. We saw a wall of sparks fly up in the air and could see the splash from the explosion. Within a second we heard the blast. We also felt the shock wave as it hit us. From what we could see it was no more than 100 meters away. With that, we ripped open the door to our tent and saw 5 people scurrying to gather their helmets, protective masks and body armor. Kenny's bed is closest to the door but there were others (who do not live in this tent) trying to get out. SFC Cross had a canteen cup of coffee in his hand and was trying not to spill it. I was trying to push past Eric Baucom and SFC Cross so I could get to my mask. It was like the Dr. Suess book where the two guys travel on the same path and neither will move out of the other's way...anyhow, I could see that he was holding his breath (so not to breath chemicals) so I let him by. SFC Cross's coffee was spilled and he was scattering to the end of the tent as I passed by. I gathered my mask, put it on and saw that everyone else had theirs on too. Fred Sullo and I helped each other get our body armor on and we were all preparing to head to our bunker...with our full chemical suits on...finally, SFC Harris yelled that it was explosive ordinance disposal (EOD) detonating something. So, we took our masks off and started telling war stories about where we were when the explosion happened. It was interesting and I know it doesn't sound funny, but to see everyone scattering for their gear was pretty funny...Eric Baucom said he tripped 3 times on the way to his tent.

Wednesday, March 19th

I have been staying up very late to keep myself on a night cycle. This morning I was sleeping in our tent and was totally shocked out of my deep sleep. I heard someone yelling and heard a horn blowing-there was a man standing in our tent yelling at us. I quickly realized that he was yelling, "GAS, GAS, GAS" and that he had his chemical protective mask on. As my friend Fred says, I levitated off of my cot and my sleeping bag flew open. I held my breath and began the search for my mask. In the background I could hear a loud marina horn being sounded as a warning that a chemical attack had taken place. I found my mask and began putting it on. It took a few seconds. I felt my eyes burning and my heart beating very fast. I was scared. Really scared. I thought, "my eyes are already burning, we are done." I got my mask on and settled down enough to realize that my eyes were burning only because I only had 4 or 5 hours of sleep and that we would be ok. I calmed down and kept hearing the alarms going off and people yelling, "Gas, Gas, Gas." I thought, Wow, Saddam did good. He gassed us and took the surprise out of our attack.

Things calmed down and we were finally given the "all clear" call. Apparently someone was wearing their mask to keep the dust out of their eyes and someone else saw it and figured we were under an attack. So, it turned out to be a false alarm but I must say that it was certainly the most scared I have ever been.

Sunday, March 23rd

3:00am: In my sleep, I heard a series of explosions that sounded pretty close by but I wasn't sure what it was and thought it may have just been a dream. I stayed sleeping then heard someone yelling, "GAS, GAS, GAS!" I grabbed for my mask. Everyone was putting their mask on and Howell was in his MOPP suit (now called JSLST) in a heartbeat. Somkovic was still sleeping so Howell kicked his bed and yelled at him, "Dude, wake up, GAS, get your mask on."

There was a flurry of activity in the tent as people put their suits on. About half the people put them on and the other half, including me, just put our masks on and stayed buttoned up inside our sleeping bags. I asked Fred if he heard a boom and he said he did so we started thinking that it may have been a Patriot shooting down a Scud. We stayed in our sleeping bags with our masks on waiting for the, "All clear" signal. It came at 3:30am and we went back to bed.

Tuesday, April 1st

At 8:55am we were all awakened by three loud booms that were fairly close. We looked at each other, a bit alarmed, but chose to fall back asleep. We figured it was another EOD explosion. A few minutes later, we heard the frantic yells of, "GAS, GAS, GAS." We all jumped up, put our masks on then our MOPP suits and stayed inside the relative protection of our tent (helps to keep some of the vapor or droplets off of us).

It's interesting to note that when you hear, "GAS, GAS, GAS" you begin to think about what is in the air that you already breathed. You yell at people for leaving the flap to your tent open because that will allow contaminants to more quickly fill your area. You look around and try to see signs of an actual chemical attack, i.e., dead animals (not many here), people acting strangely but it seems that your hearing becomes more heightened because you listen for people showing signs of duress, you listen for radio calls and you listen for signs of more attacks. It's just eerie that the air you were just breathing may not be breathable any longer.

In the event of an actual attack, we would have an interesting task ahead of us. We would have to leave our area with only the gear necessary to fly. We would leave everything here and in most cases, it would all be bull-dozed and burned to ensure the contamination didn't spread. We would then fly to an upwind, safe location and decontaminate our aircraft and personnel then wait on the supply system to kick in to replace all the stuff we lost.

We hung around for about 15 minutes before adventuring outside to see what the rest of the camp was doing. Everyone was in full protective clothing and we received word that a rocket was shot at Objective Rams (our assembly area here) and a Patriot shot it down. So now we just had to wait on the results of the chemical tests to decide whether to stay in or get out of MOPP. Within 30 minutes we heard the, "All clear." Fred and I stood and looked up the berm towards the battalion TOC and saw them take their masks off so we did too.

Wednesday, April 2nd

1:00am zulu: Woke to the sounds of, "GAS, GAS, GAS!" Put my mask on then fell back asleep until we were told to put our full protective suits on. Put the suit on then covered up and went back to sleep with the full gear on. You learn quickly how to sleep in any environment.

-Gordon Cimoli

Fighting Boredom

Sometimes you have to make the most of life no matter what the circumstances. For many, long hours of work ensure no free time and no opportunity to get bored. When one does have free time, finding something to do can be tedious. At home, one could always be with family, visit with neighbors and friends, watch TV, go shopping, piddle around in the house or yard, stay busy with a hobby, or follow one's children around the park or homework pile. In Iraq, the choices are more limited. Many spend hours watching DVDs or playing hand held games. Some read, some write and some use their imagination.

[Gordon Cimoli]

In terms of our daily lives, I have nothing incredibly noteworthy to report. We did hold the first annual Balad Dum-Dum sucker eating contest here in the Raptor camp one night about a week ago (don't worry – we promise to pass the tradition to some other poor unit for the 2nd annual event). The brave participants were allotted 2 minutes and 30 seconds to consume as many Dum-Dums as possible (including the unwrapping time). SFC Karl Cross (representing 2nd flight) held a commanding lead with a 23 sucker record until the final participant, 1LT Josh Karkalik downed a champion 28 suckers! While 1LT Karkalik (representing 1st flight) walked away the definite champion, as the official judge I awarded SFC Cross the "style" prize. It was a sight to see. Other participants included CW2(P) Gordon Cimoli, WO1 Phil Pillittere, CW2 Randy Smith, CW2 Dave Woodward and CW2 Shawn Holmes. I'm not sure if you should be proud of them or not, J but they did eat a lot of suckers. Peer pressure goes a long way (and I "suckered" them all into this challenge). Thanks to whoever sent the bag of 400 Dum-Dums — they gave us a good hour of amusement anyway.

-Gordon Cimoli

[Fred Wellman]

We are fortunate that we are busy though. Busy soldiers are happy soldiers. But, we are planning a day off in June complete with the Division Band, sports tournaments, food and the "Strongest Man in Iraq" contest. This will involve several feats of strength including the trailer lift, the big ass rock carry, pulling a HUMMV and other challenges. It should be entertaining and hopefully we will not create any hernias in the process.

-Fred Wellman

[Gordon Cimoli]

We made it through all that a little worse for wear. We hadn't shaved in 4 or 5 days and no one, not even the Command, cared because we didn't have any extra water other than what we had to drink. Prior to leaving Kuwait many of us had decided that we would go to war with a new look, so between times of suspected GAS attacks, when we were all in MOPP 4 (full chemical suits and masks) we shaved some heads. There were a few of the guys who were reluctant to get into the spirit, but after trying to dig the sand and mud of 4 days in the desert out of their hair, pretty much everybody is completely bald. So now Chad Fenner and Matt Sheridan don't feel so left out. There is still a small group of non-conformists though led by CPT "Team B that's you Smitty" Smith, the Kurdish Guerilla Fighter Kamran Gardi and their band of minions to include Ed Jewel, Todd Peterson, Kenneth Martin, Christopher Robinson, Brandon Urell, and Benito Belgrave. Even Sam "The Don/ Wookie" Denardi has lost his curly locks. Now to make up for the loss of hair on the head most of our crews are sporting some wonderful (slightly out of regulation) mustaches; although SFC Rodney Harris' looks a bit like pre-pubescent peach fuzz.

-Gordon Cimoli

[Paul Colbert]

Sanity is a precious thing, but variety isn't the spice of life, garlic is. We eventually built on our tent and built on our tent and built on our tent, to the point that we had the outer part of another tent connected to the front of our tent as a patio. During the first part of Balad's occupation, we were fortunate to make runs to the other side of the airfield to pillage and plunder. We found everything imaginable, but the one thing of note was paving stones. All the buildings and hangars were offset from the road by about a hundred feet, and each had a 6'- 7'-wide walkway leading up to them made with concrete paving stones. Well, for our tent, we would go over every day and get as many as we could steal. Eventually, we got to the point where we had run a walkway in between our tent and the Operations Sections' tent, a walkway from our tent to the taxiway (we lived on one of the main taxiways leading from the hangars to Runway 30 Left), and a patio that was and still is the envy of the company. We traded Joe Schneider's cold Pepsis for a SEE (Small Earth Excavator) for a day. That guy hauled load after load of gravel for us to put in front of our tent.

We eventually were able to spread the pad large enough to cover an area about 4 inches deep over about 400 square feet. On top of that, we leveled and evenly placed the paving stones. Beyond that, Scott Curtis got crazy and even brought in bucket loads of sand to sweep between the gaps of the blocks to hold them in place and keep them from shifting. It was about as professional as you could get in the center of Iraq, and we spent many, many mornings and nights on that patio drinking coffee, eating dinner, and telling lies. I eventually took one of the broken paving stones that was roughly shaped like a home plate and painted it black with colored writing. It said, in the best cursive I could muster at the time, "The Persian Pub, Drinks, Dancing and Tomfoolery; Angst served fresh daily – inquire within." It was our catch-phrase and a simple token at humor that always had a way to make me laugh at my own humor, scarce as it might have been in the summer heat.

The most memorable part of our "pub" was the first meal I cooked. I had brought my MSR Whisperlite stove with me from the get-go (I've since replaced it with an Optimus that my brother, Butch, bought me because the MSR was almost 10 years old and didn't fare so well in constant exposure to high heat and sand), and I finally got the first package from Mandi with pasta, sauce, and salmon. We also got garlic, which would change the face of condiments for the rest of the war. I whipped up a not-so-fancy meal that will probably be remembered by everyone in our tent.

It wasn't the best meal, nor was it the best tasting, I'm sure, but when you reach that 6-month mark and the only thing that's gone down your gullet has been MREs, chow-hall food, and MKT somewhat-lukewarm blue-green eggs, you'll welcome pasta with fresh, piping-hot sauce, and a little bit of fish (I added the salmon to the sauce for no specific reason other than its physical presence). We ate in almost total silence through the first bites. It was the first real, home-cooked meal we had had since February. I'll never forget that, and I'll never forget the Pub.

-Paul Colbert

[Gordon Cimoli]

We have many blossoming carpenters here. Every day there is a new wood project begun, and sometimes we actually finish some. We now have a horse-shoe pit and we had an improvised pool (about 8 feet in diameter), although it only lasted for one night and promptly fell apart the next morning spilling all 3000 gallons. That's okay – there is plenty of dust around here to soak it up. There is a big wooden porch/veranda/thing in construction now that shows some strong potential. CPT Dave Smith, our resident civil engineer, is our foreman. And between these things we still find time to do our job.

-Gordon Cimoli

Chapter Three
The Green Zone

[John Galt]

Wednesday, November 12, 2003

We'll bite the dog.

The CPA is divided into two groups--those working with the Iraqi Ministries and the Support Group. The military arm, known as the Joint Task Force 7 (JTF-7), reports directly to the Administrator, Paul Bremer.

I will be working with the Support Group to coordinate among the Iraqi ministries, JTF-7, Coalition government agencies and other non-government organizations (NGO). Part of the time I'll coordinate, and part of the time I'll be a referee (just without a black & white striped shirt and whistle).

My first function is to help transfer responsibility for the Iraqi guards, about 50 thousand strong, from the Coalition military to the Iraqi Ministries. The concept and breadth of this task changed significantly this weekend with the decisions to accelerate the transfer of self-government and responsibility to the Iraqis.

This type of shifting of duties and responsibilities from the CPA/Coalition Forces to the Iraqis has a key theme – the Iraqis and the world will have to really stretch to blame the Coalition for Iraqi violence upon Iraqis once they are in charge.

While walking back into the compound around the large Palace housing the CPA HQ, a female U.S. Army guard on the Green Line check point was laughing. I asked why. She said it was because her job is to guard the crack U.S. Marine anti-terrorism guards around the CPA building. ;-)

Good News!

Today I received a report from USAID, distributed widely within the CPA, that details what has happened over the course of the last few days and most of it is good! The progress may not seem fast as there's not a new hospital being built everyday or unemployment problems solved overnight, but this is progress and there are lots of people working very hard on these accomplishments. You can't walk a mile without taking the first step. Here are some examples of those first steps:

- Two hundred teachers in Baghdad were trained on how to train other teachers in student-centered learning methods and improved teaching techniques. Teachers all over the country will receive this training.

- 3,600 new jobs for Iraqis were created in Mosul, mostly helping to repair the municipality's infrastructure.

- A former Iraqi basketball star from Kirkuk will head a multi-ethnic youth basketball team formed in an effort to reduce ethnic tension among Kirkuk's youth. The team includes Arabs, Kurds, and Turkmen and is sponsored by the Local Governance Program, which will also supply jerseys and equipment. The team will play in a regional championship in Arbil and will continue to play throughout Iraq, including in Ar Ramadi and Al Fallujah.

It's a slow steady climb, but we will get to the top of the hill.

Friday, November 14, 2003

First Week Impressions

I'll brave forth with my initial impressions. Let's see what we think in six months!

The Wild, Wild East. Baghdad is a wild, wild place. Probably much like our Wild West. American pioneers built, without a blueprint, a democracy and free economy in a new land. Our Wild West had lots of law-abiding citizens, school moms and churches. It had stores and shops in an exploding economy. But our West also had some parlors of ill repute that entertained the energetic and sometimes lawless transients. Baghdad is like our Wild West. Baghdad even has an on-going shoot out between good and evil.

Pushing a String Up a Hill. There is so much to do, big and small, to rebuild a country that has been destroyed by many decades of dictatorship. The task seems inhumanely monumental. Confusion and complexity are the norm. But the Coalition forces and nations have a single, guiding star toward which they are steering: A self-governing, free Iraq.

Thousands of little decisions are made every day by the staff at CPA and individual soldiers, as we all work side by side with the Iraqi people. Thoughts and practices that are standard in little towns in USA, England, and the other democracies of the Coalition nations are unconsciously being put into practice. I admit the old hands can become very frustrated, impervious to their progress. We are pushing a string up the hill – ugly, inefficient, and sometimes exceedingly difficult, but it is being done successfully.

Perspectives. The rapid changes in Baghdad, occurring alongside the possibility of spontaneous violence, result in interesting perspectives. Was the gunfire a simple crime or terrorism? Do I get my next anthrax shot or try to skip it? Take my helmet? Flak vest?

Noises at night are very suspect. A door slamming can sound like a mortar--very muffled--or like a rocket--very sharp. You learn if tracers are close or far away by their color and trajectory. And a smile, or a hello from your co-workers, means so much more as they are a part of a small band that stands in harm's way.

Star Wars Bar. The CPA looks like the bar scene from the first Star Wars! Different characters from nations across the world, and many armed to the teeth with weird weapons.

Sit down to lunch and it's amazing what you observe: a South African guard puts his rifle on the table so he can grab a quick bite; a USAID worker focuses on and discusses child care issues; members of the British Army gather at one end of a table, with Lithuanian contactors at the other end.

Language? Take your pick.

Welcome to our World.

Sunday, November 16, 2003

And They Call It News

I was in the palace when the mortars were falling last week. I was literally simultaneously e-mailing back and forth to the US during the "attack." I was telling friends about it before it was reported.

Unfortunately, CNN blew the whole thing way out of proportion. The mortars all landed in an empty parking lot. No one was hurt. No one was killed. No one was quivering with fear in a bomb shelter. Nor did anything burn as reported by CNN, although CNN showed stock footage of a burning Iraqi personnel carrier while reporting about the "barrage." It also wasn't a barrage. A barrage is usually dozens upon dozens of shells.

Why do they have to make everything look even worse than it is?

Monday, November 17, 2003

The Missing Day

Sunday at the CPA is like Tuesday back home. Friday is the Muslim Sabbath. Friday at the CPA is more like Saturday at home, making Thursday night our Friday night. (Confused yet? Don't worry, it gets worse.)

So Friday morning is like Saturday morning. But, that means that Saturday at the CPA is a regular workday since Friday was a light workday. But it's still Saturday as we can access college football games and news via the net, so no one's fooling us.

Sunday at the CPA isn't observed like a Sabbath back home, so we work. Since it's our second day at work (remember Saturday is a workday), it's like . . . Tuesday. So Sunday at the CPA is like Tuesday, Monday is like Wednesday, Tuesday is like Thursday. Wednesday is like having another Thursday, since it's in the middle of the week. Then Thursday is again like Friday because of the Sabbath the following day.

So, what happened to my Monday? Everyone at home really hates Monday and here we've successfully eliminated Monday by screwing around with the work schedule. Who stole Monday??

We miss Monday mornings. That's your time to get a cup of coffee and complain. Complain about your job, about the Cowboys not playing better, about your spouse and kids. I miss it. Not that I don't like my job, but where is that traditional start to the workweek?

It's CPA Tuesday on Sunday.

Where's Monday? ;-)

Tuesday, November 18, 2003

D.C. Hubris

We see on the news that Senator Kennedy and others continued to show their displeasure with the U.S. Iraqi policy.

Kennedy questioned the number of security forces and implied that the Administration and, indirectly, the CPA are lying.

For real fact finding, I invite Kennedy to Iraq with no cameras, no aides. We'll give you a list, a map showing the location of every captain, sergeant and private who call Massachusetts home, and a helicopter to use. Pick any to visit. Go talk to them. Then let us know what you think, Senator.

Wednesday, November 19, 2003

Guard how?

I was just on the receiving end of a lecture from a U.S. Army officer that many of the remaining embassies in Iraq do not want (1) U.S. Army protection, (2) concrete barriers, or (3) Iraqi guards. She then demanded to know how I plan to provide for the embassies' security?

My answer – nothing changes. Nothing.

If we were to bow to those demands, they are as good as dead. They are in Baghdad, for goodness sake. Have they not been paying attention? The embassies want to wish away their physical protection and use "hope" as their security.

I have no sympathy for them if that is what they really want.

But nothing is going to change. There are too many others, mostly Americans, involved. The men and women of the 1st Armored Division (AD) are in charge of that area and feel a responsibility to the embassies.

The U.N. ordered the 1st AD to go away and removed their barriers as well as the Iraqi guards. Many of their people died due to their arrogance.

And the bad guys think they've won and they go after more of those trying to protect the rest of us. Well, not on this watch.

Thursday, November 20, 2003

How to Define What is Important

Today many innocent people lost their lives and were injured by two terrorist attacks directed at the British in Turkey. President Bush is in England, strengthening our ties with our closest ally. So, what are the new stories getting the most play in the U.S.? Michael Jackson and JFK.

Peter Jennings is trumpeting his JFK special on TV tonight and saying that was the world's worst crime. Huh? And how is a murder that occurred 40 years ago of more interest than what is happening right now, in real life?

Friday, November 21, 2003

The Donkey Cart

Terrorists made a rocket attack on the Ministry of Oil and a hotel just after 7 AM in Baghdad. They launched rockets from a donkey cart. Most of the rockets did not hit anything and the damage was rather light.

The American press painted it as a big success for the terrorists. The Chicago Tribune on 22 Nov said it was a "well-orchestrated" attack by the "tenacious insurgency" that "flew in the face of America's prowess" with a "brazen salvo."

C'mon! The rocket attack failed.

First, it was a daylight attack because the bad guys are denied the night. There have been no attacks on the CPA for 6 plus days because of aggressive Coalition night actions: AC130, Apaches, OH58's, M1, M2 and infantrymen. In desperation, the terrorists made a makeshift launcher for a day attack. And most – say again – most of the rockets did not fire. Those that did fire resulted in little damage and injury.

In military terms, we're on the offense and the bad guys are doing worse.

P.S. The Iraqi police captured the donkey and interrogated it for two hours. Nothing.

Our CPA interrogators took the donkey and questioned it for three hours. Story is that the donkey still ain't gonna talk. That donkey's one tuff customer. ;-)

Monday, November 24, 2003

If Not Now, When? If Not Here, Where?

The CPA and the Iraqis have to make decisions every day, some seemingly simple, others exceedingly hard. Many decisions may be viewed as unfair because of past practices or injustices or one's status with the previous regime.

In the last several decades difficult economic, political, and legal decisions were avoided by a dictatorship that could easily print more money, deprive citizens of basic needs, dictate action regardless of consequences or, worse, kill those who got in his way.

The CPA and the Iraqi government are trying successfully to overcome tremendous challenges without existing policies or procedures on how to accomplish these tasks. The simplest things may have to be reviewed or agreed upon by 30 different Ministries – a difficult and mind-boggling undertaking. I believe this difficulty is not understood by the American public or the various governments of the World.

For example, we need ID cards, like our drivers' licenses, for our 50K+ Facilities Protection Service (FPS) guards, and the 65K+ Iraqi Police. (The list continues but we'll start with these individuals.) We need to buy the machines that are used to make the cards, which requires that we obtain the funds to pay for the machines. Can't use Iraqi money per CPA mandate. So, we have to use CPA money. That will take at least 90 days to process. Okay, working on that.

Now, how many machines do we need? Someone must call the FPS to find out exactly how many guards are located where. FPS doesn't have permanent offices from which a quick report with the information can be generated.

How do we call them? Use cell phones. We just got 100 cell phones and are trying to link up with the appropriate Iraqis to hand them out.

Before handing them out, however, FPS wants us to make sure they have authority to do so, in writing, from their Ministry of Interior (MoI). Okay--but MoI needs a policy decision made by the CPA Senior Advisor to the MoI. All right, another step.

And this step must go through all 25 CPA Senior Advisors for approval and comment. (Okay, I "cheated" and did this before the ID card requirement was an issue.)

50

Now I have to wait to get it signed. And wait. While we are waiting, the foreign embassies tell us they want their guards to get cards first, and they want special uniforms for them.

The above consumed three long, hard days, interspersed with lunch, supper, sleep, mortars and sleep.

To accomplish the simplest tasks, we first must build the policies and procedures, within both the Iraqi Ministries and the CPA, from scratch. There is no baseline or framework from which to start as the old regime made up rules as they went along, and those rules were made to benefit them, not to establish policy or procedures.

So our requirements are do the Harder Right, not the Easier Wrong.

Do it now. Do it here. Or it won't be done right.

Tuesday, November 25, 2003

Eid al Fitr & Thanksgiving

Eid al Fitr is three days of thanksgiving after Ramadan ends to allow Muslims to benefit from and enjoy the blessings of the holy month. Muslims all over the world celebrate Eid al Fitr.

The Baghdad night sky is aglow with the total spectrum of lights as they celebrate Eid. The fast of Ramadan is broken. Day and night, the Muslims of Baghdad celebrate with their family and friends.

I was invited to a supper feast last night. Having been in the Middle East before, I prepared by not eating during the day. My host picked me up in his private car and we drove though the city. The streets were full, shops had new appliances in the windows, and the grocery stores had a bounty of fruits and vegetables that were not been seen during the last ten years of the dictatorship. People were hustling to and fro to visit their neighbors.

My host showed me old-world hospitality, serving a wide variety of dishes. Unfortunately, I can't remember all the Arabic names. We started with chickpea soup. The main course consisted of several selections, including fried flat breads with bulgur wheat stuffing, flavored with a hint of cinnamon and cardamom. Another item was a large, golden puff pastry about the size of a medium melon. It was filled with ground meat, potato, pasta and seedless raisins. For seasonings I detected nutmeg and cardamom. The main meal was rounded out by delicately fried fish, kabobs, steaks and plenty of olives and roasted vegetables.

Desert was equally delightful. My host's wife prepared her special banana pudding with a hint of coffee. Cakes, cookies and fruit flowed across the table.

Tea was served hot in small glasses with a hint of cardamom. Over tea we talked for another hour and a half, discussing Iraq culture and history.

Eid is somewhat the USA equivalent of Christmas, Easter and Thanksgiving rolled into one. (I know that not a perfect religious comparison so don't flame me for it.) Eid celebrates the joy of life. In a few days, Americans observe Thanksgiving, a celebration of the joy of life. I have been invited to another Iraqi home for Thanksgiving festivities. One of the two local Christian churches has already invited us to participate in their Christmas holidays.

Thursday, November 27, 2003

Our Strongest Ally--The View From London

I have had a tradition of spending Thanksgiving in London for the last decade with a good friend. This year, I obviously couldn't come along, so my friend's dad went with my friend. I'm glad no one had to cancel the trip. ;-)

They arrived a few days after President Bush departed England. It's normal for conversation with the locals to turn to President Bush when they learn my friend is from Texas. When a grocery clerk found out, he asked what they thought of President Bush. My friend responded honestly and candidly (not that that would surprise anyone) that he was a great President and making the right decisions. The clerk smiled and said he agreed and thanked America for taking the lead in Iraq. They received similar comments from people in pubs, as well. In fact, not a single unkind word was uttered about President Bush or what the Americans and British are doing in Iraq.

This morning they attended the Thanksgiving Day Service for the American Community in London. Over 2,000 Americans and friends attended the service. St. Paul's is closed to the public for the event. Each part of the ceremony is presided over by a different cleric from the different London churches participating. Each British cleric that commented on Thanksgiving stressed the importance of the tie between our countries and prayed for all the Americans and British in Iraq working to ensure a free and democratic society.

Friday, November 28, 2003

POTUS and . . . Who? In Baghdad

The President visited with the troops in Iraq for Thanksgiving. The troops loved it and it did the President good too. There was absolutely no advance notice except to a select handful of people in Iraq. The Thanksgiving visit by POTUS was the right thing to do.

Almost as surprising, Senator Hillary Clinton (D-NY) visited Baghdad on Friday. In fact I ran into her here at the CPA. She seemed disappointed at the cool reception she got at the CPA mess hall for lunch. Most just stared silently. A few left. I imagine she was expecting a rush of well-wishers: "Look. It's Hillary!" Sorry, Hillary but no, it ain't gonna happen here.

Given Hillary's constant trashing of the Administration's policies and the work being done in Iraq, her advance people get a flunking grade on setting up a lunch to be with the "troops" and other Americans in the CPA mess hall. That was not the right thing for Hillary to do.

Sunday, November 30, 2003

Spain's Causalities

We mourn along with the Spanish:

"Sent: Sunday, November 30, 2003 7:16 PM
"To: All Hands
"Subject: Message from the Acting CPA Senior Spanish Officer.

"Certainly, yesterday was a day of grief.

"In my name, and on behalf of all the CPA Spanish members, I would like to express to you our gratitude for your condolences and support.

"To all of you: From Ambassador Bremer, General Sanchez, Mr. Thompson,... to the JOC Military personnel, HEL Units, CPA Medical Service, 3rd Brigade HQ and Units,... All answered in unison to help us. Unfortunately these things may happen, and when occur they cause pain. But yesterday we all were comforted by your words and your warmth and affection.

"That was something never to be forgotten. Thank you very much. Spain is committed in the Iraq reconstruction and, in spite of everything, others will follow to work with us and to fight terrorism.

"Andreu, Pedro
"Brigadier General, Spanish Army
Acting CPA Senior Spanish Officer"

Monday, December 01, 2003

The Trouble with Transitions

July 2004 will mark an historic time for the CPA and Iraq – similar to when a revolution is successful. The CPA is transitioning to become something akin to an American embassy and Iraq will accept responsibility for running the country commensurate with its national sovereignty. These changes will require sudden shifts in form and function with inevitable internal friction.

The CPA's next and final steps will require establishing the initial fundamental policies and procedures for forming and ensuring the continued existence of a newly elected government. The CPA, against seemingly insurmountable challenges, has already achieved major accomplishments in the areas of basic human needs – food, water, power and access to medical services, all of which are provided at greater than pre-war levels.

The final phase, however, will present tougher challenges. To accomplish a smooth handover of power, one of the most difficult tasks may be to get some of the top CPA leadership to end its seemingly endless philosophical discussions about the more essential elements of governance. The CPA must develop final, concrete policies and procedures that are observable, measurable and sustainable.

Damn the bureaucratic torpedoes, we need to move full speed ahead!

Tuesday, December 02, 2003

Satisfying Maslow's Hierarchy at the CPA

Started the day with a good work out, grabbed a shower (luke-warm water), shaved with cold water (a co-worker tells me it's better for me that way so I'll play along), have clean undies and socks, no mortars, and to top it all off, I put on good smelling shaving stuff . . . all while singing "These are a few of my favorite things." :-)

Friday, December 05, 2003

Pushing the String

Top ten reasons why the simple can be difficult or strange in Iraq:

10. The old currency, 3,600 tons of it, needs to be destroyed.

9. A secretary and two armed expatriates with one dilapidated truck move $68 million in currency from one bank in Baghdad to another just to rebalance accounts. (There's almost no electronic transfer of money in the country.)

8. There was a run at the supply counter for small binder clips and it seems impossible to find small rubber bands. Multimillion-dollar contracts and no way to fix them together.

7. Cable TV in the Palace via Saddam's old circuits has two channels--CNN and a 7/24 porn channel from Europe.

6. It was raining and cold last night. (We're in a desert, remember. And I'm in a leaky tent.)

5. We have good riots and bad riots. (A comment made not in jest during a briefing. I guess it's like the good witch and the bad witch. I was clicking my desert boots together hoping to get out of the meeting!)

4. The PX uses paper coins as there are not enough regular coins. Then the PX ran out of paper coins. Solution? Select candy or pencils to round out the amount of the sale instead of getting change.

3. Army vs. Navy football tomorrow. (Going to be painful. Maybe I can fake a mortar attack.)

2. Printer ink is at a premium. We'll fight in the CPA to defend the last printer! (Actually, I don't have a printer so I hand write notes from the screen. I can talk via sat phone to anyone, anywhere to the world but I can't print!)

And the number 1 reason why this place is a bit crazy:

1. Two Iraqi guys threw another under one of our tanks. Guess the bad guys ran out of IEDs (improvised explosive devices) so they used a buddy. Tough recruiting technique for terrorist. And hard to write up a criminal report when the murder weapon is a tank. (Unclassified report of incident: "Three IZs were fighting, as a CF tank passed the area of the altercation, two IZs threw the third in front of the tank. IPs detained the two, charged with murder. NFI.")

(And just for grins. From the August 2003 U.K. Security Procedures – "Americans often use non-standard English. Be patient. Be aware of the language barrier.")

Sunday, December 07, 2003

Expectations and Remembrance

7 December.
11 September.
Days that will live in Infamy.
Pearl Harbor. New York.
In war, "there is no substitute for Victory."
In Peace, Berlin was raised from the ashes.
Baghdad is next.

Monday, December 08, 2003

Seek and Ye Shall Find

Today's news, once again, focuses on what some are calling America's failure to move quickly enough in Iraq or our failure to involve the Iraqis in their future. That, however, is not all the news, but it is what the major media outlets choose to report or focus upon. But it is there, if you look.

What the major media outlets aren't trumpeting is that democracy is slowly taking hold in local councils in Baghdad, the Iraqi government is setting up a war crimes tribunal for Iraqis to try their own, and the Iraqi government annulled the previous regime's decree that those of "Persian" origin were not eligible for citizenship.

These may be small steps, but they are happening all over the country and the journey will be completed by combining all these steps.

P.S.--I'm still in a tent, still 325 steps from the latrine. But I've lived in worse and I know I have it better than most of the Troops.

Tuesday, December 09, 2003

Wonder What Iraqis Think?

The Department of Sociology at Oxford University and Oxford Research International co-operated in the completion of a study on what Iraqis want. The survey consisted of 3,244 interviews in all parts of Iraq. This is the first truly representational national study in the recent history in Iraq.

They were asked about things like happiness, living standards and optimism; life areas and sense of control; trust in others; faith in institutions; the best and worst things in the past and the future; and the proper role of government.

Some of the findings:

Overwhelmingly, Iraqis want their government to represent all the main groups in society, not to exclude people (86%).

If forced to choose only one form of government to be in place within the next 12 months, respondents choose democracy (35%) over a strong Iraqi leader (29%).

A "government made up mainly of religious leaders" was chosen by only 12%, and the current Iraqi Governing Council by 8%.

Ninety five percent of Iraqis do not think that democracy is a Western construct "which will not work in Iraq."

People also rejected suggestions that democracies are bad at running the economy (83%), are "indecisive" (75%), or cannot maintain order (74%). In fact, Iraqis agreed that democracy "may have its problems but is better than any other form of government" (84%).

We are definitely on the right track doing the right thing with and for the Iraqi people.

Wednesday, December 10, 2003

Brilliant Flashes of the Obvious

An "All Hands Security" e-mail to everyone in the CPA shows the D.C. belt-way bureaucracy has been unleashed. First, there's the notice that this information is only for an "actual attack" as opposed to a non-attack – um, that's peace.

If you don't hear or notice the exploding bombs or rifle fire during an actual attack don't worry. Red strobe lights on the towers will flash. (Not sure if you can see them from the bar in the Al Rasheed hotel.)

For those who are visually impaired, after the attack starts the public address will slowly announce "Take Cover."

Besides this basic information there are five, five, other attachments:

1. Fire Guidance. 489 words. Basically says "Shout Fire." Oh, please! And "refrain from using cell phones, and Internet (their emphasis) until after the incident."

2. Direct Fire And Ground Attack. 472 words. "Get down, seek cover" if you're in your trailer. If you're at the poolside, something unique: "Get down, seek cover."

Another immortal bureaucratic utterance: "Only minimal sufficient force against clearly identified attackers is authorized (their emphasis) to stop any attack." Sorry, but I'm not stopping to read them their rights!

3. Improvised Explosive Devices Guidance. 459 words.

4. Indirect Fire Guidance. 570 words.

5. Vehicle Bomb Improvised Explosive Device (VBIED) Guidance. 531 words.

In the good ole Cold War days, "duck and cover" was good enough for ther-monuclear warfare. Plus it could double as the instructions in case of a tor-nado.

If you've never been in a very dangerous, i.e., possible combat area, like the CPA, then maybe one should carefully read it all. But, c'mon. This information is common sense.

Which takes me back to my first premise that the D.C. beltway bureaucracy mentality permeates the CPA. I guess they did bring lawyers with them – who else would use so many words to say so little?

Thursday, December 11, 2003

"TGIF" On Thursday

A baker's dozen of new people arrived to boost the manning of the ministries. Lot of work to cross the T's and dot the I's for security before July 2004. Eight recent arrivals, all officers, are working within the Ministry of Interior to help make the transfer of the FPS guards as smooth as possible, despite how the media might report it.

Since Thursday night it's our equivalent of Friday night, one of the tents has some music and cold colas. We're a wee bit heavy on guys and short a few lasses but everyone had a good time. Some breakdance contests. (?) Salsa too – which was danced brilliantly. Boot scootin' next week. (Ah, no . . . I didn't dance. I spared the kids my version of Disco.) And there was an extra patio party going on in the trailer park.

Hey! I finally got a trailer. I'm partly moved in and will finish on Friday morning. I did get to take a hot shower and it made me feel like a totally new man.

Three bangs. Okay. We had three bangs in the Green Zone. The security noise that I mentioned earlier forced me out of bed. The public address blared that there was an attack. Well, no kidding.

I came in the office to see CNN, one of the two stations we can get. It's about 1:00 a.m. so the CPA is mostly deserted. The CNN reporter states, breathlessly of course, that people "dived under their desks"--pure nonsense. I tried to get my deskmate to get under his desk so I could take a photo and send to CNN. He's too busy with the coffee machine, so maybe later.

Anyway, mortars/rockets are serious. Current estimates are that no one was hurt. First attack directed towards Green Zone in three, maybe four weeks. Baghdad Bobs are still, thankfully, not accurate.

Friday, December 12, 2003

The Daily Drudgery of Rebuilding

Rebuilding a country abandoned by a corrupt leadership for decades is difficult duty, even drudgery.

No breathless reporters stare into a camera from the top of a hotel at night to report on the rebuild of the sewage treatment plant or the water flow for 40,000 residents (below). But these acts build a country, brick by brick, farm by farm and watt by watt.

USAID daily report:

"Local Governance: The nationwide Civic Education Campaign will educate Iraqis on the democratic process in conjunction with local partners.

"Power: Iraqi power production is returning to near normal levels after a blackout caused by a transmission line failure on December 9th and 10th.

"Sweet Water Canal: A long-term solution to the canal breach has been developed. Repair of the canal is expected to cause minimal interruption of the water flow.

"Agriculture: Agricultural specialists are introducing new technologies and best practices to address urgent water needs.

"Rural Economic Development: Farmers and agribusiness experts in Arbil and As Sulaymaniyah are setting a foundation for a private-sector based agricultural system.

"Community Action: In Az Zubair, a community outside of Al Basrah, rehabilitation of water flow has benefited 40,000 residents, or 80 percent of Az Zubair.

"Sanitation: Rehabilitation of a Kerkh sewage treatment plant is making progress and will benefit 1.4 million Baghdad residents.

"Local Governance: Officials of the Baghdad city administration and interim citizen advisory council are meeting with US government officials this week to discuss local governance issues in Iraq."

This report shows the immense scope of what we are doing. Unfortunately, it's not glamorous, doesn't involve falling mortars or unhappy people. That's probably while you'll never hear about it on the news.

Sunday, December 14, 2003

Think Forward: The Talk on the Street

I just talked to some Iraqi friends in Baghdad and here's what they report about Saddam's capture.

The people are partying with celebratory fire, "just like any other civilized country, except with a few RPG's in the air." (A little war zone humor from my Iraqi friend.)

Saddam's capture is "psychologically reassuring" to the Iraqi people.

Now, Iraqis can "think forward."

The bad guys are still going to be active. In fact, they'll probably try a "few big things over the next few days just to prove a point." But with Saddam gone the Iraqi people will ask "why the bad guys are hitting us?" Answer – senseless revenge.

From the CPA, we can still hear periodic gunfire and see tracers. It's vastly different from hearing an ambush in the distance or gun ships or car bombs. Celebratory fire can gently trace the black sky and half moon with red and green shooting stars, but can be equally deadly when the bullets return to earth. But how many times will one see this? It's up to the roof to watch!

We're a little tense in the Green Zone. Happy but equally as tense as the Iraqis. The bad guys may have to make a big statement quickly. Guards are alert. The Iraqis are alert.

Something new can be a bit painful the first time around. We'll see.

By-the-By: Welcome to our Weird World!

"SECURITY NOTICE: All Hands

"There will be an unusually heavy amount of gunfire during the next 24 hours. This is due to the report of the possible capture of Saddam Hussein in Tikrit. All CPA members need to take the following measures to protect themselves:

"Stay in a hardened facility with overhead cover unless you are required by your mission to be outside. Supervisors will evaluate all outside activities and eliminate all non-essential functions.

"If you are required to go outside wear your flak vest and helmet until the 'All Clear is Given.' The all-clear signal is a fog horn blast (severe weather warning).

"Recommend that all personnel sleep in their offices or places with hardened roofs due to limited overhead protection afforded by the trailers."

Please tell CNN that I'll be celebrating under my desk (grin intended) with a beer.

Monday, December 15, 2003

SITREP: Captured + 1

Before Capture: Cut wood. Haul water.
After Capture: Cut wood. Haul water.
Saddam is in custody and a burden is lifted off the Iraqi people.
Peace continues, step by step, brick by brick:

Telecommunications: Baghdad's Al Mamoun telephone exchange officially opened for business on December 13. 11,500 active Al Mamoun subscribers are now able to call other active Al Mamoun subscribers.

Power: The 400-kV Mosul-Bayji #2 line repaired; failed last week causing a major countrywide power outage, was repaired and brought back into service this weekend.

Education: 167 teachers, supervisors, and principals, have completed the Training of Trainers program in At Tamim, Al Anbar, Salah ad Din, and Diyala' Governorates.

Community Action Program: The Al Khadhra'a Society for Productive Families--a co-op that produces textile products--is being rehabilitated. It employs 850 full and part-time Iraqis and will benefit 5,000 families.

Captured + 1: Iraq was relatively quiet. But the Coalition and Iraqis believe the hard core bad guys will try something. If today was any clue, their plans are at best spasmodic, uncoordinated.

The weather is supposed to be terrible for next few days. High winds, cold and wet. Why is that important? Bad guys don't like bad weather. Shoot a mortar at the Green Zone and it'll fly away and land in Syria. Hey! Wait a minute! Now there's a unique idea! Hmm . . . just wait a minute. . . ;-)

Friday, December 19, 2003

One Talented Mom

They are some very talented people singing the praises of the troops and what they do:

"T'was two weeks before Christmas, And all through Iraq,
The people still worried that Saddam would be back.
The soldiers went out on their nightly patrol,
Capturing the bad guys was always their goal!

"With raids seeming endless in the triangle Sunni,
We hoped that not all of Iraq was so looney!
We gathered the tribe of Saddam, in Tikrit,
And suddenly now they all started to snit!

"They told of a farm where Hussein just might be
Odierno then called on our boys - from the great 4th ID!
More rapid than Baathists our soldiers they came,
And he whistled and shouted and called them by name

"Now Delta, Now Rangers, Now Cavalry too!
On Green Hats, on Pilots, I need all of you!
Go to that farm and secure it right now!
Capture his butt – you guys know how!

"Off went our soldiers under cover of night,
So stealthy, so quiet with no trace of light
While we back at home were eating our lunches,
Our boys on the ground were following hunches!

"And then it was time for the raid to begin.
The first target came up – empty within!
Could it be our Intel was wrong once again?
No! Somewhere nearby is the wolf in his den!

"And then, in a twinkling, camouflage torn away
In a hole in the ground did their quarry lay
Dazed and confused, right at them he looked,
Did the stupid old fool know his goose was now cooked?

"He was dressed all in rags from his toes to his head,
And his beard was as matted as 12 day-old bread!
How the mighty had fallen, could this be Hussein?
One look in his eyes was to know he's insane!

"Our boys got their man – how proud we all are
The relief in our country is felt near and far
A bath he has had now – yet he'll never be clean
Forever tainted with mass torture and his Fedaheen

"To our soldiers we give our undying respect
You always give more than we ever expect
We hope you can have now a night with some fun
Your loved ones back home say - A GREAT JOB WELL DONE!"

Deborah Sandberg
Proud Army Mom (101st)
14 December 2003

Saturday, December 20, 2003

Capitalism — Good, Bad and Funny

Capitalism has its own truths. One may not like them, but ignore them only at your peril.

We watch DVDs for our principal, and sometimes only, entertainment. My British liaison sergeants brought in small, plastic envelopes I thought were promotion items for new movies. Nope. They're DVDs of very recent releases: "Matrix Revolution," "The Last Samurai," "Master and Commander," "Tomb Raider." All of these I purchased on the streets of Baghdad from enterprising individuals. That's Good. They're counterfeit. That's Bad.

The CPA is helping the Iraqis set up an FCC (Federal Communications Commission) to run the telephones and the internet. The advisor is helping the Iraqi FCC to understand that more telephone lines in a nation with only 4% market penetration of phones is profitable. That's Good. The Iraqi who's leading the FCC program doesn't have a phone. That's Bad. Or Funny if you have a wicked sense of irony.

The Iraqi Army is rebuilding. Privates get about $60 (U.S.) a month. Before the war, Iraqi Army captains made about $6 (U.S.) dollars a month. The first unit through basic training had about a 30% drop-out rate. The knee jerk reaction by the American bureaucrats is to throw money at the problem, forgetting that within the U.S. Military, pay is only a satisfier, not a self actualizing factor. In other words, no one comes into the U.S. Military to get rich, but to serve his country, to take care of the family and maybe helps the kids go to college. Still, the CPA doubles the pay for all the Iraqi Army and the police and the border police, calling it not a pay increase but a hazardous duty payment. That's Good. But it puts into place an instant inflation by increasing pay without commensurate productivity. That's Bad.

I got a haircut today. It's free through the CPA. That's Good. I paid the barber an extra $2 (U.S.) dollars as a tip. That's ridiculous! That's Bad. But when a barber is using a straight razor around your head and neck, I gleefully contribute to keep him happy. ;-) I want to make sure that barber is happy.

Sorta like the most trusted man in Europe in the early 1800s was Napoleon's barber.

Monday, December 22, 2003

Winter's First Night

The seasons change in this ancient cradle of civilization as booming clouds bring cold rain.

Finishing late at night, we run from our CPA offices in a marble palace built from the tears of its people through a maze of sandbag walls to our small little rooms. Distant booms we hope are cloudbursts. Darkness has a cold bite to our ears and nose while our eyes see a spectacular array of stars. But you dare not linger as the night is marred by arching red tracings of spent bullets.

A small radio sings out the local Armed Forces station. A bunch of kids from Los Angeles work in a little office in the Green Zone to push Christmas songs throughout Iraq for those pining for home. We're warm. We're safe.

Winter's first night was celebrated by prehistoric peoples across the world. These primitive people sat around fires and watched the vast expansion of the heavens. The stars spoke of the beginning of spring, a physical manifestation of hope. Winter's first night is the first step in a long cold march to the rebirth of spring.

Tuesday, December 23, 2003

CPA Holiday Spirits

"David Letterman and Paul Schaffer will be visiting the Palace Pool area on 24 Dec between the hours of 1500-1600hrs for a CPA version of 'The Late Show with David Letterman'."

Watch for this wild and wacky CPA group on TV on 24th. Letterman is always good and this place is a treasure trove of funny stuff. At least I think so.

1. Lebanese money is flowing into Baghdad. Seems the radical Lebanese groups are holding meetings, electing leaders and worrying about pension plans and medical coverage. Heck – they're unionized! Now, what kind of friggin' suicide bomber group is that? Can you imagine the meeting in the union hall?

2. How much is enough? $6.3 million is a footlocker full of money. I've seen it. $150,000 easily fills a small backpack. Seen it, too. $1.3 billion is in the vault downstairs. Gonna see it. And my checking account has been balanced only three times: Sinai Multinational Force and Observers (MFO) tour, Desert Storm/Desert Shield tour, and CPA/Baghdad tour. Believe it.

3. We just approved a rush order for ammunition for a ministry. The Religious (Moslem) Ministry! I hope they only plan celebratory fire for tomorrow. Geeze!

4. No Smoking signs inside the CPA. Can't smoke here because it's too dangerous. So, go stand outside to smoke. Get mortared.

5. No "bomb shelters" here. Rather, the new language is "Attack Shelters." I wonder, is attack supposed to be a noun or verb[?] Somehow when I see it, I see the verb: Attack! Just in case the bad guys get lost?

Humor. We have it in Baghdad. I'll admit, however, it's probably a wee bit unusual. I'm sure David Letterman will be much, much better.

Wednesday, December 24, 2003

Silent Night

Last night our guardian angel was an AC 130. About 1:30a.m. I woke up to hear it firing its main gun, a 105 U.S. Army artillery piece with an automatic loader. I quit counting at thirty. Rapid fire. Probably was at about 3,000 feet but no more as the bang to bang was less than seconds. Almost one long bang! Then the Vulcan kicked in. Went on for about an hour. No moon and no clouds. I got up but couldn't see it because it was so low, just behind the palace, away from my view.

The U.S. Air Force watched over us last night.

Pray for a Silent Night to all of Good Will. No bombs, no bangs. At your home. Everywhere.

We are home for Christmas. In our dreams, in our hearts.

UPDATE: 2010 Hours, Local Baghdad time. Two explosions--Rocket Propelled Grenades (RPG's). Low level explosives. Dangerous but not "big." No injuries reported. Midnight service continued with Christmas carols. CNN (our favorite) reports "insurgents try to make a spectacular statement." Thank goodness no one is hurt. And I've heard louder noises during Texas/OU weekend.

Thursday, December 25, 2003

Merry Christmas!

The future is bright.

My thank you to all the men and women serving in the Middle East and those standing watch in the USA over our families and friends.

...no greater love than those who stand watch.

Saturday, December 27, 2003

Small Police Successes

The Iraqi Police caught three suspected terrorists who were filming the sight of the recent rocket attacks. Their video zoomed from the point of impact to the firing position. One particular firing position was not used when the

Police chased the terrorists away, averting possible serious catastrophe. They were video taping new missile trajectories to hit the Water Ministry when caught.

Sunday, December 28, 2003

New Money Flowing

The New Year brings in the new money--U.S. Government money--over $18 billion allocated for the rebuilding of Iraq.

All U.S. Government contracts will be completed under open and public competition under appropriate Federal regulations. This is to help cut down on any real or imagined waste, fraud and abuse, in the U.S., Iraq and other Coalition countries.

The CPA and the Coalition have already made big impacts in upgrading basic services and providing food, water and power. Yes, there are long lines for gas in Baghdad. One key reason is that freedom has tripled the number of privately owned cars in Baghdad and the supply capacity is having trouble catching up! Overall the basic welfare is equal to or better than what existed before the war.

Spending billions of U.S. taxpayer money is a tremendous emotional issue, and should be. The CPA will have to work every program, every day and watch every dime to do the right things. I'm sure you'll be watching. (And you should be.)

Thursday, January 01, 2004

New Year's Parallax

Honest differences exist (see below) in the direction of the work in Iraq. The preponderance of journalists say the U.S. led Coalition is all wrong. Good news is rarely reported as it lacks the requisite sensationalism to attract readership.

Some in the U.S. blame the CPA for responding too slowly. My view – the Coalition has been working for 8 months to overcome two-plus decades of neglect and lack of infrastructure while terrorists shoot at us.

Some Iraqis blame the Coalition for all their troubles. My view – They do not accept personal responsibility. Instead, they look for someone to blame. The

CPA doesn't cut power lines, doesn't steal copper cable, doesn't steal petrol, and doesn't steal food. It's just the opposite, as we are paying to buy, import and install the stuff. Then the "bad guys" destroy it all over again and the some of the "good" Iraqis blame the U.S. /CPA /Jews /Christians /Iranians /anyone else instead of trying to fix it or identify the bad guys.

Some views are true, some only partly true. Somewhere among all the views, mine included, is the real truth. And we'll find that only many decades from now.

Friday, January 02, 2004

A Typical "Day in the Life" at the CPA

Prayer call over the speakers of Baghdad's ancient mosques at 5:45 a.m. usually wakes me up a little earlier than I'd prefer to get up. I'm a light sleeper so I stay awake. The faintest fingers of the sunrise begin to wiggle through the window.

My half of the trailer is about ten by seven feet with an AC/heater unit and a double locker. I sleep half in and half out of the modern sleeping bag. Works like the old one.

I'm warm and dry, unlike many soldiers. There are no chairs or tables in the trailer but I don't need them and can't fit them inside.

The biggest luxury I have is a (shared) bathroom with a shower and hot water, as long as you're careful about synchronizing with the three other people in the unit.

By 6:30 a.m. I head to my office in the palace.

Huge sand-bag walls create a winding pathway through the gravel covering the winter's mud. Walls are continually going up around our trailer park. They are eight to ten feet tall and about six feet wide at the base. It's like a maze for mice looking for cheese. Or maybe there's a beast in here waiting to attack. ;-) Either way, the lanes are too thin for mice or men.

I cut through one of the northern gate guard posts. Two marines stand and check everyone. It's the same guards every morning and the same me but they dutifully check my badge. If you have a weapon, you have to clear it by taking out the rounds and then pulling the trigger into a sand barrel. And yes, a shot is occasionally launched into the barrels. Huge embarrassment for the one that did it.

The palace is as huge as a Hollywood set and it's pretty but without function-- pure fantasy. Inside it is huge, empty, non-functional halls of polished marble and vaulted ceilings.

The CPA has been forced to build anther maze of plywood offices inside the palace to try to make it functional. Solid construction, but carefully crafted so it doesn't damage the building. Only a few holes were drilled into remote places in the walls, away from the artwork, for the communication cables.

And the palace is cold. Someone once asked what's made of marble, dark and cold? A mausoleum. Gee, thanks. We needed that. (But it was funny.)

I zip into my little office in the north wing, west side. The west side is the rocket side but Baghdad Bob usually manages to overshoot and land in the river. We share computers as I'm temporarily staffed with two soldiers from each major command, referred to as MSCs (lingo for Major Subordinate Command). A huge chandelier hangs from an ornate imprinted ceiling over polished (and slick) marble floors that stand in stark contrast to the plywood walls of the maze.

About 1,500 people work in the palace. That may seem like a large group, but it is pitifully small given the task of repairing the entire country after so much neglect, building the infrastructure, and creating policy and procedure, all while trying to stay safe. As with any headquarters, we have many special conferences, meetings and other shenanigans. Wires run all around the building--down the halls, across the ceilings and under the floors. You trip on them, pull at them and tangle with them. The computers that we never seem to have enough and the wires that seem to multiply supernaturally leverage the work of our small work force.

I check the computer for the news. Our early morning is 9 hours ahead of Dallas so we get your late evening news shortly after we begin working. The latest updates are usually provided by CNN or Armed Forces Europe TV.

I generally skip breakfast. Maybe a real cup of coffee and a banana. Then the day begins in earnest – work, meetings, suspense items, missed suspense items, budgets and more budgets!

You know everything's important and immediate but you have the unknowns and the unknowable. But, you must make a decision and go to the next point.

Lunch is big. One of the receiving hall swells with visitors by this time. Another huge chandelier hangs about twenty feet down and thirty feet across in the mess hall. It's so big that although most of the lights have gone out, no one seems to have the nerve or time to get up there and replace them. The food is cafeteria style with a nice selection. It's actually very good cafeteria food. Meals are hot and plentiful, almost too plentiful. This is office work and the calories can stay with you. ;-)

I use lunch to ambush my fellow workers. Even with the proliferation of e-mail, it's hard to connect with people. If you're patient, the old lion taught me, you can catch the swiftest gazelle at the watering hole. I may only eat a quick sandwich, but I get my staff work done by capturing the unsuspecting gazelles.

Spliced within the day are the routines of life anywhere. Laundry – two days max to get it back, folded and washed with clean water.

Mail–APO, taking about two weeks to get here from home. Free outbound letters but you have to go to Baghdad International Airport to send boxes and that's a real pain.

Physical Training–two new gyms with equipment better than most gyms at home. Open 24 hours. You can even log some miles around the Green Zone.

Shopping–Post Exchange (PX) with all the necessities as well as electronic equipment, CDs, and candy. Even a small souk (Arab open air shops) along the road. Cheap tourist junk as well as quality goods.

Barber–works for tips.

Beauty Shop–there's one here but otherwise, ya got me.

Around 6 p.m. you check in with those at home. It's now 9 a.m. at home. Read the Wall Street Journal, New York Times and even catch some morning shows on Armed Forces TV via your computer. Staying connected--that's what helps keep us sane.

The workday doesn't end as it continues well past 7 p.m., with dinner in the mess hall squeezed in at some point during the evening. I suspect the majority of us work at least twelve hours a day, six or 7 days a week. My office has been working until 9 p.m. recently on the budget. It's going to get worse too before it gets better.

While we had some time off during the holidays, my office was open and we worked part of each day. The soldiers in the field don't get long breaks so we old troopers won't stop either.

By late night, we zone out. Catch some news when it's the beginning of your day back home. See how the market is doing, exchange emails with home folks. Double check the calendar over the desk to make sure I know what the next day is. Watch some DVDs and visit in the office. After all, the trailer is too small to do any entertaining there, so free time is usually spent hanging out in the office, unless you want to be alone.

This is Ground Hog country. Every day can easily be indistinguishable from the other days before and after. Progress through days and days of hard work can be measured in inches at the CPA HQ, knowing that it causes huge and hopefully positive changes in the safety and lives of our citizens in uniform and for the newly freed Iraqi people.

At the end of each long day we weave our way home through the maze, looking for new twists and turns. And we hope there are no mortars tonight. Random or "celebratory" rifle fire is not even noticed anymore. The MP company sends out armed motorized patrols to protect us in our wee trailers. And soldiers of a mechanized brigade put armored patrols into the really bad parts of the city. My flack vest and helmet are still right next to my bed. I'll read and listen to radio a bit before drifting off.

AC130 was very busy last night. The 105 Artillery piece was on automatic. It was working the southeast locations and hard to see with the night fog from the river. I can go to sleep with outgoing fire. Incoming fire is a wee bit different!

And I'll start over again when prayer call wakes me.

Sunday, January 04, 2004

Homecoming for the Next Great Generation

They're coming home soon. The ground troops who won the war and are building the new paradigm for peace are coming home.

Just wait. Over 75,000 are rotating back home. Young Americans who left as kids. They return as adults, hardened by their duty to face and beat evil. They join those who recently returned from Afghanistan's burnt mountains, the Gulf's green waves and the Sky's blue horizons.

And they have a story that's worth telling. I just hope we listen.

Politicians and journalists who want to strike and criticize from the sidelines with "questions" will have to scrap with these new, hardened citizens who bring answers.

These Americans will tell you about Ground Truth. Ask and these Americans will tell you the truth from having their boots in the sand.

They'll talk around the family dining room table, their old school rooms, the community meetings, churches and even a pub or two. These young adults will tell, in their own words, the story of the liberation of Iraq.

They will speak of valor of their friends, some who were wounded or died, the honor of their sergeants, and the camaraderie of their peers that kept them going when they moved together into harm's way. They will speak of the horrors of the dictators that murdered Iraq. They will speak of giving food to the hungry, rebuilding schools, providing clean water, replenishing hospitals and, for the first time in a long time, seeing hope in the eyes of a noble people.

They won't speak of their Duty, of their Honor, of their Courage. For that is what they say they found in their friends. They will shun those titles for themselves. But in your hearts, let there be no doubt that these garlands should also fall upon their young shoulders.

They won't speak of being role models for those who were deprived of freedom for decades. They can't see in themselves the traits of honor, personal responsibility and the drive to do what is right that they learned at home and at schools that have made America a beacon to the world.

They will not see their greatest gift to a yearning world - themselves.

They refresh anew the dwindling ranks of World War II Americans honored upon their triumphant return. Another truth is reborn –The tree of freedom is renewed by the sweat and blood of each generation.

Just wait. They are coming. And they will become impatient. They'll see hungry American children, broken American schools, aged water and power systems, inefficient medical care. They fixed it here and they know it can be done. They will accept no less in America.

The Homecoming of a Next Great Generation. Welcome them and listen to them, watch them. Their greatness is to come.

Wednesday, January 07, 2004

Perfect Storm

It's ugly but we'll work through it.

The Diplomatic Protection Service, guards at the embassies, has a similar problem. A few hundred were hired in an unknown and improper manner. So, they should be removed from payroll. Things normally move slowly in the Middle East, but not this time. The Iraqi Ministry of Interior sent the Iraqi police to fire the guards currently on duty at the embassies. Not just those improperly hired. They fire all they can find.

The embassies are unprotected and perturbed.

The Russians file a protest in DC. (I wonder if the protest would have been made if it was night time in DC.) We scramble and get guards to the embassies, eventually. Another growing pain develops into a crisis and is then cured.

And – I can't make this up – It's RAINING here in Baghdad. A real storm.

Welcome to my world, the Wild, Wild Middle East.

Update: Had a small riot by some people who were laid off after caught ghosting as police. They were padding the payroll and we caught them. The riot was only "fair" by our standards--only a few windows broken.

Saturday, January 10, 2004

A Strange New Sound

We've got a lot of different sounds over here. Some wouldn't cause any concern for civilians. A lot do. Today there was a new sound--a strange and distant honk. Not a car. Nor an alarm for incoming.

It was geese.

Heading north along the migration routes outlined by the ancient rivers.

Honking at us humans with our petty existence.

They've probably been following that migration route since before we discovered fire.

It's a nice sound. A sound of life.

Thursday, January 15, 2004

Signs on the Trail

Along the lengthy trail to normalcy, small signs stand out.

During an essential but boring conference with our Iraqi counterparts, our eyes wandered out the window and observed an old man cutting the yard on a riding mower. He wasn't cutting it in long straight lines. He would stop, stand and look at the lawn, then mow a bit in unusual patterns. Soon most of were watching him intently. During a tea break, we westerners were at the window watching this mystery unfold.

One of our counterparts came out of curiosity of what was capturing the westerners' attention. He laughed and pointed out that the old man was doing what he had been told to do and would continue until told otherwise. In beautiful Arabic script, he was writing "Long Live (the) President."

I'm sure he'll be told to change it. And then change it to something else on 1 July.

Suits. Saw more suits today than I have since I was home in corporate America. Two "assessment teams" from America, a delegation from an Eastern European country, and an Assistant Secretary of State. I guess I'll have to start shaving closer for the growing flow of VIP visitors.

Talk about cleaning up, the ladies' hairdresser has new prices and services: (from the sign outside the salon)

- Hair, Style: $20
- Manicure: $10
- Pedicure: $15
- Wax Legs: $10
  - Arms: $10
  - Bikini: $20

I guess we're winning the battle for hearts and minds... and looking good while we do it, too.

Monday, January 19, 2004

We Will Not Forget Them

A terrorist struck again at CPA in the Green Zone. It was a deliberate attack on the Iraqi people, not the members of the Coalition.

It could have been much worse.

As the car jumped out of line to speed through the gate and thereby inflict more casualties, especially on Coalition members, two Iraqi civilians swung their cars out to block it. Two Iraqi police approached the terrorist's car. Then the car blew up.

Without the immediate and unselfish act of two Iraqi civilians and two police, the carnage would have been worse.

Iraqis are defending their country.

And we will remember the courage of those who stood up to the terrorists.

Sunday, January 25, 2004

The Third Wave

They went right past the guards at the gate. In broad daylight. They came in buses. They came in convoys. They came in airplanes. They are among us.

The Suits from D.C. have arrived—the Assessment Teams, looking at security, personnel, and finance. (Quick hint to the teams — we need more security, more people and the release of funds.)

The first wave to arrive in Baghdad was the OHRA people. Remember those brave few who tried to take charge of a seemingly impossible situation, the complete collapse of a nation?

OHRA started with one guard at the doors of the Palace in a hostile environment. Sleep accommodations were wherever you dropped. Food consisted of military MREs.

The second wave started with Bremer. A shifting of political tactics, if not strategy, to meet the deteriorating environment. With Gurka guards on the perimeter, tents and trailers for housing, hot water, cell phones, mortars at night, rockets into the Al Rasheed.

But the CPA is still under-manned and under-talented for the huge mission of building a country. Senior Advisors to Iraqi ministries arrive for 90 days then head back to D.C. to tell their war stories. The new 90-day wonders take time to learn. Or, there is no one official from D.C. to take the lead so the U.S. Military must take over. Isn't it a shame that the largest and most successful free market democracy has a reserve lieutenant colonel as the Senior Advisor to the Ministry of Trade of potentially one of the richest nations in the world? Where are the icons of the American free market?

The second wave ended with the capture of Saddam.

The third wave is the crystallization of the creation of what precedes the distribution of $18 billion aid and will eventually result in creation of a formal U.S. Embassy.

The Assessment Teams ask questions. Then they want the computer to print documents. Oops, sorry, no printer. They then need to make copies. Oops, don't have a copier either.

Then they dine with the masses rather than in an executive dining room, which we don't have anyway. Welcome to our world.

One member of one of the Teams remarks his Secretary pushed them out of D.C. to find out what's happening. The CPA isn't what's happening. The Ground Truth out there in the field with the women and men of the Coalition is what's happening. Accountants want three bids for small municipality work in the field. Three bids? And then the follow up paper work which barely makes sense in English has to be translated.

A regional team can only do a few key projects as others must be delayed pending the completion of endless documentation.

Bottom Line? The budget process so carefully crafted for confusion by Congress and the OMB perchance for business as usual is not meeting the needs of the unusual business of Baghdad. We need more economic and capitalist talent, not bureaucracy. We've got more than enough of that.

I hope the Assessment Teams get that message, and soon.

Wednesday, January 28, 2004

The U.N. Is Coming. The U.N. Is Coming.

U.N. personnel have been in Baghdad since Friday to assess the security situation.

Mr. Annan said, "As soon as we have signs that the practical arrangements and the security arrangements are ready, and that they are ready to protect my people, we are ready to send the mission." (NY Times International, 28 Jan 04)

Months ago, the U.N. Iraqi mission was attacked and twenty-two people were killed.

Sergio Vieira De Mello was the U.N. mission chief. I remember watching his presentation to the U.N. Security Council. He was quite full of himself. Flowing and flowering congratulations for the U.N. presence in Iraq which could do no wrong and a thinly veiled condemnation of the Coalition, especially of the U.S., which could do no right.

De Mello removed the Coalition guards and disregarded security recommendations for his mission and people in Baghdad. He and twenty-one people died in a preventable car-bomb attack. These deaths were due to negligence in ignoring the security recommendations and the arrogance which sprang from that negligence.

As usual, the U.N. cannot make a real security assessment without what we in America referred to as being "Politically Correct." They do not recognize the situation as it is but rather as they wish it to be when viewed from cocktail circuit in Manhattan.

Maybe the blood of the innocent people with the U.N. will provide a sobering appraisal this time around. Security is better in Baghdad than when the U.N. turned tail and ran. But everyone and every organization must have situational awareness and put into place appropriate security procedures as Baghdad and parts of Iraq are still dangerous places.

Annan has to make a decision on whether to support the acceleration of mass elections. Is it possible? Yes. Is it dangerous? Yes. Can the Coalition and the U.N. take precautions to prevent most terrorist activities that would stop a national election? Yes.

However, the U.N. will probably declare Iraq peaceful for national elections before 1 July, then withdraw to Manhattan, issue edicts about their love of peace and criticize any security measures put into place by the Coalition in order to allow the elections to take place.

Then the U.N. representatives will buy another round of congratulatory drinks at their favorite Manhattan cocktail bars, paid for by the U.S. taxpayer.

Thursday, January 29, 2004

The Weird, Wacky World of John Galt

Periodically the CPA issues "All Hands Notices" for information purposes. I have posted some in the past. The latest two, however, truly illustrate what a strange place the CPA in Baghdad is.

The first notice is about the closing hours of the bars and restaurants at the Al Rasheed hotel. The rules, about which everyone is reminded, include "personnel will not handle weapons while under the influence. Weapons are not authorized in the disco or sports bar."

That's probably a good rule as it must be difficult to do the Hustle while worrying about your M-16.

The second notice is even stranger. So strange, that I'll just post it rather than try to explain it:

"ADMINISTRATIVE NOTICE
"NO. 01-A047
"DATE: 29 JAN 04
"*****************************

"Looking for "Original" Nooses from Abu Gharaib execution chamber

"The Ministry of Human Rights has been asked to establish a memorial museum at Abu Gharaib prison. Cafeteria grapevine says there is an individual in one of the trailer camps that has one of the original nooses, and intends to take it home as a souvenir. Such an item is actually property that belongs to the Iraqi people, and would be an excellent addition to the memorial museum.

We are asking for an anonymous return of the noose, no questions asked."

Friday, February 06, 2004

"One thing Iraqis agree on: We are the enemy."

This is the title of an article published in a major U.S. newspaper: "One thing Iraqis agree on: We are the enemy."

Not all Iraqis agree we are the enemy. As a matter of fact, not all Iraqis agree on anything!

To disprove this broad assumption, all I have to do is find some Iraqis that have options other that labeling us the "enemy" and that's not difficult.

I talked to one Iraqi who says that most of the Iraqi people want us to do what we came to do and then leave so they can take charge and get on with their lives. But, he says, most Iraqis think they need time to ensure their basic safety, set up a preliminary government, and start working on economic development. I doubt anyone working here doubts this sentiment is held by many, including those of us working here to give them their country back.

This Iraqi lives outside of the glare of the TV camera or the self-importance of the by-line's author. And he doesn't know every Iraqi. He's just an Iraqi working like many other Iraqis to build a future.

Enemy? No, definitely not enemy. But let's not fool ourselves; we are the enemy to some. But to a far, far greater number of Iraqis, we are not.

Not to the 86 diplomatic guards that recently graduated nor the additional 91 that graduated the following week. Nor to the guards that ran off the last rocket attack even when they didn't have any more ammunition.

I'm not blind – some hate us, but not the majority.

So, don't think that there are dozens of millions of Iraqis that think "we" are the enemy. It just ain't so. And I hope most people can recognize the difference between shoe polish and this stuff.

Tuesday, February 10, 2004

Incursion into the Red Zone

Took a trip into the Red Zone, escaping from the Green Zone. We went to the 82d Abn Division Headquarters at Ar Ramadi.

I made sure to keep a low profile. Jumped into a mid-80's BMW--unwashed with a bump or two. Had a four-wheel drive beat up Nissan as a follow up car. The drivers were Iraqi-Americans.

Although I sat in the front seat, I put on a hat and tried to blend in. Maybe I'd look like a Canadian journalist so they'd take pity on me.

Before the trip we didn't know exactly when we would leave or the route we would take. We went due west on Route 10. West Baghdad is not a good side of the town. Not the worst, but I'd prefer not to be there after sundown--even if it were in the U.S.!

By mid-morning the markets were open and full and there were lots of families in town.

We were noticed. They waved. We waved. We were not a target, at least not a high priority target for bad guys who want to create a reputation.

The 82d Abn HQ is on the Euphrates River (Nahr Al Furat) that is a beautiful dark blue, with hint of turquoise. After our business concluded, we talked outside near the circular garden. I chatted and tossed bluebonnet seeds. Maybe next year, they'll grow for the 1 Marine Division HQ.

It was a perfect spring day. The slight breeze kept the dust down rather than swirling it everywhere. Puffs of clouds sailed along the blue sky.

Monday, February 16, 2004

The Other Transition of Authority (TOA)

There's another TOA. The CPA's internal time line is to have an Embassy set up by 1 June. That's only 106 days left to Transition of Authority (TOA - the new verb to get used to) from a CPA to an Embassy.

CPA has about 3,500 people, give or take a few bakers dozen. And I'd say we're understaffed. Lots of work still to be accomplished before IT hits.

We had a small "it" under CPA control in 2003. "It" was the proper stewardship of $4 billion in immediate aide. For restoring the necessities of life and security.

The big IT on the horizon is a huge tsunami of $18 billion in aid. For rebuilding the infrastructure of a country.

The CPA worked hard and, in my humble opinion, is almost overwhelmed by the $4 billion in aid. The $18 billion may crush whatever is left when the CPA morphs into the US Embassy. We'll need more people, not less.

Noah rode out the Great Flood. Hope post-CPA can ride out the $18 Billion tsunami.

Saturday, February 21, 2004

Escape from CPA Geo-Politics

We escaped to enjoy a beautiful Spring day. Went rug shopping on Friday. Very, very low key/visibility. Old car. No convoys. With Iraqi friends. (Note: Anyone reading this at CPA, don't try it!)

The boulevards were clean and open. Most locals were at religious services when we went out. We got to the rug market about mid-day. The first little shop we visited was run by young brothers.

Carpets were folded square and piled to the rather tall ceiling. I picked out some of my favorite types – rich golden threads highlighted by a medium, bright blue. I crawled all over the rugs on my hands and knees, looking for imperfections in each hand made rug, tied one knot at a time. Perfection.

Prices? Way below unbelievable levels. The rug market has not been impacted by the new expatriate community of the CPA or some of the other Non-Government Organizations employees. The prices seem frozen in the 60's. I didn't have the heart to bargain. But I did – it's a contact sport and expected. Little cups of super hot and sweet tea were served as we looked at the various rugs. I knew what I wanted but needed to act disinterested.

Found a little unique 4X4 silk on silk rug. Price? I'm ashamed to say what it was priced. Price in USA? Yikes.

We went driving around to show my VIP CPA guest the city. He's been out and about a bit but always in a very protective bubble. We just went here and there without any preconceived plan. We accidentally got into a wedding caravan and joined the honking and waving at the wedding party. I suspect they knew we weren't part of the official guest list.

The shops were open. With such beautiful weather, everyone seemed to be at the cafes. Terrific little cafes. And we saw two new pushcarts selling, of all things, hot dogs! Very popular (and there are no Americans around).

My VIP pointed out a new toy store. A big one full of toys. Think what we were seeing. Toys are purely luxury items, not necessities. Someone, without any CPA or Coalition money, purchased a load of toys, brought them in country and is selling them to make a profit. Micro-economics at it's best.

Toys are for children. And children have been said to be God's physical manifestation of hope for humanity.

Hope.

Not a bad day.

Tuesday, March 02, 2004

Your News. Our News

We have a new constitution over here. Two key facts – it was done and it was unanimous. But the devil is in the details. One key detail was a decision on a single word: "the" or "a." Is Islam "the" basis for law or "a" basis for law? "A" was chosen.

I sat with some senior people in the government, in a social setting, and they made light of the serious issue saying that the Council recognized that there are so many different interpretations of Islam, that there is no hope of really saying "the" Islam. Sunnis and Shiites separately claim to be "the" Islam. So it was more a matter of practicality for the group. That's one way to approach the issue rather than killing each other. Two steps forward.

But there was death in Iraq today. During the holy days, some radicals struck. One step back.

The leading cleric said the attackers couldn't be true Moslems. Our ears instantly went up. Is this a code to blame the Coalition?

The cleric said that the terrorists may claim to be Moslems but they were just terrorists and fanatics, hiding behind a peaceful faith.

That's one of the best things I've heard in a long time.

Monday, March 08, 2004

Constitution

Iraq has a Constitution, unanimously signed. Iraq's Construction has a Bill of Rights, federal structure and direct elections.

IMHO, Iraq's Constitution will have to be debated, defended and championed as long as people continue to live in the Fertile Crescent. Today's signing is a successful event and the official first day of an ongoing challenge of freedom.

I hope the Iraqis celebrate their accomplishment today. And get back to work building their country and its democracy in spite of inevitable hardships.

Tuesday, March 09, 2004

The Fundamental Principles of the Law include the following:

(The following is an announcement from the CPA.)

"The system of government in Iraq will be republican, federal, democratic, and pluralistic. Federalism will be based on geography, history, and the separation of powers and not on ethnicity or sect.

"The Iraqi Armed Forces will fall under the control of Iraq's civilian political leadership.

"Islam will be the official religion of the State and will be considered a source of legislation. The Law will respect the Islamic identity of the majority of the Iraqi people and guarantee the freedom of religious belief and practice.

"Arabic and Kurdish will be the official languages of Iraq.

"The people of Iraq are sovereign and free. All Iraqis are equal in their rights and without regard to gender, nationality, religion, or ethnic origin and they are equal before the law. Those unjustly deprived of their citizenship by previous Iraqi regimes will have the right to reclaim their citizenship. The government will respect the rights of the people.

"The Transitional Iraqi Government will contain checks, balances, and the separation of powers. The federal government will have the exclusive right to exercise sovereign power in a number of critical areas, including the management and control of the following national security policy; foreign policy, diplomatic representation, border control, monetary policy, commerce, and natural resources.

"The Transitional Executive Authority will consist of the Presidency and the Council of Ministers, including the Prime Minister.

"The Presidency Council will consist of the President and two Deputy Presidents, and will be elected by the National Assembly as a group. The Presidency Council will represent the sovereignty of Iraq, may veto laws, and make appointments. All decisions of the Presidency Council will be taken unanimously.

"The Presidency Council will nominate the Prime Minister and, on the recommendation of the Prime Minister, will also nominate the Council of Ministers. All ministers will need to be confirmed in a vote of confidence by the National Assembly.

"The Prime Minister and the Council of Ministers will oversee the day-to-day management of the government.

"The Federal Judicial Authority will be independent. A Federal Supreme Court will be created to hear judicial appeals and to ensure that all laws in Iraq are consistent with the Transitional Administrative Law. It will consist of nine members, who will be appointed by the Presidency Council upon the recommendation of an impartial Higher Juridical Council.

"Federalism and local government will ensure a unified Iraq and prevent the concentration of power in the central government that enabled decades of tyranny and oppression. This will encourage the exercise of local authority in which all citizens are able to participate actively in political life.

"The Kurdistan Regional Government will be recognized as an official regional government within a unified Iraq, and will continue to exercise many of the functions it currently exercises. Groups of governorates elsewhere in Iraq will be permitted to form regions, and take on additional authorities.

"The governorates will have Governors and Governorate Councils, in addition to municipal, local, and city councils as appropriate.

"All authorities not reserved to the Federal Government may be exercised as appropriate by the governorates and the Kurdistan Regional Government.

"Elections for Governorate Councils throughout Iraq, and also for the Kurdistan National Assembly will be held at the same time as elections for the National Assembly, no later than 31 January 2005.

"Iraq's security will be defended by Iraqi Armed Forces, working together with the Coalition. Consistent with Iraq's sovereign status, the Iraqi Armed Forces will play a leading role as a partner in the multinational force helping to bring security to Iraq in the transitional period. The Iraqi Transitional

Government will also have the authority to negotiate a security agreement with Coalition forces.

"The National Assembly will be responsible for drafting the permanent constitution.

After consulting with the Iraqi people and completing a draft, the proposed constitution will be submitted to the public in a referendum, which will occur no later than 15 October 2005. If the constitution is adopted, elections for a new government under the constitution will be held, and the new government will take office no later than 31 December 2005."

Thursday, March 18, 2004

Bombs are the Anomaly

Bombs make the news but are decreasing in volume and regularity. The good news is emerging but slowly, losing journalistic coverage to the bombs of a few maniacs.

"An http://news.bbc.co.uk/2/hi/middle_east/3514504.stm opinion poll suggests most Iraqis feel their lives have improved since the war in Iraq began about a year ago. The survey, carried out for the BBC and other broadcasters, also suggests many are optimistic about the next 12 months and opposed to violence. But of the 2,500 people questioned, 85% said the restoration of public security must be a major priority. Opinion was split about who should be responsible, with an Iraqi government scoring highest. Creating job opportunities was rated more likely to improve security effectively than hiring more police."

The allocated $18 billion in economic aid is just starting. Once it catches, employment will soar and people will have a true vested interest in their jobs and their country. Those who threaten the economic recovery will be seen as a personal threat, not some theoretical anomaly that hurts others. Right now, even the friendly Iraqis seem to think that the violence affects others, not themselves.

But then that's about the same with Spain, I guess.

Turning your eye from evil does not prevent evil but promulgates evil.

Sunday, March 28, 2004

Last year, the US only spent $4 billion in economic aid. Starting this summer, it will begin spending $18 billion. Every contact will require 10% be spent for self-protection. That'll put a lot more protection forces which will at least slow if not prevent the bad guys.

And the footprint of that huge, huge amount will create a lot of employment. Unemployment here is high and a huge cause of discontent, regardless of religion or politics. We can see where we literally spend money for contacts and compare that to the sharp decrease in violence. Frustrated people will turn their eye to those few that want to create violence and hatred. That's not a nice thing to say but it is also not uncommon through out the world.

So, with a big economic program to get this country going, unemployment already is dropping very quickly. Contactors are finding it difficult to hire talented people on the cheap. Then the contractors are teaching skills to a population that is willing to learn. Adults going to school are good. Kids going to school are better. And workers feeling a sense of pride in themselves and their town, their province and their country are good.

Wednesday, April 07, 2004

al-Sadr Ants

al-Sadr is a dangerous man. And the Iraqis and Coalition will decisively deal with him and his insurgents. Journalists should not elevate al-Sadr as an irrevocable challenge.

al-Sadr is a petty cleric with delusions of grandeur, garnered from his father who was assassinated by Saddam. He is an intellectual lightweight and over his head in politics. He is wanted for murdering a cleric competitor of the same schism of Islamic faith, a weird personal vendetta even in the crazy Middle East.

al-Sadr has motivated to violence a small part (10%) of a minority schism of Islam. He has about 3,000 hard-core followers, maybe 5-8,000 cheerleaders. His core locations are slums with high unemployment and the perception of disenfranchisement by simple democracy. Many of his thugs are suspected to be remnants of the secret police or Republic Guards.

US Marines appear to have an anaconda strategy in the Falluja, deliberately and relentlessly squeezing this key al-Sadr sympathetic city to rout out the terrorists while causing minimal damage. House-to-house fighting is difficult and time-consuming. The Marines are relentless.

My analysis.

Power Grab. Everyone expected a challenge to the legitimate transfer of authority to the Iraqi government and to the sovereignty of the Iraqi government and its procedures for democratic elections. al-Sadr is a power grab, plain and simple. He makes his move at a key religious time.

Slow Motion Tet Offensive. Combat has moved from terrorism to an insurgency. The terrorists have changed tactics from attacking soft, civilian targets to hitting the Coalition military. Most Iraqis and Coalition states do not doubt the outcome of the battle.

But the terrorists are buoyed by the successful retrenchment of the Spanish government as a reaction to a single attack in Spain. Terrorists are attacking in force the Ukrainian, Spanish and Polish forces in the Coalition. Like the Tet offensive, al-Sadr does not expect to have a military win but to permanently damage the will of the Iraqis and the Coalition.

al-Sadr has miscalculated. The Coalition is attacking, not defending. We are killing the terrorists while avoiding collateral damage or indiscriminate attacks.

Ants. A wise man once told me about the ant theory to control people. You put some sugar on the table. The ants will gather around it and look. One ant will eventually venture forth and go for the sugar. You take a huge hammer and smash that ant. The others get the message and go elsewhere. It's a bumbling homily but fairly correct.

al-Sadr is an ant and will be smashed. Completely and finally. The Iraqis and the Coalition knew the challenge would come eventually. Now the Iraqis and Coalition are decisively dealing with it.

Friday, April 09, 2004

Friday

Well. Very quiet. The bad guys promised to attack and occupy the Green Zone, take over the major cities and storm the Sheraton hotel.

I was on the back veranda of the Palace after supper when we heard the mortar fired across the river to our right. Stood there for a bit & then heard it land off to our left. Later we determined that it landed near the Sheraton. So all last night we saw repeated film of one darn mortar hole at the tennis courts next to the Sheraton. Over & over. Then the announcers ask various talking heads – Is it over? Have we failed?

One mortar produces a lot of gloom & doom.

The 1AD reacted well to the threats yesterday in Baghdad. First, they went around with loud speakers & said that there would be no rallies, etc. The Coalition militaries cordoned off the key center where Saddam's statue was toppled. That is a big PR place for all the western news although it's really a minor location. Same with the Sheraton hotel. The foreign press is at the Sheraton so the bad guys were going to storm it. New principle of war: Don't attack the military – attack the press.

Also the Iraqi police were broadcasting from their cars that anyone seen on the streets with an AK would be shot. No warning. Gee – no one on the streets.

Marines are clobbering the bad guys at Falluja. The Marines offered a unilateral cease of hostilities but the bad guys keep shooting, even shooting their own humanitarian vehicles. The Marines resumed offensive operations.

This weekend is also a big anniversary when the Moslems remember a martyr. There will be a traditional march to the main mosque. Again, threats by the hot heads about a big rally to throw out the Coalition. Should be interesting to see how it plays out.

Coalition has retaken many cities. Some interesting sights as the main population is glad to get rid of the thugs that brought about the latest violence.

Anyway, it was a good Friday.

Friday, April 23, 2004

1 July Defined

The Transition of Authority to an Iraqi sovereign government is only 69 days away. In practical matters, it will be only a date on the calendar. In philosophical matters, it is a brave voyage in a region mired in centuries of darkness.

The press and even some lazy politicians seem to believe Iraqi Sovereignty is an on-off switch, controlled by one all-powerful person. Suddenly on 1

July 04 there is a something evil or wonderful, according to one's preconceptions.

The Transition has already started and is a continual project. The Transition is the collaborative effort of multiple individuals, governments, religions, ethnic groups and non-government agencies.

The UN is probably one of the least respected foreign organizations by the Iraqi people. Saddam cleverly circumvented with the help of the UN ten years of sanctions. The Oil For Food (OFF) project will be the keynote program of collaboration that impoverished the Iraqi people, built hundreds of palaces for Saddam's group and lined the pockets of the UN administrators and several foreign national governments, such as France and Russia. Iraqis consider the UN a collaborator with Saddam.

1 July will squarely set the mantle of responsibility upon the Iraqi people for the conduct of their own affairs. The blame game by pundits of the rebuild of Iraq will no longer be an automatic referral the US and the Coalition. There is no perfect time to shift the burden of self-government. But 1 July is a good day within a long process.

Sunday, May 02, 2004

Show Me The Money

The single greatest error in the Rebuild of Iraq is the lack of speed in processing the US Congress mandated funding ($18 billion in 04) for the Iraqi Rebuild. The Washington DC professional bureaucrats considered the disbursement of approved funds as just "Business As Usual" that has lead to slow political and economic progress, even delaying building security forces.

On 02 November 2003, I posted: "The Center for Strategic & International Studies (CSIS), a D.C. think tank, was asked by the Pentagon to study the progress in Iraq. CSIS was in Iraq on June 27 - July 7 and filed its report: 'Iraq's Post-Conflict Reconstruction', downloadable at their site. One of the key CSIS criticisms is that DC treats the rebuilding of Iraq rebuild as business-as-usual rather than a priority project. 'Business As Usual'--regardless of where the errors or delays lie, it's a sad commentary on our ability to win the peace. The U.S. Military won, not once, but twice. U.S. Troops are still in harm's way in Iraq. The rebuilding of Iraq falls prey to government bureaucrats, Byzantine contracting rules and politically-correct contractor preferences."

I personally worked two programs, one for $110 million and one for $15 million, for security forces for six months. The $110 million was nickled and dimed, bits and pieces according to the desires of accountants, not the people building the security forces. Heck, the $15 million for weapons security, a usable program in Iraq, has still not been spent due to financial bureaucratic bungling. Rather than rant, I will say only that accounts and the bureaucracy delayed the implementation of the program.

The real failure in Iraq is in the lack of timely disbursement of funds that allowed chronic unemployment and disrupted services to demoralize a liberated people.

One year after the war, the initial funding has put in more electricity and water capacity than Iraq ever had even before the war. The $18 billion has not yet hit Iraq. The rebuild was not to restore Iraq infrastructure but to have an overwhelming, visionary program to create a representative government within a free economy.

Mistreatment of Iraqi POW's

Wrong behavior of a very, very small group of people. Arab press has splashy coverage. But when we dig up another mass grave from Saddam days, no Arab press coverage.

The US will show that we are people of law by objectively prosecuting the people in open court and punishing them.

The future trials of the horror under Saddam will be more a defining point to the Iraqi and Middle East situation. Will they try to blame the Zionists, the US, the (fill-in-the-blank) again? Surely.

And the horrors of Saddam on his own people will overshadow disgusting behavior by a few soldiers.

Wednesday, May 05, 2004

EndEx

EndEx is "End Exercise." I am no longer at CPA and am rapidly losing the boots-on-ground view. Without that, I'm just another passenger in life trying to describe a distant truth and probably fabricating truth in the process.

Freedom is winning more than losing in Iraq.

The liberation and rebuilding of Iraq is a huge and positive opportunity in the Middle East that has been held captive for hundreds of years to ignorance and intolerance.

Deeds will fade away in a week or so.

Thank you for your interest, your support and the meaningful dialogue.

-John Galt

Chapter Four
The Stories

The daily life of living in Iraq is certainly different to daily life back home in the U.S. The most obvious difference, and not to be taken lightly, is that this is a combat zone. And being in a combat zone there is the ever-present threat of being attacked. During the official hostilities it was war, the U.S. was on the offensive and it was very intense. Before and after that period of constant danger, little sleep and always on the go with high adrenaline, anxiety and fear, there is a whole another pace to life.

The daily life of living in a tent city, a trailer, or if lucky, a real structure, is not home. Simple things are not simple: always under threat of an ambush, walking a half mile to a chow hall or eating cold MREs, not being able to bath regularly, being attacked by strange "bugs" like camel spiders and scorpions, surviving intense sandstorms, under pressure of extended tours and second tours in a rapid succession, and finding something meaningful to pass the few hours of off duty time. Through all this people live interesting lives.

[Fred Wellman]

When most of the fighting stopped we ended up just south of Baghdad in a little town called Iskandariyah and it was one of the worst for dirt and misery. We had hoped to head south but the Division began conducting stabilization operations in the Mosul area and we ended up with 11 aircraft spread all over northern Iraq supporting the Apaches, flying the General Officers and providing support to the higher headquarters. So, last Sunday we got the word for me to take our TAC (Tactical Command Post) and a couple of aviation maintenance guys up to Mosul to support all of our helicopters which were up there.

Mosul is about 260 miles north of where we were, just south of Baghdad in Iskandariyah. The boss decided I should go up there with my small tactical command post, which is myself and three soldiers, a small tent and my HUMMV with a trailer. So, we headed out Monday morning at about 9:00 and started going north.

Right away it was hilarious. We had four total vehicles in our little convoy. As soon as we left camp we had to turn on to Highway 8, which is a lot like Campbell Boulevard in Clarksville, Highway 74 in PTC or Manchester in St. Louis at rush hour. But there was no traffic light so we could not get on. I waited a minute and in a second there were little kids trying to sell us Iraqi money for dollars. It is a big business here. I was not digging it though because we needed to go.

I got fed up and jumped out of the truck and marched out in the street, holding my rifle in the air and stopping traffic. I did the same thing in the other direction and waved my guys out. They were crying with laughter. They had no idea what the hell I was doing. I guess I just said, "Screw this" and jumped out into the traffic. They could barely drive and my NCO, SSG Swett, was taking pictures. I got in and looked at them and they were dumbfounded... I explained my theory that, "Not everyone speaks English but everybody speaks Machine Gun." They lost it. It was pretty funny I guess...but at least we were on our way. They decided right then that riding with me on one of these trips was going to be more fun than it usually was with my Assistant.

So, we immediately got stuck in this huge traffic jam in the town there south of Baghdad. People were walking up and touching our arms and talking to us. It was a little stressful because a week before a convoy had a grenade thrown in the window of a truck the same way. I just held my weapon out the window and pointed it up to let them know I wasn't playing. But, everyone was so nice. One man walked up and in his best English said "It is good to have you here"...I just said we are glad to be here. It was kind of touching to hear the sincerity in his voice. That ended up being a sign of how most of our day would go.

Interestingly, I know why they must have been happy. About every other block there was a T-72 tank wedged into the alleys amongst the houses. Most of them were very blown up. What amazed us is that they were all destroyed and there was hardly any damage to the buildings around them. I don't know if they were bombed or we destroyed them afterwards.

Once out of Baghdad I brought the convoy to a stop in an area that had lots of trees and grass. Which was one big change around Baghdad and north. It was kind of weird to march out and pee amongst the green....lol. I picked the spot because we had two females in the convoy and I always try to find them a spot with some privacy. Otherwise it is a big pain for them because they have to hang ponchos up between the truck and trailer...and I imagine that it just sucks for them. They seemed to appreciate the thought.

So, as we sat there I noticed in the grove of trees there was a woman and some small children. They were off about 50 yards and hiding from us a little. After a short while a man crossed the highway on a tractor and gathered them under a tree to watch us from a distance. I had put a big bag of assorted hard candy in the front seat of my vehicle before we left hoping to see some kids. I couldn't resist so I grabbed a big handful and walked over to them. I showed the father what I had and sort of gestured to him if it was okay if I approached. He waved me over and the kids started walking to me. They were so cute with big brown eyes, curly brown hair and the biggest cheeks.

It was two boys and a girl and the boys marched right up but the little girl was about 3 and held back. So, I gave them each like three or four pieces. They were so excited. I turned around and two of my guys were standing there with their weapons at the ready. I asked them what was up and they were telling me they had no idea what the hell I was doing. They were starting to think I am a little unpredictable but I am just not scared of speeding cars or poor farmers and their families. I told them that if those three kids remember that an American officer gave them candy instead of the vile stories they hear at the Mosque then maybe that was three less suicide bombers someday. So, it is worth the risk.

So, we mounted up and headed north again. Before long we saw a bunch of trucks on the other side of the median heading south with a ton of people in back waving and yelling. As we got closer I saw they had AK-47's and pictures of Saddam. I realized that they were Saddam supporters celebrating his birthday and trying to be tough. There must have been 10 trucks and over a hundred men. As we passed they started shooting. I assume in the air because we didn't take any rounds as far as we could tell.

I just told my driver to step on it and if he slowed down I would shoot him! I had briefed everyone before we left that since we did not have any heavy weapons in the convoy that if we were ambushed we were driving through and rallying up the road. We just did not have the firepower to put up a fight or try to arrest a hundred people...no way. So we drove through and kept going with our eyes locked on the rearview mirrors for about 20 kilometers.

After that it was fortunately uneventful for about 150 miles. We finally got to Mosul and it is beautiful. The last fifty miles of the route was all rolling hills and grass as far as the eye can see. It looks like Oklahoma or what the American prairie must have looked like. As you drop down into Mosul it is all steep hills and cliffs overlooking the Tigris. We were all stunned. Then as we approached the little airport the kids were all lined up along the road.

They were waving like mad and cheering. They didn't look like Arab children. I think they were probably Kurds or Turks. They came right up to the truck and were handing us little bundles of wildflowers they had made. One little boy handed me some and said, "I love America!". I swear I almost cried. It was amazing. They weren't begging for food or candy... just happy to see us. It was cool. Everyone had been waving at us the whole way. All of the goat herders and shepherds, that are everywhere; all of the people passing us in cars. As a matter fact, SSG Swett, my 23-year-old female Sergeant, was having the time of her life.

All the men were blowing her kisses and telling her they loved her. She was dying and turning all kinds of shades of red. She is so funny. She is a little blonde haired, blue-eyed Maine girl and she really stood out in the back of the truck I guess. She was like "Sir, how come they don't do this to me at home?" I explained to her that in America it is called sexual harassment and American men get sued for it.

Anyway, so we dropped down into the airport only to be told that our entire unit has been ordered to move to the air base 35 miles south at Qayyarah West shortly after we left. I just said okay...but we are sleeping here tonight because after seven hours on the road we were smoked. They let us bed down right in the terminal and I had hot COFFEE and a hot SHOWER!!! Yes, an actual shower. I have not had a "porcelain" shower since we left Kuwait. I had actually only had three washings of any kind...and that is not good numbers in a month and a half of combat ops. (Note: thanks to all for the baby wipes... don't need anymore)

I had wandered into the Terminal's old bathrooms hoping for a sink to shave in and there was a shower room. I was like "oh yeah"...stripped my dusty crappy uniform off and jumped in. Unfortunately, I had to put the same dusty crappy uniform on when I was done but I got the funk off of me after a week and a half without a shower of any kind.

-Fred Wellman

Lieutenant Colonel Matt Gapinski is in the U.S. Army Corps of Engineers living in Jacksonville, Florida with his family. Matt made the local paper when he came home early and surprised his son by showing up at his elementary school.

[Matt Gapinski]

I have spent the last 3 weeks in the city of Hillah about an hour south of Baghdad. Leaving the luxury of Camp Commando, Kuwait was hard, especially when they installed (but did not turn on) air conditioning in all the sleeping tents there. It was an all day drive (350 + miles) through the desert. As we went further north, the scenery actually started turning green.

We are staying at on of Saddam's former palaces. Since anything of value or that was not nailed down is gone, it is difficult to imagine life here with Saddam. The locals say nobody was allowed near the place. It is on the outskirts of town and is actually a pretty nice place. There are flowers and birds here. Of course, since everything was looted, there is no power or running water. We do have generator power for our offices and all our water comes from the river. It is purified and is technically clean but tastes chloriney(?). Before we came here, we all started taking (and continue to take) doxycycline, an antibiotic, because of the sanitary conditions (or lack thereof) in Iraq.

My living quarters appear to be a guesthouse of some type. I live in what used to be a bathroom complex. There are 4 of us. I took the outer, open room with the window so I wouldn't be sleeping in an enclosed room with the fumes and whatever was left in the pipes. The other guys don't seem to complain though. There is also a sink in one bathroom that is unoccupied. I think the Seabees put it in. No running water, but it drains so you can shave and brush your teeth there. The walls and floors are all marble. Rough to sleep on until I procured a cot. The bugs get bad at night so I rigged a mosquito net over my cot. It has not been cooling down as much in the evenings, so it is tough going to sleep. Or once you do fall asleep, you wake up drenched in sweat.

When we first got here, the shower tent was open every other day. Now, we get showers every day. The water is either hot or really hot, but it still feels good getting clean. It is nowhere near as dusty as Commando and not quite as hot, but it is more humid here. I have been able to run fairly regularly in the evenings. My running partner is semi-famous. He is an Elementary school principal in Delaware and was quoted by the President in his radio address about a month ago ("I did not come here to conquer. I came here to help."). He also had an article about running in the desert published in Runner's World magazine. We have to wash our own clothes in buckets and hang them out to dry. The good thing is it is so hot that everything dries pretty quick. Yesterday, it was 108F.

The food here is terrible. We actually prefer to eat MREs (Meals Ready to Eat) that we get for lunch and/or breakfast. The hot food out of the mess hall is called tray packs. Huge trays placed in boiling water to cook the food or whatever it is inside. Somebody didn't do a good job of ordering as we usually have the same thing for 3-5 days in a row. They usually supplement the tray packs with fresh fruit and/or HDL milk (in a box). Luckily, the mail truck arrived a few days ago with mail and lots of packages. (If I didn't send you an e-mail, I didn't get your package or letter. Sorry!)

The ruins of the ancient city of Babylon are right on the grounds here. I was able to go on an hour or so long tour. It was pretty interesting. It was first settled in 2340 B.C. King Nebuchadnezzer, circa 600 B.C, built the famous Hanging Gardens of Babylon, one of the ancient 7 wonders (and no longer here), and the Tower of Babylon. Apparently the Book of Daniel, in the Old Testament, references this same time period. Alexander the Great conquered Babylon around 300 B.C. You can actually see the original stone of the city because it is contrasted by the "Saddam Stones" where he built right on top of the ancient structure.

On Mother's Day, they flew in a Marine Band for a Concert in the Amphitheater near the Ruins. In addition to playing a routine of patriotic songs, they also played some New Orleans Ragtime, which was pretty fun. That was followed by a cookout where we had the best food since we were here. Hot dogs, hamburgers, steak, and cold sodas! We had all forgotten about having hot dogs and hamburgers every day for lunch just a few weeks earlier at Commando.

Hillah is a typical Iraqi town. Practically all Shia (Shi'te). It was probably in the news recently because they uncovered several mass graves there. Unfortunately, there will probably be more crimes against humanity uncovered. I have read an interesting book, "Saddam's Bombmaker" by Mohammed Hamza. He writes about many similar happenings. It also clearly illustrates why France and Germany took the position that they did towards this conflict. It was all about money - lots of money. The attached picture shows a "Saddam wall" in Hillah that has since been covered over.

Everyday life in Hillah seems to be back to normal. The kids are returning to school, which was a very uplifting and welcome site. We visited a local fish farm, where they grow Carp (like our Catfish farms). I know, but apparently it is similar to a favorite local fish. Anyway, the head guy gladly gave us a tour and even offered us a milk crate full of carp. We politely refused saying we had no way to cook it. We had the traditional Iraqi tea in his office. He had even brought some to our drivers who were outside guarding our vehicles.

We have several translators that we use - some Kuwaiti, some civilian American contractors, and some Iraqi ex-patriots. On a recent excursion into Baghdad, we took an extra interpreter (ex-pat) because his son was supposedly in a hospital there. It turns out that he was a Brigadier (full colonel) and band director in the Iraqi Army until he defected to Germany 3 years ago. He hadn't seen his family since. Well, we took a little detour to his house (that's were the attached photo of me with the kids is from) to reunite him with his family. His wife, whom we never did get to meet, was expecting her brother-in-law to visit, so we were served all this food she had prepared for him - Rolled grape leaves, eggplants, fresh pita bread, fresh fruit. Technically, we are not supposed to eat locally prepared food, but in this case, we made an exception. After nervously looking at each other, we even drank the "bottled water" he served us. Luckily, all of our gastrointestinal tracts survived without harm! Of course, we didn't get the full story until afterwards, thinking that he had seen his family since he returned to Iraq. His son was OK, also.

On this same trip to Baghdad, we made it center city, which was/is strictly controlled by heavy (armored) U.S. forces. We visited the Al Rasheed Hotel, which always used to be shown on CNN where everyone steps on a tile picture of George Bush (the elder) as they enter the lobby. Somebody even carved out George's face, as it was no longer there. We also had the opportunity to visit the Ba'ath Party National Headquarters (don't ask). I don't know why, but it had not been looted. Talk about extravagant - mahogany doors, gold fixtures and trim in all the bathrooms. The furniture was still there, also. Plush chairs. We even went on top of the roof for a complete view of the city (snipers weren't out that day).

Still did not see a lot of war damage - other than the destroyed Iraqi tanks and tracked vehicles along the highway. The people are all going about their business. Although major offensive operations have officially ceased, there are still plenty of bad guys around. So when we go out the gate, we are still security conscious (and locked and loaded) which makes it hard to take good pictures. They have traffic jams in Baghdad - we must have hit morning rush hour. Although it may have been caused by people in line to buy gas. It is very ironic that a country with such a vast oil supply is short of fuel (probably due to existing UN sanctions). I think the price for the equivalent of a gallon of gas is $.05 (depending on the exchange rate), which is more than double from before the war. But if I only made $7/month, I wouldn't be happy either. Capitalism took hold pretty quick...

The whole time, we were in Baghdad, I saw maybe 5 women wearing western clothes. The rest were all covered up in black. Although in open society, Iraqi women may be treated like second-class citizens (it is a cultural thing), my guess is that the matriarch still runs the family. One of our other interpreters left Iraq and has lived in San Diego for a number of years. He says he will move back here, but I'd like to hear what his wife has to say about that.

-Matt Gapinski

[Fred Wellman]

We moved into several large "fest" tents. The largest held sixty-five soldiers and the smaller ones about eighteen. We ended up with a few of each and no cots the first couple of nights. Fortunately, they had wooden floors so it was not too bad. It was also cold as hell. The temperatures were getting down in the low fifties but it felt like the thirties and we were bundled up in our sleeping bags every night.

We would have to wait at least a week or more for our ships to arrive before we could do much of anything other than sit around and start coordinating with the other units already there. It was like a reunion of aviators. There were eight Apache battalions, two Cavalry Squadrons and three Blackhawk battalions separated amongst three different Brigades on one airfield. You couldn't walk five feet without seeing someone you knew from a previous assignment.

Every time we went to the Mess Hall I spent half the time shaking hands and getting back-slapped from someone. It was really the highlight of our day to go to meals at breakfast and dinner. It was great chow. Fresh eggs, French toast and bacon every morning and something original and fresh for dinner at night. We were living like kings. So, on the third day God burned down the chow hall.

Well, not God, but a little crappy refrigerator that shorted out and burned down all three tents in one monstrous conflagration. Fortunately, no one was hurt but there went our one joy on the whole post. Udairi did not have phones, internet, or recreation facilities to speak of...but we had a great chow hall.

Without it we resorted to a few days of MRE's before they could organize the resident unit's mobile kitchens into a new dining facility for all of us. Once they got it up we were once again eating fresh if not comfortable. The first breakfast consisted of hard-boiled eggs, lots of bacon and white rice. This was a little different but not bad at all.

The second breakfast was the same thing. As a matter of fact, every breakfast for the next three weeks was the same damn thing. Now, I don't want to seem ungrateful but imagine eating hard boiled eggs, bacon and rice every day. It became a mantra...eggs, bacon and rice. I even made up a Dr. Seuss rhyme:

I do not like eggs, bacon and rice,
They make me not nice,
When I eat them more than twice.

I wrote Crystal that with the diet we were on I would probably have a heart attack instead of getting killed by the enemy. I explained that if I dropped dead I would have one of my Captains put a bullet in me so it is a heroic combat death and she can get on Oprah and cry. She didn't seem thrilled with the plan.

-Fred Wellman

Mark Maddox is a doctor in Bend, Oregon. When he found out he was about to be deployed he and his fiancée quickly got married. Mark has been back home for only a couple of months and expects to be sent over again before the end of the year.

[Mark Maddox]

The Army and being deployed to Iraq changed my life more than I ever imagined when I signed up for the Reserves back in 2000, in my fourth year of residency. My father had been a surgeon in Vietnam and something told me that this was something I needed to do to give back to me country. It really didn't seem like too big a sacrifice at the time – ninety days once every 36 months. That is 90 days in country; travel time and admin time in route don't count. My 90 days turned out to be closer to seven months. This is a long time to be away from my practice. It's also hard on my patients since I'm the only colonrectal surgeon in Bend, Oregon. Now the 36 months is changed to twelve and I know I'll be going back in a few months. I'll do what I have to do and I would never trade my experience in Iraq for anything.

A day a soldier came in to the Combat Surgical Hospital bleeding badly from a early morning HUMVEE wreck. His spleen and liver wore torn and he was in bad shape. We operated that morning and then again that evening as the bleeding still had not stopped. This soldier ended up needing 50 units of blood including eight units of whole blood. It was the first time in my life that I had ever seen a warm blood transfusion. That night as I was making my rounds he ask me if I was the surgeon who operating on him. I said, "Yes." And he said, "I want to thank you for saving my life." That one moment made everything worthwhile. All my previous thoughts and feelings didn't matter any more. After we stabilize our patients we send them to Germany for further treatment. I never knew what happened to that soldier.

Besides being a surgeon for the 31st CSH I also did about six weeks at Abu Graib where we took care of the security detainees. Here we were a target for the bad guys. Not the hospital per se but the detainees in the compound. We received 12-15 mortar rounds every day. I was living in a concrete building but the detainees were living in tents. One afternoon the mortars hit their target. It was overwhelming. We had 92 into surgery in four hours. We couldn't handle it all; we'd triage and send by helicopter to other hospitals. Everything we had was in use. There were only four physicians and some nurses and medics. It took seventeen hours to tidy up the mess.

The one thing that did not sit well with me was having to take care of the enemy. It is an ethical issue. I've sworn to be a doctor and still it doesn't makes sense to try to save the guys who were moments earlier were firing on Americans. I spent many off duty hours trying to address this issue in my mind. Then one day at 3:00 A.M. I'm operating on a seventeen your old boy who had been shot in the back after dropping grenades off an overpass onto a U.S. convoy. I kept thinking that he could have been trying to kill me.

As it turned out he wasn't a bad kid. He needed money and someone offered him cash to attack the Americans. He didn't hate us; he was just financially motivated. In the end I did what I had to do and that is to be a doctor.

While I was there I met a translator who was a dentist. He once was forced to give his wife up to be used by Saddam Hussein or be killed. He was given a choice: his wife or his life. He gave his wife up. What kind of place is it to have to make that kind of choice? Everybody suffered while he built 380 palaces for himself. Iraq is a long way from Bend.

If there is one thing that I wish I could impact on society that would be to highlight the reality of this war. Every night on the news we hear the body counts of the dead. What we don't hear is what about the wounded. We ignore these folks and these are the ones most affected. These are the ones who had their lives taken from them at a very young age and now they have to live with crippling wounds. Some are paralyzed, many are missing arms and legs, and we don't ever hear about these people. Their lives are forever changed. I wish I could draw more attention to helping these folks; they need our support.

- Mark Maddox

[Jim Gilson]

Back before the new dinars were put into circulation, the CPA was paying all the Iraqi workers in U.S. dollars. And I mean cash, there wasn't a system for direct deposit. This meant that with thousands of Iraqi workers there was a considerable amount of cash needing to be distributed on a regular basis.

Because my normal job as a protocol officer was a bit slow at times, I would volunteer to help out where needed. A couple of times I volunteered to help out in the process of cash exchange. The normal process was to go to a bank and sign for the payroll in dinars and then take this money to a second bank and exchange for dollars. Then it was simply to bring the dollars back to the Green Zone.

We did these money runs very low profile. Just a couple of guys to sign for the money and three contract security personnel. We'd go in with a couple of casual cars to not attract attention. One key was to make sure the timing was smooth. That is the bank was ready at the exact time you arrived. Quickly in and out.

On this one particular day, the bank was not expecting us. Somehow they didn't communicate internally that point. That left me and one other volunteer like me. After some wait we were able to leave the bank with the cash. Now with an exchange rate of one dollar equals two thousand dinars, a few million dollars worth of dinars is a lot of cash. We left with duffle bags of money. If anyone could ever imagine what was in our duffle bags as we drug them back to our car, they'd be dumbstruck.

We then proceeded to the next bank and when we got there the bank wasn't there. It was just an empty building. At this point the private security guards got frustrated and left. We continued with mission and found another bank that could help us.

The bank manager realized the task and ordered every bank employee to work every available counting machine. The whole place was overwhelmed with that sound of money being shuffled by these machines. We are almost done when the bombs started going off outside. The tellers ceased counting and ducked.

My partner and I just started grapping bundles of $100,000 and stuffing them in pockets. It was utterly crazy. Luckily I was wearing pants with cargo pockets and a jacket with extra pockets. As quick as we could we just stuffed all the money in pockets and ran. We made it out of the bank and happened onto a convoy of tanks and Bradleys so we just joined in. We made it back to the Green Zone without a problem. In the danger of exploding bombs and our haste to leave we never were asked to sign for any receipts. When we got back it was a miracle because all the cash balanced to the penny.

Sometimes I wonder how crazy it was to be running down the sidewalk with a few million dollars in cash. If I wasn't so honest this could have been the greatest bank robbery ever.

-Jim Gilson

First Lieutenant Scott Travis returned from a 14-month deployment in Iraq in July 2004. Scott was involved in a lot of reconstruction and renovations in central Baghdad between August '03 and Jan '04. After that Scott spent some time on battalion staff. Scott is a member of 2d Brigade of the 1st Armored Division from Baumholder, Germany.

[Scott Travis]

In early July, our company was tasked with facilitating the payment of former members of the Iraqi Army. They gave us a location and they gave us the people with the money and we made it happen. It was a company mission that lasted about 4 weeks. My platoon was tasked with night security on site to guard the money. My guys said there were firefights (Iraqi on Iraqi) every night out there. That mission really didn't involve much on my part aside from ensuring the guard force was prepared and properly rested up. It was a nice break from the usual running around town.

The night that Uday and Qusay were killed was a pretty exciting evening. All of the sudden, at 10:30 PM, gunfire erupted all over the city. My whole Platoon and I hopped up on the roof of our building with our rifles and watched the night sky, tracer fire coming up 360 degrees around us in the distance. At first we thought it was some kind of coordinated attack, but we figured after about 5 minutes of was just celebratory fire. Apparently falling bullets killed a lot of Iraqis that night.

Once the pay site mission ended, we received a new Battalion Commander. He brought to the table a whole new concept for Combat Engineers in a peacekeeping role.

-Scott Travis

Patrick was a Bradley Platoon leader for Task Force 1-30 from Ft. Benning, Georgia. Unfortunately, Patrick's marriage became a casualty of the deployment.

[Patrick]

My observation is that most of the Iraqi army did not want to fight. Many just deserted when the time came. Sometimes we'd come upon a fighting position and we'd find the weapons and uniforms and no people. They must have packed a bag of civilian clothes with them, then when the time came they would change and leave all the military stuff. They'd take the food and cigarettes, of course.

Once our platoon was manning a checkpoint to make sure the convoys made the right turn. This was just after that unit that got lost and shot up, so more emphasis was put in place to prevent that from happening again. Our position was exposed and not well defended. That afternoon the mayor of the village came to us and told us that that night the bad guys were gong to mortar us. We took his advice and left. It was really strange. This guy was petrified that if he did not warn us that he'd be in serious trouble. He was much more concerned about us than the bad guys with the mortars.

-Patrick

Captain Ben Wallen was an engineer company commander who spent three months in Iraq. Ben is now at the University of Texas getting a masters in engineering which will further benefit the Army in future projects.

[Ben Wallen]

Our third and fourth week began our real world mission focus. We began with driving up to Baghdad. The convoy of 368 miles took a mere 36 hours to make due to numerous stops due to maintenance, refueling, and rest stops. Our company did a great job on the convoy. We kept focused and safe. We originally headed out with 33 vehicles and by the end of the trip we had 43 vehicles as a result of picking up vehicles from other units that had broken down along the way and were fixed and just waiting for someone to gain control of them to bring them forward. We had the pleasure of experiencing crowds of kids rushing up to the vehicles to try to grab stuff off off them as we slowed down going through border towns in Iraq. Anytime we stopped, we also had Iraqis try to sell us a variety of items...from turbans to soda to ice to their money (Dinars) in order to get some American dollars to help out their family.

We had most of the company in Baghdad by 19 May. We have a variety of missions right now. We are guarding Enemy Prisoners of War (EPW) (yesterday we had one of the highest secretaries of the interior for Saddam in our EPW cage). We are assuming responsibility for monitoring the progress of water, waste water, electricity, trash, and the standards of living within our Forward Operating Base (FOB). We also have an EOD (Explosive Ordinance Detachment) team that we support heavily with our soldiers supporting the mission of eliminating/removing UXOs (unexploded ordinance) from our area in Baghdad. We are keeping busy and doing what we can to help enable the Iraqi people to get back on their feet.

Our living conditions here are not too shabby. We have a shower area with running water. There is a haircut place and a place to drop off laundry. Both cost $1 and the laundry is ready for pick up in 2 days. Many of our soldiers still cut their own hair and do their own laundry; however, it is nice to have it available. We have a PX trailer that comes to our area three times a week for us. We also have a dining facility that provides one hot meal a day (either dinner or breakfast). Our building does not have electricity or water; however, it is certainly better than living in a tent in the dirt...yes indeed.

-Ben Wallen

[Anonymous 1]

My husband and I were both serving in OIF at the same time. I was back in the rear and he was part of the advance guard to the Baghdad Airport, in the thick of the fighting. It was strange being close but not being able to see each other. Still it was better than living half a world apart.

We did see each other once in Iraq when a patrol he was on took him close to our camp. He convinced the major with him to stay in my camp for the night. That was crazy. I was standing outside my tent and next thing I know my husband is standing behind me.

All I'd seen of him up until that point were the spray painted "Baghdad or Bust" signs that soldiers from his company sprayed on Iraqi Guard shacks while heading north. I knew it was his unit because they would leave their unit designation. You probably know that mail was all but stopped for the first month after we crossed the berm so we didn't even know how each other were doing. When the mail system did come back online it only took about three days for us to get in country mail.

We saw each other one more time down in Kuwait. My unit was redeploying in July but Billy's was told they could be there for another three or four months. Of course I wasn't in a hurry to get to an empty home so I volunteered to work at the Shuiaba Port in Kuwait (which extended me about an extra month, bringing me home in August). Once again, out of nowhere Billy was in my camp in Kuwait. This one totally took me by surprise because his unit was still in Baghdad. His Chain of Command allowed him to fly down on a four day pass (that's the easiest way to explain it I guess) and say goodbye since they were suppose to be there till December.

We now have a baby boy who is four months old. I've only been back for 12 months. Yeah :) The mayor of the port (a Reserve Major who was pushing 65 yrs, funniest guy) helped us out. Billy needed to find a ride to the Kuwait Airport and we thought the Port would have a run out there each day to the airport. Turns out they didn't. But, when we walked in, both LTs with the same last name, he thought it was cool that we were married and deployed. He handed my husband the key to the visiting Generals' quarters and winked. Hahaha. That was the first time in eight months I'd slept inside. There was AC and a shower too. That was almost as cool as spending time with my husband!! It was nice also just to get a break from cramped living with so many other people.

Ended up my husband caught a ride back to the Kuwait Airport with some of the Spanish troops. They were on their way to Basra.

-Anonymous 1

[Fred Wellman]

While doing that we have had some interesting missions. I personally was able to fly in support of the new ORHA (Office of Reconstruction and Humanitarian Assistance) chief, Ambassador Bremer, last week when he visited Mosul for the first time. I ended up with all of the camera crews on my aircraft so if you saw film of a bunch of helicopters flying around that was my aircraft. Hopefully it was smooth footage and not bouncing all over the place.

Yesterday I flew a recon for our Long Range Surveillance Detachment up towards the border with Iran in the mountains. It was absolutely beautiful up there. The mountains are incredible with rivers winding their way through and little villages dotting the valleys. I took half a roll of film of the area and the snow capped peaks.

With that flight we are now flying missions all the way from Kuwait in the south to the Turkish border in the north and from the Syrian border in the west to the Iranian border in the east. Try keeping track of that many moving pieces and you will know why I have an extra large bottle of Tylenol on my desk.

-Fred Wellman

Heather Grodin-Putman is currently in Iraq and keeps up with friends through her web site. Her husband Jeremy has been very helpful in getting Heather's stories included here.

[Heather Grodin-Putman]

The first few weeks here days stretched on forever and weeks whipped by at breakneck speed. My days started around 4 am and ended around 10 or 11 pm. Sundays offered the opportunity to sleep in until 7 am or so. We were all rather worn out. In late April/early May, we began having one day off per week. This holiday, and no more 0730 briefings, has made way for a schedule that is bearable, and even allows me the chance to do some PT!! I run about 3-4 times a week as the sun is rising and the temperature hasn't risen above 75 or 80.

Time still flies and our Ground Hog days are a reasonable 14 hours. Meals at the chow hall with my friends and co-workers break up the monotony. Good days involve good briefs and jello without fruit in it. This experience has made me appreciate the small things, and realize what is really important in life.

We have now moved to a closer mess hall, (Black Jack) but I have not been inside. I normally eat grilled cheese, potato wedges with ranch dressing, and a salad. Sometimes the main meal looks edible – so I will feast on greasy chicken, rice, and over-steamed broccoli. The heat, not the food, is the best weight loss program—it's either greasy fast food or nothing. The potato bar (when stocked) is wonderful with bacon bits and broccoli. I cannot complain, it is undoubtedly better than MREs (meals ready to eat-out of a bag). (lots of smiles (Ingrid and Keith)...we're away from the TOC!)

Speaking of the TOC--since we arrived in country, the Soldiers of the Division staff operated out of the tent farm on the left while we waited for the completion of our building on the right. We just, within the last few days completed moving into the building. The cement floors and drop ceilings with florescent lighting are reminiscent of an office building, minus dividers segmenting us into cubicles. It is unusual to operate without the buzz of generators, constant blowing dust, and the sounds of the tent flapping in the wind!

Trips off Camp Victory. Though Camp Victory is relatively safe, the reality is that no member of the Coalition Forces is truly safe in this country. 'I do not laugh in the face of danger', and seek out less safe conditions, but I do take the opportunity about once monthly to get off post. The first time I had a meeting to attend in the Green Zone. I drove, which heightened the excitement of the trip. I did not know that military tactical vehicles could move that fast!! Thanks to my Mom's driving lessons on Route 128 and 93 all those years ago, I had no problem cutting off civilian traffic at break-neck speeds. I had a lot of fun, despite the constant concerns of IEDs (improvised explosive devices) on the roads. I relaxed a bit more on the return trip – my knuckles weren't white due to my death grip on the steering wheel!

Camp Victory is full of juxtapositions....western and Muslim, peace and war. It is hard for me to visualize what this place looked like with the ousted dictator strolling along the lakes or hunting in the swamps of where I live now--what is now North Camp Victory. It is also humbling to see the damage of the bombs that fell during the war. Here is a destroyed bridge, and in some areas around this building the stone shows more damage from the bombs. We have repaired some of the buildings.

In some areas along the main routes, there is more evidence of the war once fought on this ground: a memorial left by Iraqi soldiers for their fallen.

About three weeks ago, the PX opened. I am happy they are here, but I can see that most Soldiers' plans to save money (to include mine) went out the window. Though I have not invested in a fridge, large screen TV, or any video games, I have increased my movie and music collection a bit. Ah, I suppose it's not a bad vice. Likewise, when the same old chow gets boring, we head for Burger King (as does everyone else--it's mobbed!). ... and the line is still 20 minutes long (three weeks after opening!) I am waiting desperately for the Starbucks (but I will not hold my breath!!)

Today on my day off and I am always happy, also, to have had an unlimited amount of time to talk with Jeremy, though the connection was far worse than normal today. I heard his voice--and that is almost as important as whatever trivial thing we were discussing. Again, the simple things that must be appreciated!

It is like ground hog day here – not much ever changes.

I am relatively safe here, but those folks who need prayers the most are the ones patrolling daily--always on the road or manning checkpoints. That being said, I constantly feel a wall of safeness around me – thank you, and keep it up!!

The news makes everything sound horrible – just remember all the things you do not hear – about the sewer projects designed to eliminate the sewage flowing down the streets or the water improvements to bring fresh water to the people in Baghdad. We are rebuilding this country one project at a time in order to provide jobs and improve the quality of life – not an easy task for a bunch of individuals who studied military history and have been maneuvering tanks for the last 5-30 years.

-Heather Grodin-Putman

[Fred Wellman]

This is a subject of many conversations amongst us. I actually have a theory on soldiers in combat. It seems that most conversations usually turn to one of several subjects. These include but are not limited to the following:

• Food (both the relative merits of various MRE menus and the desire for real food)
• Bowel functions (both the relative merits of these and the desire for more or less)
• Human relations (do I really have to elaborate on what I mean here?)
• Going home.

Generally speaking the conversation will eventually arrive at one of these four subjects. I personally don't have a problem with this but my Intel officer gets very upset with the whole bowel functions subject during meals. I don't understand why but she really gets warped when this comes up during a lovely dinner of beef stew. Some people are more sensitive than others I guess.

-Fred Wellman

[Matt Gapinski]

I have been back in Babylon, Iraq for the past month (after a two-week vacation in Camp Commando, Kuwait) so it's time for another update.

Much has changed at Camp Babylon. There are a lot more units here now. Our unit is now living in the Palace up on the hill. At first, it was a pain walking up and down the hill, but you get used to it. The mess hall is now air-conditioned and the same contractor that is at Camp Commando now provides the food. They started on the 4th of July with a special dinner (lobster tails, shrimp and steak). Everyday, they have plenty of fresh fruit in the mess hall - so it is a big improvement.

We now have two laundry facilities, so no more washing clothes in a bucket. A second shower point opened up and the hours are a lot more flexible. No improvement on the heat though. The high is between 110-120 degrees F and the low is 80-90 degrees F. Only about 6 weeks or so of summer weather left. All of the offices now have air conditioning. Ours works about 50% of the time but we kept our fans, which do a decent job of cooling the office. There is no A/C in the Palace where we sleep. Sleeping in the heat is no fun. We have learned a few tricks for trying to keep cool like sleeping in a wet T-shirt, which works for a few hours before it dries out, or keeping a wet sock over your water bottle, which actually makes the water cooler (not cold) and drinkable. We have local ice delivered just about every day, so that helps.

Our supposed replacements, a Polish Division, have started to arrive here. I haven't run into any Gapinskis from the fatherland. The problem is that once they take over in the next few months, no one seems to know whether we will begin redeployment back to the States or get relocated to somewhere else in Iraq.

Our work effort has stabilized with most of our efforts being computer work, compiling data and reports. We work more with the Coalition Provisional Authority (CPA) Ministries in Baghdad and serve as the go-between the local governorates (provinces) and the different offices that deal with Public Facilities. One of my team's new missions is irrigation. I went to a meeting with the local irrigation office to discuss a project that would irrigate over 25,000 acres of farmland. It has been in the works for over ten years. The engineer in charge of the project, a guy who must have been in his 60s, only spoke a few words of English so it took awhile to get sufficient detail to be able to submit the project for funding. He really knew his stuff and was eager to get the project started.

On a recent trip to Baghdad, I ran into an old friend from the Savannah District of the Corps of Engineers, who is here on temporary assignment and in charge of garbage removal in Baghdad. It is interesting how relevant everyone's perspective on their living conditions is. He was working in Saddam's former main palace with A/C and a full dining room, but complained about the lack of electricity and running water in the hotel he was living in. Our living conditions here aren't the greatest, but pale in comparison to the troops who are out manning checkpoints all day in the heat in full battle rattle (helmet, body armor, etc.). We only wear ours when we go outside the Palace grounds.

I am sure the news reports detail the daily attacks on the military here. But of the literally hundreds of convoys that are run everyday, only one or two get fired upon. We don't take any chances and have our weapons at the ready once we are out the gate. We joke about the irony of having one finger on the trigger while we are waving to the Iraqi kids with the other.

In addition to our special meal, we celebrated Independence Day with a 5K run (definitely not my best time, but OK considering the conditions) and a volleyball tournament (we lost our first match). One of the pools here is now open which provided a refreshing dip. We did not have any fireworks though (scheduled or unscheduled). We were able to reflect on our own nation's struggle for independence, which, anyway you look at it, did not happen overnight (either from 1776 to 1783 or to the Civil War). So, it is not unreasonable that things will take awhile to sort out over here. It just isn't easy going from a brutal dictatorship to freedom, especially in this culture where "God willing" (meaning: it isn't up to me) is the mantra.

We did have a treat the other night when Lee Ermey paid a visit to the camp. He hosts his own show on the History Channel called "Mail Call." He was a former Marine and played a drill instructor in the movie "Full Metal Jacket." He also did a bunch of beer commercials for Coors Light where John Wayne's image was dubbed in. He has been traveling around Iraq and taped an episode for his show, but just talked to us for about 45 minutes. He accomplished his goal of letting us forget about where we were for a while.

-Matt Gapinski

[Fred Wellman]

I really can't complain too much though. I have an amazing staff that has things completely under control. Mostly I sit around giving guidance and putting out little fires as they pop up. Unfortunately, that means actually putting out little fires as they pop up because the beautiful green grass I mentioned in my last letter is now lovely brown kindling with the onset of 100-degree temperatures.

Hardly a day goes by when somebody's garbage or poop fire doesn't catch the grass on fire and the entire battalion pours out with shovels and water jugs. We have met all of our neighbor units this way but it is not a great way to make friends amongst units when they try to burn your buildings down. Imagine that in your neighborhood at home and you can see how this might cause problems here. We are yet to lose any equipment but have lost a little bit of rear end following each incident. Fortunately, I have plenty to spare. As my boss is fond of saying "They will run out of teeth before I run out of ass!"

Incidentally, I did say, "poop fire." One of the pleasures of field living is the inauspicious duty of poop burning. Our portable toilets consist of a seat on top of half a 55-gallon drum. When poop levels reach critical the can is dragged out, jet fuel is applied in copious amounts and a match is added. This is very glamorous duty needless to say and soldiers are volunteering left and right for this detail. (That is sarcasm, incidentally).

-Fred Wellman

[Gordon Cimoli]

3:56am Woke up out of a weird dream. I dreamt that CPT Hester was opening and closing the door to our tent and was slamming it each time. After the fourth slam I realized that this wasn't a dream and no one was slamming my door. In the darkness, I laid quietly in my bed listening and heard more distinct BOOMs from incoming mortar fire. I counted 11 explosions (while I was awake). They seemed to come in series of 4 or 5. I sat up and yelled to Dave and Billy, "Mortars!" They didn't move. My body tensed up as I heard the next series of explosions. I closed my eyes and listened to the last few hit then fell asleep while concentrating on listening for more.

-Gordon Cimoli

[Fred Wellman]

Today is a beautiful sunny day here. The doves are cooing in the eucalyptus trees in the front yard of our headquarters and I am sitting writing you in my little office/room. I have to say that this is about as good as it gets for living in a combat zone. I wanted you all to know I was thinking of you and home.

As a matter of fact, on Sunday I am leading a delegation to one of the local villages to our west, which has been asking for our help with their water supply, which was damaged during the war. So, we are going out to assess it and have some sort of a feast. Hopefully we can help these folks and do some good here.

-Fred Wellman

Bob Ohls is a Field Artillery Battery Commander in the Pennsylvania National Guard. Since his unit went after the declared fighting, they have been doing Military Police duty, working closely with the new Iraqi Police.

[Bob Ohls]

August has been pretty good to us. It is still hot, but the guys continue to drive forward. This month has been our best month so far at maintaining 100% uptime of our generator. This may not seem like much but imagine if everyday in the middle of the afternoon you would lose power at your home. This loss of power made it even more of a burden on our soldiers who worked the night shift. They would be 3-4 hours into their sleep and would wake when the air conditioning would go out. Many times by the time the generator would come back on line those soldiers who barely slept were getting ready to go back out to work for another night shift. This is how we struggled through June and July, but in August the generator ran consistently for us so our air conditioners, refrigerators, fans, etc. were able to run and make our daily lives a little more bearable.

Our meals have also been the best ever and each week we continue to get new meals that are similar to the ones that Kellogg, Brown, and Root (KBR) provide all of the other dining facilities in the Iraqi Theater. Our cooks are working hard with the limited facility, equipment, and rations that they have to prepare meals in order to keep the morale high. As we get a full-time civilian staff providing the meals, our new dining facility and a new kitchen the meals will only get better.

We have also been utilizing our recreational tent more the past few weeks. The 2004 Olympics have been broadcasted on our satellite system, so we always have a small crowd in there. We are anticipating the TV pastime to gain momentum as we approach the football season. This will be our last major sporting event while we are in Iraq. It would be great to make it home for the Super Bowl but if we don't, at least we know we can watch it here.

The final note that I wanted to pass on from Iraq is the difference that we have noticed in the Iraqi Security Forces. We don't travel to Baghdad much but three days ago on our trip to our old forward operating base, Camp Cuervo, we saw a much stronger Iraqi National Guard working the various checkpoints. They appeared more attentive, dressed in a complete uniform, and they portrayed a sense of pride. Along the same route the Iraqi Policemen (IP) were patrolling the highways in their SUVs. IPs patrolling the highway is similar to our state policemen at home. There were at least six separate vehicles on the hour trip. Their presence on the highways help to eliminate any potential crime.

A few months ago, our soldiers witnessed three separate incidents of a carjacking just outside of our main gate. On one of the occasions while we were working the main gate, a car circled back for our protection. This particular car-jacking attempt was on a young Iraqi engineer who was working in Kirkuk. They were heading south on their way home to Baghdad. His wife was in the passenger seat and their two young children were in the back seat. He was able to turn the car around and get his family to the safety of American camp entrance. As a husband and a father, I would never want to be in his situation. Fortunately this is not a major worry back home in the states. Now the IPs conduct check point operations not far from our main gate to deter any criminal activity. The local police are becoming more present and a stronger force to protect the Iraqi citizens. These changes and improvements have been in the past six weeks. I'm sure that the improvements will grow exponentially the next six months and six years.

-Bob Ohls

[Fred Wellman]

I am a little anxious because I got some bad tea out there two days ago and have been suffering from what some are calling the "Pesh Merga's" or as my very clever mother of a toddler Flight Surgeon calls "poopy-tummy". I have had a whole heck of a lot of "poopy-tummy." So, I am not looking for any more.

I am happy to report that I did finally get my first official day off yesterday. Unfortunately, it was directly tied to the previously mentioned intestinal malady so it was not much of a day off spent on my cot or in the latrine. But, hey, a day off is a day off.

-Fred Wellman

[Gordon Cimoli]

The internet situation has gotten better over the last couple of days. The brigade has established an "internet café" of sorts in a tent with about 5 terminals supported by good bandwidth. The word is quickly spreading throughout the brigade so I anticipate that the lines will be substantial before long, but it has not been bad so far. It is located on the other side of the airfield, so not completely convenient to us, but it is doable and much better than what we had before. I don't predict any improvement in the phone situation for quite some time.

-Gordon Cimoli

[Fred Wellman]

The media keeps telling you how they already hate us here. It is a lie and a bunch of crap. The people here are thrilled and show it daily. You can't walk the streets of Mosul or drive 100 yards on a road without being waved at or told thanks. The truth is that we are finding the torture chambers, the mass graves and the chemicals that the Hussein regime hid from the world and the horrors are too much to show to you at home so you get the opinion of a bunch of idiots staying in the middle of Baghdad where all his rich cronies lived and tell the reporters what they want to hear. You know who they are because they have nice cars and good clothes. It wasn't free enterprise that got them all that money.

The truth is in the eyes of a child who isn't afraid of his father disappearing in the middle of the night. I have seen the scars on men's arms as they point at them and say "Saddam...bad...America...good". Nope, the nightly news won't show that. Just my opinion as a humble ex-politician soldier.

-Fred Wellman

Major Carlos C. Huerta is the Jewish Chaplain at the United States Military Academy. He wrote this paper as a summary of his experiences in Iraq for his boss. Chaplain Huerta shares his paper for this book.

[Carlos Huerta]

Is an Army Chaplain's ministry, really ministry? Does his or her kind of service bring any honor to G-d? When I think about these questions I think of Moses, Jesus, and Mohammed. Moses who gave up the palace of Pharaoh to lead the Children of Israel, gave one of his last sermons standing on the wilderness on the Plain of Arabah to a congregation that spent their last forty

117

years in the desert sands of the Middle East.[8] Jesus gave his famous Sermon on the Mount sitting on a mountain, perhaps using a pile of rocks for his lectern and chair.[9] The Prophet Mohammed gave his last sermon out in the open in the Uranah Valley of Mount Arafat. [10]

It seems that an army chaplain's service has more in common with these three great spiritual leaders than it has with most of today's clergy. When I realize that, I begin to understand just how special what we do is. We meet our congregants wherever they are, in whatever foxhole or firing position they are assigned. On the battlefield, we preach our sermons, sometimes to two, three, maybe ten. But there is more to our work than just counseling, giving sermons, and performing worship opportunities for our soldiers. Sometimes we are lucky enough, to set the oppressed free, share our food with the hungry, and clothe the naked. [11]

I was assigned battalion chaplain to 1st Battalion, 320th Field Artillery, 2nd Brigade Combat Team of the 101st Airborne Division (Air Assault) during Operation Iraqi Freedom. The Division fought its way up from Kuwait to the Turkish border. During the battle, I with my Chaplain Assistant, SPC Will Rodriguez, would visit soldiers after all night fire missions, give services on the gun line using expended ammo boxes as my pulpit, sharing the word of G-d with soldiers who were fighting in the desert, without hot showers or hot chow for months. We would come into the firing position during the late morning or early afternoon. Often the soldiers were sleeping after nighttime battles. Instead of announcing there would be a service, I would play my saxophone softly. I would play hymns, and as I was playing one soldier would come and pull up an ammo box. As I continued, that one would turn into ten, then twenty. Sometimes during the playing they would ask request which I would play if I knew them. After playing for about an hour, rather than have a sermon, I would ask those who wish to pray and open their hearts to G-d to do so. Their prayers would often talk about their loved ones back home, their safety and the safety of their buddies, their loneliness but yet, pride in what they were doing. We knew then that perhaps these prayers they were offering would be some of the most meaningful prayers we would ever hear in my life. After this "service" they would go back to sleep, to guard duty, or prepare for the next battle, and myself and SPC Rodriguez would go away knowing that our life was forever changed by this service in the chapel of the sand and sky.

After the war the 2nd Brigade Combat Team of the 101st ABN DIV, commanded by COL Joseph Anderson arrived in Mosul, Iraq at the end of April

2003. The city was pretty torn up due to the war. COL Anderson, who was now acting as the defunct mayor of the city, divided the city and gave each battalion a section to manage. He also assigned different tasks to his staff officers. Some were responsible for security, some for, gas and propane, others for water garbage removal. All city functions had ceased to operate since the start of the war. He assigned the chaplains and their chaplain assistants the task of visiting, and rebuilding the Iraqi school system. There were over twenty schools in the sector that the 1st BN, 320th FA, commanded by LTC Mark A. Murray, was responsible for and it had over 18,000 students in attendance.

As the project officer, it was our job, with the LTC Murray's approval and guidance, to plan and organize various elements of the battalion to get the schools up and running. It was also our job to plan and fund the rebuilding of schools as monies came available from Brigade or Divarty. I remember the first school we visited in our sector. It was Wednesday, 23 April 03 and the school was Al-Yarmook High School for boys. It was a day that changed our lives and our perception of Iraqis forever.

This is a story of a Jewish chaplain, his Christian Chaplain Assistant and Iraqi Christian translator Mr. Khalid Toma, and an Iraqi Muslim English high school teacher working together to take care of the "least of these", the Iraqi children. When we walked into the high school we were met by a group of teachers who were not sure what an American was. We were the first American any of them had seen. They had come to work but had no students, because the school was totally destroyed. All the glass windows were broken, the doors stolen, blackboards ripped off the walls, the light fixtures ripped of the ceiling, no functioning toilets or running water, and the school was not painted in over ten years. As they told us all the things they needed to get the school up and running, we knew the only thing we could offer them at that time was some paper and pencils for the students. SPC Rodriguez and I felt powerless walking into a totally destroyed structure offering only pencils. It was there that we met Mr. Mohammed Mushraff Mohammed, the father of five daughters. He was the high school English teacher and he sat next to me and talked to me in English and helped our translator relay the messages of the principal and other teachers.

With subsequent visits to the schools, we and Abu Nur (what Mr. Mohammed was called by his fellow teachers and friends) became friends. We would talk to him about the other primary schools we had visited and tell him about their condition. He told us that the war was not totally responsible for their condition. He said that the education system received almost no money from the Saddam regime in over 15 years. The schools went unpainted and that toilets and running water were rare at most elementary schools in Mosul. The young elementary school students were forced to defecate in hall ways or the school yard. If they wanted to wash or drink water they would have to run home, if they lived close enough, or do without water. The teacher's salaries were on the average the equivalent of Five Dollars ($5) a month. Even by Iraqi standards they were almost poverty wages. He told us that Saddam had no need for education and needed very few educated people.

As the weeks and months passed, money came to fix the schools. The obvious problem for us was, now that we had money, how do spend it wisely. Where do we find plumbers, glaciers, carpenters, painters, builders? We were strangers in a strange land and we needed contacts to help us rebuild the infrastructure. We knew that there were many corrupt and unscrupulous people out there that would not only steal from the Americans or fellow Iraqi citizens, but would also steal from their own children. How do we meet the honest ones? How do we get the most bang for the buck? We knew that if we could do this right that we would be fulfilling our mission in "winning the hearts and minds of the Iraqi people". Mr. Mohammed made us shine. He for nothing else than love of the children, not only pointed us in the right direction, but spent all of his summer supervising the rebuilding of all the schools in our sector, and then some. [12]

Cement was the key to our program, and it was also in high demand. Because of the battalion's reputation in its aggressive school rebuilding program, the Mayor of Mosul made Mr. Mohammed his only exception to policy in acquiring cement. He had the ability to acquire the cement directly from the factory at cost. His high ethical standard and hard work made us trusted by the Mayor's office and staff. He was single handedly responsible for turning a mud brick, dirt floor, thatched roof, one room school house into a modern 16 room facility in the village of Halabya. Part of the facility was turned into the first high school that village and the surrounding ones have ever had.

In terms of school supplies, we were able to purchase some locally, but hundreds and hundreds of pounds of pencils, erasers, sharpeners, crayons, paper, rulers, stuffed animals, etc., were sent to us from many different church and school organizations in the States. LTC Murray personally made an appeal, through his wife Betsy, to his church back home and managed to receive boxes and boxes of the kind of "stuff" that made the Iraqi children smile when he passed them out at school dedications.

The Catholic chapel at West Point, with the help of Chp (MAJ) Jerry De-
ponai, shipped over 40 boxes of school supplies. This was primarily through
the effort of Mrs. Carolyn Tiger, who works with families of returning soldiers at West Point, her husband LTC Tiger who is stationed there and is
on the Catholic Council and SPC Paul Alexander the Chaplain Assistant at
the Catholic Chapel. Needless to say that the USMA Chaplain, Chp (COL)
Scott McChrystal was the ever present in the background greasing the skids
when they needed greasing. What is important to note is how the religious
community back home, through their chaplains and chaplain assistants, and
the soldiers on the battlefield were connected together spiritually and tactical-
ly, through their chaplains and chaplain assistants, to help with the mission of
building a nation and winning the hearts of the children.

Mr. Mohammed, Khalid, I and SPC Rodriguez, a Muslim, Christians and
Jew, would spend hours in meetings with the Mayor, with the cement factory,
with the principal of the schools to plan their reconstruction. When we finished a group of schools that were within one location we would have a school
dedication ceremony. We would invite the Division Commander, Brigade
Commander, Divarty Commander, the Chancellor of Mosul University, the
Mayor, and the acting Minister of Education in Mosul for a ribbon cutting. It
was a joyous community event and the parents, teachers, and children of the
schools would prepare food and the camera crews from Iraqi television would
come to film it for broadcast. The Iraqis, being a very religious people, would
always open the event with the reading of a passage of the Holy Qur'an. At
one event, I, a rabbi, even was blessed with reading a chapter of the Holy Koran in Arabic. The one I read was Surat Ma'un. It read;

Who is he who denies Judgment,
Such is the man who repulses the orphan,
And encourages not the feeding of the poor,
So woe to the worshipers
Who are neglectful of their prayers,
Those who wish to be seen
But refuse to supply even the needs of their neighbors. [13]

We learned more about faith, love, and service to G-d from a Muslim and
Christian while we were in Iraq than we had for years serving in America.
We learned that in the service of our Creat-r, a Jew, a Christian, and a Mus-

lim, are all G-d's creatures, capable of doing great things together, capable of changing the world, one bathroom at a time, one classroom at a time, one school at a time. When we left Iraq, we knew that we were privileged to do a ministry that very few are privileged to do. We knew that being an UMT, an army chaplain and a chaplain assistant, allowed us not to just minister to our soldiers, but together with our soldiers, minister to an oppressed people, a great and wonderful people, a people who had much to teach us about the ways of G-d.

On 15 November 2003, Charlie Battery of the 1st BN, 320th Field Artillery lost five soldiers when a Blackhawk went down responding to enemy fire in Mosul, Iraq. One of the soldiers killed was a PFC Sheldon Hawk Eagle. He was a Christian, Native American from the Lakota Nation. I, years before, was given a medicine pouch by the head of the Lakota Council and I brought that pouch to battle with me. It contained some sweet grass and sage. Before we went to battle in Kuwait, I gave PFC Hawk Eagle some sage and sweet grass to burn before war. After we arrived in Mosul, PFC Hawk Eagle often went with me on my school missions.

After he was killed, we went through his belongings to send home. He had many pictures of his experience in Iraq. What struck me the most was what the pictures were of. Out of all the things he could show his loved ones at home about his wartime experience, the thing that he wanted to show them the most were the children. He took pictures of the children whose schools we were fixing. To PFC Hawk Eagle, an artilleryman, working with his chaplain in helping kids get a better shot in life was something he was proud of.

Mr. Mohammed taught me a religious poem written by a great Muslim Imam, Ibn Arabi. I now have these words on my office wall, written on a sign wall in Arabic so I can remember them every day I come to work. The words are,

There was a time when I took it amiss in my companion if his religion was not near to mine;
But now my heart takes on every form: it is a pasture for gazelles, a monastery for monks,
A temple for idols and a Ka'ba for pilgrims, the tables of the Torah and the holy book of the Qur'an.
Love is my religion, and whichever way it's riding beasts turn, that way lies my religion and belief. [14]

Note: I dedicate this all Chaplain Assistants, without whose presence G-d's blessings on the battlefield would be greatly diminished. In particular, I dedicate this to my Chaplain Assistant, SPC Will Rodriguez, who, because of his sense to Duty, Honor, Country, missed the birth of both of his children due to deployments. His willingness to serve G-d and Country, and the countless times he threw me to the ground covering my body with his during incoming enemy fire, has taught me more about Christian love and faith than a thousand words. May our Nation and Leaders only understand their tremendous self sacrifice and service to the Corps, to the Army and to their G-d. [15]

-Carlos Huerta

Michael Hanes served eight and half years in the Marine Corps. Mike has served as an embassy guard in Cairo and El Salvador. His last four years was in an elite Force Recon platoon where he was on the SCUBA dive team.

[Michael Hanes]

We spent three to four weeks patrolling Baghdad. We would drive around in our Hummers and maintain order in our assigned sector, like cops patrolling the streets. I was the .50 gunner on top of one of the Hummers. It was a good view. Sometimes people would throw roses at us and other times we'd see some shady characters lurking in the shadows. The bad guys stayed clear of us because of our special attire. We didn't look like ordinary Marines. We had the black masks over our heads and we wore dark sunglasses. Sometimes we'd see people running away yelling, "Commandoes, commandoes!"

One morning we were on vehicle patrol in the streets of Baghdad, suddenly civilians, fathers with daughters in their arms, etc., begin to point down a certain road and everyone joins in. They are pointing and yelling. We begin to go down the road in our Hummers with all our weapons covering every direction. When we came to another road everyone was pointing and yelling at us to turn down this road. We turn down the road and it leads us straight to the bank that was being robbed. As we pulled up about six people ran out and got away, the other, about six, inside we captured.

I stayed outside covering one of the streets. Others went inside the bank and found it deserted and burning with smoke everywhere. There was a blown hole in the wall. As we were securing the bank, to put the money in a safer place, a crowd of spectators begin to form. I remember standing on my Hummer with my .50 cal machine gun pointing down the road for security against any enemy vehicle. At first I was nervous, as a crowd began to form. Normally we would use "flash bangs," grenade simulators, to keep them back. A lot of old ladies with shopping bags seemed to care less of everything and we'd let them go by. Soon the police showed up and shooed away the crowd.

The kids were harder to control. I had a lot of kids begin to start hanging around my vehicle; we were giving them Skittles and M&Ms from our MRE packets. They asked my name and I told them, "Michael." They are began chanting, "Michael Bush, Michael Bush, Michael Bush..." It was kind of funny and all the Marines got a kick out of it. I was impressed with the Iraqi civilians. They pointed out the evil doers.

The next day we were on another vehicle patrol and we began to drive by a gas station. People began pointing again, they were pointing at a group of people and a car. We captured the people and seized the car, when we opened the trunk, to our amazement; it was full with AK-47 rifles. By this time a crowd began to form, my buddy, Big Moe, a huge intimidating Samoan guy, grabbed a rifle in each hand, went to the curb side walk and began busting the rifles and shattering them on the concrete, the people began cheering and honking their horns. Everyone was very happy to see these devices of death being destroyed.

-Michael Hanes

[Kristen Lewis]

This is another LRP story. I was up at the LRP again when I ran into one of my classmates, Nicole Dieso. We had a Systems Engineering class together. She was part of the 1AD, taking our (3ID) place. We were standing around talking when one of her soldiers brought her a Burger King bag. I just stared at it. Where did that come from? AAFES set up a Burger King on the other side of BIAP! I couldn't believe that. Nicole gave me one of her Whoppers and fries, which was probably one of the best meals I'd had ever. I took it back to my HMMVEE and split it with my driver (you always take care of your driver!). Every convoy after that we went to Burger King. I would tell my drivers that as soon as they downloaded their trucks they could drive around to the other side of the airport and visit the PX they set up and eat at the Burger King. As long as everyone was ready to go at 1500 I would keep allowing them to go. They were never late. Every morning, the soldiers who weren't going out on the road would put in orders with the drivers who were and they would bring back dozens of Whoppers for them. We would wait in line for 3 hours just to get a hamburger. It was such a morale boost.

Lieutenant Colonel Chris Gehler commanded an Aviation Task Force in the 82nd Airborne Division. Chris is now at the Army War College in Pennsylvania with his wife and three children.

[Chris Gehler]

Once we crossed the border, it all became very intense. For three and half weeks I never felt relaxed. I was always concerned, concerned about my men in the air supporting the ground troops with supporting fires from our attack helos, concerned about our air assault operations, and especially concerned about our ground patrol operations. We put parameters on the missions to try to keep my guys safe while accomplishing the mission. We took no undue risks. Still the ground troops needed us. In the urban areas we were their best over-the-shoulder fire support. We were quick, light, nimble and accurate. They did not like to go at it without us.

To keep pace with all the demand we ran the same aircraft all day. We ran three shifts of flight crews. The maintenance teams were like pit crews in a NASCAR race. We never took a day off that first month. I didn't feel I had the luxury of time to even take a black bag shower. For the first three and half weeks I never took one shower; I'd feel like I couldn't or shouldn't relax too much; the pace was too intense.

I also did my time as a pilot also. Flying over the countryside, I saw the same scene over and over. Kids, families and everyone would run out of their houses and wave, showing their gratitude. Driving through the towns, I saw the same reaction. I think people really appreciated their new freedoms, like the chance to participate in the pilgrimage to Karbala which had not been allowed for over 20 years. Everyone was happy to see us and yet I never heard this view ever on the news. The vast majority of people I encountered supported us wholeheartedly.

There were isolated pockets that were dangerous though. We had numerous firefights and engagements with the Fedayeen. You never really get used to seeing an RPG blow up in front of you or bullets flying by, but you do get used to reacting and reengaging quickly. We were blessed that no one was hurt during those early fights.

After I got back, I thought everything was so negative. Most news commentary on the war did not have a clue as to what's going on, with the exception of journalists like Karl Zinsmeister who did a great job as our embedded correspondent. He was open-minded and did not come with a pre-conceived agenda.

Another thing I noticed was how backward parts of the country were. There was little to no infrastructure in the small towns and villages. All the houses had little streams behind them where the family would draw their water. They didn't have running water – electricity was hit and miss. I think most people at home thought that was a result of the war, but there wasn't much to begin with. This was the product of thirty-five years of no investment.

-Chris Gehler

Kelly Thrasher was in the Individual Ready Reserve when he decided he could be more active in helping his country. He then volunteered to join a Civil Affairs reserve unit. His first six months was at a high level staff position and his second six months in Iraq he had a CAT-A, 4 man team, that operated doing CA type missions with the coalition soldiers.

[Kelly Thrasher]

I'm in the reserves and was activated as part of a four man Civil Affairs Team from Norristown, Pennsylvania. I came over before the war started and was working with the Marines, interesting lot. They are extremely focused and great executers of the close fight but have no real resources to deal with the long haul. They are like a SWAT team – they come in, kick in the doors, shoot the bad guys, and leave the mess to the Army. I loved them and hated them.

The last six months I was there, things got better, but at first it was difficult fighting bureaucracy to get the proper funding to do the job. We lived downtown with our Dutch counterparts. A big part of our day was shaking hands. We would carry weapons and wear flak vests though we would take our helmets off – they would scare the children. Of course we would give out gifts and candy; the surprising thing was when we would receive gifts back - flowers and candy. Making friends is not hard if you smile, act friendly and above all respect their religion.

Some of the other coalition soldiers would not smile and wave. We worked with the Italians, the Dutch, the Poles, the Filipinos. The ones that were not friendly were mostly the ones from the former Soviet countries. The Iraqis were most concerned about the Marines. They were always on the lookout for them.

The translators were always a great resource. We got most of our ideas for projects from them. One in particular I remember well. He was twenty-two, college educated with a computer science degree, but no training. He was very religious and always drawing parallels between Islam and Christianity. He wanted to learn about the world and genuinely wanted to make his country better. He had strange notions of history based on what he was taught. To add to the confusion right after Saddam fell, the religious schools started teaching we were Crusaders - Butchers.

Once we came to negotiations with one of the Shia groups, SCIRI, the Supreme Council for the Isalmic Revolution in Iraq. We came into a firefight and backed the police up in a town called Suk ash Shuyuk. The town was under Italian "control" but SCIRI was enforcing the laws. This group was heavily armed. On that day we negotiated with the police to help SCIRI apprehend looters. It was an interesting and exciting time. At the day of the incident, I sat down with the local SCIRI commander. We talked mostly about his history of fighting Saddam for 20 years and now he wanted to get back to his life before that. Although he was supported by Iran, he was Iraqi and wanted nothing more than for his small are to return to its potential. He was not pro-American, but anti-war. We negotiated over his possessing automatic medium and heavy weapons. He eventually surrendered an anti-tank system and a medium machine gun to me as a sign of faith. As I left with my 4 man team, we noticed that he had over 50 men and heavy weapons.

-Kelly Thrasher

[Paul Colbert]

The series of compounds and palaces Saddam, Uday, and Qusay Hussein built in the western part (Abu Graib) of Baghdad was immense, lavish, and occupied by thousands of Americans, Brits, Aussies, Bulgarians, Koreans, Mongolians, Spaniards, Italians, Dutch, and Poles as the headquarters of CJTF-7.

The Hussein family had built this "oasis" in the middle of the desert, along with other palatial complexes in Tikrit, downtown Baghdad, and Mosul, as a distinct slap-in-the-face to the Iraqi people living mere feet from the walls, dividing those with the money and power and those without.

I was extremely impressed, despite their original intent, with the architecture and lavish surroundings, especially inside the buildings. The most impressive buildings and palaces were on the inside of the inside. All the palace complexes were built with complete over-watch in mind. In the palace compound we lived in, Saddam had built a city inside a city – two sets of walls with an interior and exterior. We soon found out that the entirety of the compound housed his close allies and his family, limiting the inside ring to just his family and the outside to the Ba'ath party member he wanted to keep close, but not too close. For instance, our house (I lived with the C3 Air section) sat just outside the inner wall and it was quite apparent that Saddam wanted to keep his political party members within arm's reach, but at their expense – the nearby gate still has a guard shack, huge electrically operated metal gates and a retractable spike-strip in the ground just outside the gate. This was full-proof to me that Saddam was a man who meant business, even with his closest allies. On the inside complex, the big house (literally), was Saddam's and contained as many houses and complexes and palaces of every known size, shape, configuration, stature, material, and spacing any architectural firm could possibly conceive. The big palace has about 6,000 square feet of living space; some houses on the north side of the lake might have 500. Two separate houses on the east side of the complex were side-by-side and housed Uday and Qusay at one point, and all three, including Saddam's big house were bombed, efficiently and precisely with JDAM laser-guided bombs based on intelligence at the beginning of April when the USAF kept the Iraqi Army and its leaders' heads down with every known piece of ordnance in the inventory.

The JOC (Joint Operations Center) is where I worked. Situated directly across from the big house, the building the JOC was in used to be a brothel or a party house for the Hussein family and Ba'ath Party members, each possibility different depending on who you asked. On the west side of the lake is JVB (Joint Visitors' Bureau – wine and dine for all the higher-ups that come into country like Senators and Congressmen, Secretaries, and Foreign Dignitaries), which is one of the most ornate and beautiful buildings of all the palaces on the compound. The list goes on and on for each of the different buildings, but all have similar features – marble, granite, and polished sandstone in any place that has a horizontal or vertical surface, gold fixtures, doorknobs, and even toilets, and ornate chandeliers. The big house, of course, is the most ornate and lavish of them all, though.

In the center of Saddam's palace is a huge 200-foot-diameter rotunda, supporting the weight of the largest chandelier I have ever seen. At least thirty feet tall and over sixty feet in diameter, his chandelier must weigh in excess of a ton. Around the base of the rotunda are massive granite pillars supporting the weight of the heavy roof. The palace is two levels, each about sixty feet, floor to ceiling. The floor is inlaid dark wood (walnut, maybe?) and granite, and the off-shoots on the bottom floor are banquet rooms, dance floors, meeting rooms, a theater, and the master bedroom. The second floor few have seen, but is equally as large with numerous rooms above the rooms below. On the outside, large buttresses support the exterior walls and each has walkways connecting the entire second floor. Once you peer inside, though, you have to be impressed with the gold, most of all – toilets, gold; faucets, gold; doorknobs, gold; intricate molding in and around the doors, gold; emblems all over the house, gold; connecting structures of the chandeliers, gold; Arabic writing on the walls, gold; stairs, gold; chairs, gold; any other place any human being could potentially put gold, gold.

As for our own house, we got lucky. I will never, nor have I up to this day, complain about our living arrangements. I went from a drafty, hot, dusty tent to a house with the same gold toilets and sinks with hot and cold running water, indoor plumbing, a real shower, full kitchen with stove, and consistent electricity without the drone of a generator nearby. I sleep in my own room – dark and cozy with heating and air conditioning. We were never too sure who lived here, but they were obviously one of high wealth and power. We never truly realized this wealth until Andy Tierre-Slough (Squadron Leader from the Royal Air Force) noticed that we were all eating off of serial-numbered Limoge china with a platinum border. Limoge china, as I'm told, is one of the most expensive brands of china world-wide, and, in most cases, the most expensive outside of the country for which the dinnerware was named. The house has four bathrooms, four fireplaces, and two massive bedrooms on either end of an expansive sitting room in the middle, overlooking the turquoise-colored lake through wall-to-wall, seven-foot high glass doors. Outside is a huge porch, about ten-foot deep and running the entire length of the house, covered with the expanse of the roof above. We had green grass, trees, date palms, roses, daisies, and several boats.

-Paul Colbert

[Michael Hanes]

We had a secure compound in Baghdad, guarded by Marines, that we could go back to and rest. One day an Iraqi citizen tried and tried to get in claiming he wants to volunteer to be a translator. He knows English very well and when I asked him why he wants to do that he replied, "I want to do something good, among what is happening here."

During that month I had two canteen baths. I was ready to get back to Kuwait and a little more calm life. Back there we got our mail. Everyone got a whole bundle of stuff except I got nothing. I was upset. The mail is important; it keeps you going. A hand written letter means so much. It's a piece of heart to us. Letters and care packages mean a lot. Many times we got them from people we didn't know like from kids from schools. That day without mail really upset me after being gone a month. Then the next day I got my big pile of mail!

-Michael Hanes

[Paul Colbert]

The next few weeks saw many celebrities and dignitaries visiting the country to see how the troops were doing. Most notably were David Letterman and the World Wrestling Entertainment "Smackdown" troupe. Others, like Robin Williams and Paul Wolfowitz (Deputy Secretary of Defense) also came to the country, but went to other places.

Christmas was definitely different for all of us this year. Although this time last year was some of the most hectic of my life (7-day work weeks at 14-16-hour days) getting the company ready for war, I was at least home. I could come home to a wife and a warm bed, grab a beer and sit on the couch for a little bit, and even relax because I knew I was away from work.

The winters in the desert are wet, so we had to contend with pudding-like mud for weeks. In fact, even right now, there's nothing but mud outside. Being away from your family is worse, though. But all things considered, it wasn't too bad. I missed everyone's cheer and laughter, and the boyish anticipation of being with family, opening gifts with each other on Christmas morning. Angela got me, though, the night prior with a Christmas eve gift in both e-mail and on the phone (I'll get you back...). Mandi got to spend the holidays in Birmingham, and was able to see all of her family and all of mine.

We had a great Christmas dinner. Coupled with Butch and Johanna's gracious 15-pounder (which we're still eating on, oh, by the way), we had a great brunch at the chow hall, with a four-piece brass section belting out everything from Sinatra to New Orleans' Jazz. Ice sculptures were everywhere and cheer was in the air.

But, behind every sun, there's a shadow, and behind my bright spot was definitely a dark one. I've never been away from family for this long, and despite the fact that Thanksgiving was great and I will never forget my opportunity to spend that with my wife, I do long for next Christmas to make up for time lost. I still have that anxiety in my chest as to what I missed. What this war has taken away from my time with my family, and what it continues to take away, even as I sit here and type this, will never be replaced. Although I'm now a "vet," I've not done anything more than my job. I laugh sometimes at the things that do sadden me and think of those men who were gone from their loved ones from 1942 to 1945, some less, some more. These men are the true heroes and they're still around us today. I've done my time over here and I want to go home to be with my family. No one should be away from their families this long, but I do have to admit that even though there might be a little dark to go along with the light, it's normal. Additionally, I also have to admit that with some of the veterans that are still walking around from WWII, Korea, and Vietnam, their darkness is probably much larger and more foreboding than mine. And, lastly, I'm glad that I still have a light shining. I've lost friends and classmates in this war, people I knew, and people I sort of knew. I've got a friend, John Fernandez, who doesn't have any legs, and I've got some friends that I don't know if I'll ever see again, even though I know they're alive now. God Speed to all of us. Someday soon, we will reunite...

-Paul Colbert

[Gordon Cimoli]

Anyhow, on the way back we rolled through a small village of about 4 mud brick homes. There were some kids playing outside (the ones you see in this picture). We stopped to give them some candy that we had. The kids were apprehensive to come near us but the adults came out to chat. An old man came out and apparently he had many wives and his children numbered in the teens...he was at least 80. He asked us for some Viagra. You talk about a successful marketing campaign – how did Viagra get word all the way out here? haha

-Gordon Cimoli

Major Kim Darby is currently serving in Iraq as part of 1st Infantry Division, as the Executive Officer for the 601st Aviation Support Battalion. As the XO for an Aviation Support Bn, her dealings with the local Iraqis are limited to those who come on base and work for her battalion.

[Kim Darby]

One of my most vivid memories from this deployment occurred in Kuwait. We were in the final preparations for the movement north into Iraq. My unit was out in the middle of the Kuwaiti desert conducting convoy live fire and close quarters marksmanship training. After the day's training, everyone just pulled out their MRE (package Meal-Ready-to Eat) and broke open a cot right next to their vehicle in order to bed down for the night. The sky was crystal clear, not a bit of light pollution, with more stars visible than you could ever imagine. I can remember trying to get my cot set up and my poncho liner arrayed, when the soldiers in the 5-ton truck next to my vehicle brought out their portable radio. And the next thing you know, the desert air was filled with the strains of Toby Keith singing "American Soldier," a very poignant song with a lot of meaning for a bunch of soldiers getting ready to drive 500 miles north into Iraq to start a year long deployment away from their family and friends.

-Kim Darby

[Fred Wellman]

The Army is the strangest of careers. One day we are attacking and my focus is on rescuing downed aviators and providing ammo to the Apaches as far forward as possible. The next day I am handing out candy to kids and trying to get potable water to a village of 200 people. It is an unusual life. But, there is no kind of job satisfaction than when a child hands you a bundle of flowers and thanks you freeing his country. Nothing I have done in my life outside of the Army can compare to having that kind of impact on someone's life. Not politics and not business. So, I guess it is worth the sacrifice and pain.

-Fred Wellman

Chapter Five
The Iraqi Americans

Over the years under Saddam Hussein's misrule many people left their homes in Iraq and moved elsewhere. This was not always easy to do. If you were working for the government at the time, you had to get permission from your employer saying it was okay for you to go. Then getting a passport was a long ordeal and usually involved having to bribe somebody.

Still many left. The Jewish population, which was once almost half of the population of Baghdad (during 1920's), has dwindled to almost nothing. Those who stayed generally declared that they had converted to Islam whether they truly had or not. Many Christians also left. During the 1990's, a great many professionals, doctors and professors, left just because of the economic conditions. When the Iraqis left most would go to Europe, Australia and America. For those coming to the United States, many would settle in Detroit.

Below are six stories from natives of Iraq:

Fayrouz Hancock shared with me her story of growing up and living in Basra between 1966 and 1988. By the time she emigrated most of her family had already left. Now she is married and living in Dallas.

Fayrouz Hancock lives what she calls a boring life; that is, no bombs are going off, no one is spying on her and she has no fear of arrest and torture. Little things like job hunting are mundane after growing up in Basra where she was in the middle of a war for eight years. She is now happy to be living in the United States where she has an equal opportunity to excel. She loves her country, and wants the best for it. She writes a blog, "Living in Dallas," in which she educates the readers about the culture and latest news in Iraq.

She was fifteen when Saddam Hussein attacked Iran. Basra was in the middle of the combat zone. She hid under the bed when the bombing first started. Later she and everyone else in Basra would get used to it and live life as best as they could. It was constant bombing everyday. Through it, she was able to study and get accepted into college. Mrs. Hancock earned her degree from the university in Basra in computer science.

Over the years, Fay's family left its country. Her older sister left Iraq during the 70's, her youngest brother left during the 80's, and the rest of her siblings began emigrating after 1991. Her parents left their homeland in the first part of this decade.

Fay was living in Baghdad when Saddam Hussein attacked Kuwait. When Desert Storm kicked off they would huddle next to the battery-powered radio since there was no electricity. For safety, Fay and her sister went to live with her uncle in Ammara.

As you all know, Saddam lost that war (as usual). After three days, the Iraqi soldiers started pouring into the city. They were dirty, tired and hungry. Most of them walked from Kuwait to Ammara on their way to their hometowns.

She reports, "My uncle asked the women with magic hands to cook a big amount of Byriani as fast as possible. We cooked the food and drove to Ammara's main road, where the soldiers were arriving. You had to be there to feel what it means to lose your pride. I hated Saddam at that moment. I hated what he did to those soldiers. I hated being an Iraqi."

Fay soon found herself in another war zone right in the middle of the Shia uprising. "The uprisers burned government buildings and took control of public transportation." In a few days the Iraqi army came thorough and stopped the uprising. Fay returned to Baghdad where she was serving her obligatory service to her country, working in a hospital.

After college Fay worked for Ministry of Education. Every female government employee with non-engineering, teaching, or medical backgrounds is required to serve for twelve months in a hospital. Fay's twelve months were right before Desert Storm and the following uprising. She witnessed the tragedy and suffering of the effects of war as each employee worked long hours to help those wounded receive proper and caring treatment.

Working for the government in information technology had its risks. Fay could never really trust everyone. Anyone could be a spy for Saddam Hussein. One always had to be very careful about what one said and only to those closest of friends. Some they all knew were spies and there were many others that one could not know for sure. A few years later, she had had enough and resigned her job and left the country.

Fay is a Chaldean Catholic. During the 80's there were about 500,000 Christians living in Basra. Now there are about 100,000. Chaldean Catholics are Eastern-rite Catholics, with autonomy from Rome.

She grew up speaking Chaldean, a language which is the modern version of Aramaic, the language Jesus spoke. From watching the "The Passion of The Christ," Fay learned that Chaldean is similar to Hebrew. Today there are very few Jews living in Basra. Those who remained usually openly declared that they are converts to Islam.

Today Fay is hopeful for a new way of life for Iraq. She supports Father Yousif Thomas Mirkis efforts to start a new university dedicated to Human Sciences Studies.

Another gentleman I talked to grew up in Iraq, moved to Virginia, and then in 2003 moved back to Iraq to help his country. His father was thrown in jail for competing against Uday Hussein in business. The son submitted the second story.

[Anonymous 2]

On the day I had to leave Mosul I was curious to discover that most of the city's citizens were still optimistic regarding Iraq's future, and although weary from the war, they were not yet displeased with the American occupation. However there were those who did harbor twisted feelings. Those were mostly ex-regime loyalists and since the border control was virtually non-existent, some were foreign terrorists. Some have come to settle old scores, others to join a holy war. As our car pulled into the taxi service office, the driver saluted me with smiles and congratulations upon my return to Iraq. I immediately sank into the torn mystery-colored sofa while the ceiling fan above our heads swirled loosely as if trying to exit its own orbit. Our driver resumed his routine tire check for the trip while I downed half a cup of tea and quietly listened to the owner of the taxi service office with the white moustache. He formed a few rather conservative conspiracy theories by Iraqi standards and paused for reaction as the Al-Jazeera reporter whined about the situation in Iraq on the television set above his head.

Suddenly a blue Volks Wagon (or as Iraqis say: Brazili) pulled up and from it emerged a small man in a dishdasha (a long white Arab garb). The man looked as if he'd just woken up a few minutes ago. He immediately withdrew a pipe on a tripod, set it on the ground and produced a few shells which he then dropped into the pipe. The sound was loud enough to attract us out of the shop. When the folks around the shops saw that it was a man firing off a few shells, they immediately disassociated themselves from the scene. Those who didn't make it inside in time waved to the man while he returned his equipment back into the car as if he'd just dropped by to ask for directions. "Al-Salam Alikum," said the man, the audience answered: "Walaikum Salam." By then the man, the blue Brazili and the weapons were gone. The scene was so quick and disorienting that my mouth and body decided to lose coordination for a few moments, which apparently wasn't very abnormal in that part of Mosul as no one paid attention, but then again someone just fired a few missiles seconds ago.

My mouth decided to catch up with my brain, and I said something to the effect of: "Stop him!" The men in the shop looked at me as if I'd just asked them to commit seppuku. One of them insisted that he didn't want any trouble, and soon quickly the rest of the men in the shop attached themselves to this noble cause.

One could draw many conclusions as to the nature of why Iraqis refuse to report crimes. One reason could be Fitnah. Fitnah is an Arabic term that delineates the act of instigating mischief between two parties; the outside party being the Fatan or instigator. In Islam Fitnah is worse than killing. "Perhaps it is like starting Fitnah," said one of the old men at the shop offering another reason. What he had meant was that he was starting trouble between the man who had just fired the missiles and the Americans. But the old man missed the big picture: it was obvious that the man firing the missiles was the one starting Fitnah between the Americans and the innocent owners of the nearby shops. "But what if the Americans show up and start shooting up the place as this was the point of origin? Doesn't that make the terrorist the Fatan?" This new concept of Fitnah did not sit too well with the old Iraqi men as it put Allah on the side of the Iraqis and Americans rather than on the side of the terrorist, who was most likely not American. In my mind however, a terrorist is a Fatan, for although he might have not injured anybody, he is starting trouble.

As we were exiting Mosul to go to Baghdad, I asked the driver to pull over by some HUM-Vs that were arresting black market sellers of gasoline. I informed a corporal (I don't remember his rank) about what had just happened and he immediately radioed another company. As we took off the driver was very upset and asked me this question: "The Americans were not going to go there until you told them." I answered: "So?" He lit up a cigarette and smiled while saying: "You just started Fitnah!"

-Anonymous 2

The third story is a selected number of blog entries from Omar Masry. Omar's mother is from Saudi Arabia and his father is Lebanese. Omar, with an Arabic background, served in Iraq as a Civil Affairs expert and his observations are enlightening. Omar's mother is right now the first female Saudi American running for state legislature in California.

[Omar Masry]

Sunday, December 28, 2003

Gas Lines

Gas lines seemed a bit shorter today, still ridiculously long though. Everyone shares the blame for it though. Halliburton for not getting the refineries up to standard fast enough and then price gouging the military. Smugglers stealing oil and charging ridiculous markups for gas, and most importantly the insurgents. One Iraqi at the convention center (where CPA has briefings) told me rumor on the street was the attackers were justifying harming Iraqi people by claiming they were blowing up pipelines going to Israel. Only one problem the pipeline that used to run to Haifa 40+ years ago is ruined. Now if the U.S. is really "stealing oil" to give to Israelis why would it be importing oil from Turkey, Kuwait, and now Iran and why would insurgents be blowing up pipelines coming from refineries in the North and South INTO Baghdad?

The fuel situation is a prime example of how devastated Iraqi society has become. People fear that the next day there won't be any fuel, just like they might fear civil war or revolution, and start hoarding fuel or constantly keeping their tanks full and getting back in line all the time which only adds to the fuel lines. When a people have little faith in their government or its stability, they are reluctant to focus on improving civil society, and corrupt practices become necessary to ensure survival. Its interesting how more Iraqis go to the fuel stations guarded by Americans, apparently they have more trust in the lines and fuel quality, and not being gouged when we are in charge.

On the brighter side got to see some women's groups working with CPA on starting women's centers throughout Iraq. Another focus is going to be on getting more women to run for elections on the national level and the neighborhood/district advisory councils the military has helped form in just about every village in Iraq. There's also a need for books (Arabic preferred) to place in libraries in these women's centers (help would be appreciated). Also got some huge boxes of supplies donated by Americans back home to give out to Iraqi children. While I was happy to see everything I noticed none of the food products included pork or anything that might be deemed offensive, except I did find a bunch of toy guns. Sorry guys, Iraqi kids ABSOLUTELY do not need to be carrying around toy guns, send them toothpaste or toothbrushes instead. Thanks anyways.

Friday, January 2, 2004

Just another day...

Today as I drove around the Airport and over to the Green Zone downtown I pondered some of the little things that have changed since I've been here. When we first got to Baghdad I was sleeping in Terminal B of the Airport on the baggage conveyor belt. Taking showers on the aircraft ramps, practicing Close Quarter Combat in the scrap Iraqi Airways Tupolev and chasing my laundry down the runway when a Blackhawk helicopter landed close by. The airport hadn't really been used much after the '91 war and still felt like it was stuck in some quasi French/Intercontinental 70's time warp. The terminal had been trashed, aircraft wreckage littered the runways, the duty free shop was looted, and the basements were flooded with sewage. Now the terminals have been cleaned up and the airport is unofficially open for business. Everyday there are more and more Iraqis working at the airport and there's been thousands spent renovating Iraqi airways buildings that will be turned over to the Iraqis in June. One of our teams cleaned up the area around the main mosque for airport employees (non Muslims aren't allowed to enter it). Apparently some Iraqi Airways planes are still in airports in places like Pakistan/ Libya/Iran, left there since the initial UN sanctions, and Iraqi Civil Aviation officials are fighting to get them back since they are the rightful property of the Iraqis. I hope they get all the money in Syrian banks, add that to the money released by the UN the other day and that's a lot of reconstruction money that will be a little better spent (thank you, congress, for imposing oversight over wasteful contractors).

I remember kicking it once with some Iraqi Americans who would toast "Next year in Baghdad" and then break down in tears because they couldn't return to see their families, many of them being political asylum refugees. Now they will.

Monday, January 5, 2004

What you don't see...

Watching TV news about Iraq, you're usually subjected to three main themes: raids, soldiers standing around a street, and aftermath of a car bomb or road-side explosion. What you don't see is maneuver commander (someone in charge of an area) of units running tankers in front of others in line for fuel at refineries so they can get more supplies for their respective neighborhoods. You don't see captains normally trained to drive the most advanced tanks in the world pulling over a trash truck to see if it really is being used to clean up trash in the neighborhood he's working in. You don't see a Major normally assigned to a Cavalry Regiment giving a presentation on how he's working to move internal refugees out of buildings to be handed over to Iraqi ministries with slide graphics that consist mostly of pictures of Iraqi kids. Normally his graphics would be infantry formations or flanking moves, instead there's a picture of him giving a male sheikh the traditional Arab customary kiss on the cheek. Briefings that would normally be preceded by a call to attention as the commander walks in are sometimes replaced with the Iraqi transla-tor giving his/her "5 Arabic phrases to learn today" lesson. I don't think they could ever really make a good American movie about Iraq because so much here isn't black and white (good vs. evil) like American movies tend to por-tray; it's infinite shades of gray, where so many decent and honorable Iraqis are paralyzed by fear and too many of the corrupt minority fashion themselves as sheep's in wolf's clothing.

Monday, January 12, 2004

Where's the party at...

Driving back from CPA we came upon a traffic jam. I saw people running around on the side median and my first thought was an attack had taken place, yet I heard no gunfire and saw no smoke, or even other military in the area. As we crept closer we came upon an impromptu wedding caravan stopped on the side of the road with a couple Iraqis dancing to Kadhem Saher. I looked over and yelled congratulations, the groom realized I was Arab and started yelling, "now we can get married, thank you." Now since I didn't get them any presents I'm only guessing there was probably some restriction on them getting married over Ba'ath party rules. It seems Mondays are the days for weddings around here since we passed two other caravans just on the way to the airport.

After I left, I showed a DVD to some of the soldiers in our convoy, it was about the Rebuilding of Iraq. I setup my laptop on the hood of my Humvee and a little Iraqi girl selling candies came by and then called over some other Iraqis. They were like mesmerized just seeing scenes from the Kurdish areas to the ports in Umm Qasr, but when it showed the mass graves every one of them had tears in their eyes. They asked me to play it again, and by that time I had 30 Iraqis standing in front of my Humvee watching this 7 minute video of their country over and over till the battery died. I still don't understand why the kid's first guess of where I'm from is Egypt. I know it's a big country and all but there's a few more nations out there. They laugh if I say Yemeni, though.

Friday, January 16, 2004

Driving around Baghdad I saw a lot of streets being torn up as inadequately small sewer lines get replaced, and not just in areas that were more supportive of the former regime. You see a lot more ICDC troops (Iraqi Civil Defense Corps) around as well, manning checkpoints, nabbing suspects in raids, and setting up cordons around suspected roadside bombs. They actually seem pretty sharp, and carry an air about them that they actually care about their jobs. It's amazing how the same young men you wanted to cast off as hard headed and lost can change just by giving them a job, a decent salary, some training, and a modicum of respect. Most of the ICDC serve in areas on purpose close to where they live. This is done so they have a vested interest in protecting their neighborhoods. A lot of projects that have good intentions will not survive here if people are not invested in the project and feel an incumbent responsibility in it. People would show their discontent by sheer negligence and occasional vandalism of public property and spaces because it was the only form of expression left against a totalitarian regime. Companies in the states would probably donate thousands of computers to schools here, but they know the next day most of them would be stolen, so you have to find Iraqi-run community groups that have a purely philanthropic interest in the welfare of their respective communities. Usually the only ones that fit that description are the women's groups (secular and religious, multi faith and single-issue focused).

-Omar Masry

The fourth story is about a Kurd who left Iraq as a young boy and as an adult became a helicopter pilot for the U.S. Army. He just recently had his first visit home in nearly three decades.

Chief Warrant Officer Kamran Gardi of the 5-158th Aviation Battalion is an Iraqi born Kurd who spent the first eight years of his life (1965-1973) living in the combat zone of the Kurdish fight for independence.

Since age 12, Kamran has lived in the United States. In June 2003, he was able to return to his home in the hills near Irbil for a long-awaited homecoming. It had been thirty years since he had seen his grandmother, cousins and many others of his family and childhood friends. "I was lucky and happy to see my Grandmother. She passed away less than a year later."

Kamran's father, originally a soldier in Saddam's Army who later turned against him and joined up to fight with the Kurds, knew Marsaud Barzani, the Kurdistan Democratic Party (KDP) President. It was President Barzani who organized the homecoming. Kamran and fifty-four soldiers from his unit were welcomed to the KDP Guest House and treated to a huge meal of Kurdish cuisine.

In 1985, Kamran joined the Marines, from "a sense of loyalty, and wanting to pay America back for kindness she offered my family." For Desert Storm, he was called on active duty and served in northern Iraq though was not able to get home for security reasons. Kamran was hopeful that they would have gotten rid of Saddam Hussein at that time.

From 1985 to 1992, Kamran continued to serve in the United States Marine Reserves. Kamran left the Marines and joined the Army in 1993 to become a Blackhawk pilot. To the people who never left the war-torn Kurdistan, Kamran's life is difficult to imagine. "When I told my cousins (the Girls) that they could be pilots, they were blown away. As if how could this be?"

Kamran wanted his military comrades to make the trip with him so they could see what life has been like for the Kurds. "People just can't imagine," said Gardi." That's why I wanted to set a trip like this up. So that these guys could get out with these people who are so grateful and so they can see and realize what a difference they've made in these people's lives."

Kamran recalls moving frequently and constantly evading bombs and bullets from Saddam's planes. "We were always going from village to village, dodging his planes and their indiscriminate bombing of towns, villages, schools and mosques. This has been a prayer answered. Not just for me, but for a lot of the citizens of Iraq."

To seek safety for his family, Kamran's father moved them to Iran in 1974. Then with the help of a friend living in North Dakota, Kamran 's father was able to get asylum for them. They arrived in New York City in August 1977. A local sheriff and his church became their sponsor. Later, in 1982, the family moved to Dallas, Texas.

At the homecoming, his father, a Peshmarga – "those who face death" - who is still alive, gave the aviators a tour of the area where they had cataclysmic battles with Saddam's Divisions.

President Barzani made sure any time one of these soldiers had business in the area, they were treated as VIPS with a bus, a driver and were taken to the markets or to some historical sites like the mountain fortress and boundaries of Saladin--a strong warrior in that area many centuries ago.

Kamran summarized his homecoming. "It was wonderful. I spent all of my time there visiting family and friends, or they would come see me at my dad's house. It was very nice, hard to put into words.

"Life is slower and more laid back then here in America. People spend most of their free time visiting family and friends. Irbeal is hot like Texas without air conditioning. When you arrive at someone's house at eating times or if you are invited, they put on a feast. Most of my relatives have large families, i.e., 12-15 children. That is very typical in Kurdish culture although I think that is changing. They are like anyone else, wanting to provide for their family and to enjoy life." [16]

[Gordon Cimoli]

Monday, June 23rd

Woke up at 5am and got dressed so we could go to breakfast. The contractor-run dining facility is scheduled to open today. It is run by Brown and Root. I have only heard of them and all I have heard was praise. The dining facility is inside of many prefabricated trailers that are joined together to form a large dining area. There are air conditioners inside. I got a hot meal here in Balad--one that did not come out of cans. I had bacon, eggs, potatoes and toast.

Then were set to take off at 7:50am. We departed ahead of schedule and flew to Mosul. We landed in Mosul and were refueled while running (hot gas). We lined up on the runway and departed for Salab ad din (we just called it Saladin). The terrain was rising and leaving the desert floor in exchange for mountains and river valleys. The approach to the landing zone was marked by a prominent road though wound up the mountain. We could see the road approaching. It was very black and stood about amongst the brown hills. There were cars slowly driving up and down the road. We followed the road and were looking for a soccer field on the right side of the road.

We were over the small but beautiful city and did not see a soccer field. We circled and then, by luck, passed over the soccer field that was marked for our landing. We let it pass out the right side and could see large H's painted on the ground--a symbol for a helicopter landing site. We circled, then set up to land. We were the first aircraft in and as we approached, we heard someone calling us on the emergency frequency. It was a Special Forces unit that set up the landing area for us. They briefed us on the field and obstacles then we turned to land. We landed all 5 helicopters in the soccer field and still had room for 1 more. As we were landing we could see a lot of soldiers around the perimeter of the field. They were not U.S. soldiers so we assumed that they were Kurdish Pershmarga. This entire area has been controlled by the Kurdish Democratic Party (KDP) since 1991 after the Gulf War ended. Since then, this region has enjoyed many freedoms that they previously did not. For them, our liberation was just another step in their freedom. The biggest differences would be noticed by the people in the central and southern regions of Iraq.

We shut down and immediately noticed that it was only 89 degrees and, as sick as it sounds, it was cool and comfortable to us! We were immediately greeted by Kamran's father and cousin and many Kurdish soldiers. It was amazing to see an actual uniformed military other than our own. These guys have been defending theses very hills for decades!

We were loaded up into small busses and driven to the KDP Guesthouse. One thing to note: we were in a very wealthy town. We were told that it is a place that people go to vacation. It seemed that every car we saw was a BMW, Mercedes or something that was new and nice. The houses looked great although ethnically different.

Once there, we were treated like royalty. We were served tea and water on silver platters by men dressed in very nice suits! We were given free run of the grounds. We walked around enjoying the smell of the beautiful flowers that were all in bloom, the look of the mountain valley thousands of feet below us and the feel of the green grass! There were Peshmerga fighters all over the grounds and there were many men dressed in nice suits also. We walked around enjoying the mountain retreat.

After an hour, we all took our seats under a grass-roofed gazebo and waited for the President of the KDP to arrive. We first saw many more guards, then we saw a TV camera. We all stood up as President Marsaud Barzani walked down the steps to our gazebo. He was greeted by our Brigade and Battalion Commanders and then by Kamran Gardi. The President then walked around and shook each of our hands. He sat down then we all took our seats, the TV camera capturing the event as it happened and we all joked about being on Al Jezeera news that night.

We then watched as there were trays of food brought out for about 30 minutes. We all "ooh'ed and ahh'ed" and talked about the food is it came out. We took pictures of the food and then were finally allowed to eat.

The President went first. We all joined in and were amazed at a 30 foot table filled with trays of food, cold soft drinks and water. They had nice plates and silverware (this is normal for the people reading this, but was a shocker to what we have lived with for the past 5 months). I ate rice, pita bread, beef kabob, chicken kabob and kufta (potato roll with rice and beef in it). The food was amazing and I am boasting that it was the best meal I ever had in my life. While we ate, the food kept coming for 30 more minutes and then they changed gears and started bringing out desert. I saw them bring 2 huge cakes, baskets of peaches, plums, grapes and platters of watermelon and cantaloupe with the rinds cut off! WOW! While we ate, a man came around with an ice bucket and, using tongs, put ice into each of our glasses! After eating we got up and went to the desert table and enjoyed what we could fit on our plates. I have a white cake with chocolate frosting, coconut and banana inside. It was to die for! I also had some melon and a fresh peach that dripped down my chin as I bit into it. While we ate dessert, a man came around and served us some more tea! I just ate everything that I wanted and I felt totally comfortable afterwards.

At some point during our dinner, we were presented with the patches that the Peshmarga wear on their arms! We gave them some of our patches in return.

After we were done eating, we posed for a picture with the President, then were put back in the buses. We drove for a little more than an hour, through valleys and over mountain passes where the Kurds battled the Iraqi Army for many years. We arrived at a beautiful waterfall that appeared from the side of the mountain. We got out and took pictures of the beautiful sight. There were Kurdish civilians there who we walked around and shook hands with as well. We loaded the bus and went to another waterfall. This waterfall just happened to be on the face of the Kurdish 5 dinar bill! I took a picture of me holding the bill with the waterfall in the background.

While we drove around, Kamran's father told us about the history in the area. His dad was in the Iraqi Army but left it to join the Kurdish fighters in the early 1960's so he had a very unique perspective on the Kurds!

We took a company photo on top of a cliff overlooking a river valley thousands of feet below, then continued our drive back to the aircraft. We were already well behind schedule so things were a little rushed to leave.

Some more of Kamran's family showed up. His Grandma and many nieces, nephews and cousins arrived. He hadn't seen his Grandma since 1973 when his family fled the country! It was an awesome homecoming.

We took off and arrived back in Balad a few hours later. Everyone had smiles on their faces! It was a great day!

-Gordon Cimoli

The fifth story is about a woman, Salwa Ali Al-Oumaishi, who was murdered this year along with Fern Holland and Bob Zangis. Salwa was an advocate of women's rights in Iraq whose life was dedicated to defending women economically, socially and politically. This story was written by her sister, Suhair Al-Oumaishi.

[Suhair Al-Oumaishi]

It is not easy to describe Salwa's character; she was a witty and smart woman who faced lots of difficulties and trials in her life. Her merciful personality consists of many aspects and abilities. She was known among everybody by her excessively shrewd mind and her exceptional ability to understand people's minds, motives, deeds and what they hide.

Being born in Iraq in 1966 from Iraqi secular Muslim father and a Christian mother in a house that held together two religions peacefully made Salwa's alert mind aware of the kinds of discriminations in her society and at the same time she was studying both sides at home neutrally.

During her childhood she was active, lovely and so friendly. She entered private elementary school and finished her high school in her neighborhood area. Her enthusiasm for woman's rights began since that time, joking a lot at beginning then she became much more serious when she entered college of English arts in Baghdad.

At her twenties and thirties, she couldn't stop helping people around her, sensing their misery during the hard times of sanctions and standing with them in their weakness. She lifted their spirits and stood against tyranny and injustice. Merciful Salwa, who never, never gave up hope believing in the ability and strength of her people.

In college, she was highly nervous, her brother was assassinated two years ago by Saddam's regime and she responded to the call of freedom. Influenced by western civilization Salwa began to develop the idea: I WANT TO GO TO U.S.A.

After graduating from university, she faced the most disappointing future that can ever happen, the embargo on Iraq left her jobless and totally without freedom for long and endless years...with some temporary, low income, jobs sometimes. Spending these years at home helping her two retarded siblings in their crises and disorders, forcing herself to give up her dreams, she collapsed in 1998 and decided finally to leave Iraq.

Her sister Jinan (who lived in America and died of cancer later on in 2002) helped her along with her father to find a job and settle in Syria. Those years were her happiest times among relatives and friends in Syria, but her destiny decided to send her another problem: Her dearest and eldest sister is sick with cancer...Salwa, come and help me please.

Leaving for U.S. late 2002, Salwa stayed there and returned to Baghdad in February 2003 after the shock of the death of both her father and sister. She came back immediately to be with her family again during the third war on Iraq.

The debate of women's rights in the Middle East is thorough among its own societies but on the surface everything seems calm and all the problems do not exist. Salwa cared for human dignity since her early teenage time.

As usual understanding perfectly and accurately the hidden problems, the unspoken ideas, the real tendencies of women, the genuine force of her society and she had a vision...All kinds of problems in this society are formed and strengthened by its suppressed women and if you educate and set them free you can create another world in the Middle East.

Her main concern and anxiety for women's rights is the law of Honor Killing in Iraq, this law permits the male to kill a female on suspecting her having an affair. Salwa kept discussing this law and stood fiercely against it: "THE MAN HERE HAVE AN IMPORTANT AUTHORITY, THE AUTHORITY TO KILL," those were her words four days before she was gone forever.

The word (religion) in its Greek origin means: Re-uniting people. You should have seen Salwa's religion in this respect, her concern was to bring people together and help them understand and forgive each other.

For this reason she went to live with Americans in their own place and tried to form understanding between the two cultures. Bringing people together is her dream and ideal.

Salwa loved Fern from her heart, she calls her, "The Real Lady." How much were they twins in spirit? I don't know.

In America, Salwa met and liked many American saying they are helpful and simple.

During the war, Salwa waited impatiently for the Americans, for Democracy, for rebuilding and for work, work, and work. In that critical time, Ms. Fern Holland needed a woman secretary...Salwa ran for the job and gave many things up for it so that she can make her dreams come true, and now was the perfect time, women liberation? Women in parliament? Is this the door of heaven opened to her? Yes, I think it is.

Both Fern and Salwa believed sincerely that Iraq can achieve democracy; they thought the Iraqis want democracy and will sacrifice for it. Fern too believed in human dignity and Iraqi women began responding to them without hesitation.

So, the lovely two serious dreamers coming together encouraging each other, completing each other, doing and saying what the rest feared to do or say.

Sing for Salwa: "The Girl with April in Her Eyes," by Chris De Burgh, it was her favorite song during her twenties.

And what can I sing for you, courageous Fern? You sacrificed your life for other country and other people's problems.

-Suhair Al-Oumaishi

The sixth story was written about an Iraqi American family living in Florida. Though they came to the U.S. long before Saddam Hussein, I still find their story enlightening. Four families from Mosul came to Florida together in the early 1930's and started a grocery business together. Soon after arriving, one of the men died of appendicitis. The other encouraged the wife and children to go back as they cut her out of the partnership. She stayed and survived. She pulled her eldest son out of high school so he could start his own grocery store, she sent her middle son to an orphanage, and she worked sewing clothes and roasting peanuts. The youngest son, starting at age 5, would sell the peanuts. When World War II started, the eldest son was drafted, made a cook in the Army and fought in Africa and Italy. The middle son came back to run the store. The younger son's job was to make sure the mayor received his payments. He grew up, went to college, married a local girl and together they raised seven daughters. This story is about one of the daughters. [17]

[Anonymous 4]

How many have seen the movie, "My Big Fat Greek Wedding"? If I'd known such a story could have been a hit, I'd have scooped them with my "Big Fat Iraqi Wedding." After all, my story begins well before that movie was ever made.

Lynn (not her real name), and I came to that time in our relationship which is known as time to meet the parents. We were both living in Atlanta and we picked Easter to make the drive down to Florida where she grew up.

As we exited off the I-95, we stopped to see her sister along the way, mind you I say one of her sisters as she has five others. One of her sisters is only nine months older than Lynn. Her dad jokes, "I got her mother in the hospital." As we neared the complex, I noticed a few signs for buildings leased by Zeyadi [not the actual name] Management Company. "Oh, they are my dad's cousins."

Our next stop was her dad's pharmacy, where he worked everyday for thirty years. On the way we passed a Zeyadi (her maiden name) pharmacy. "No, that's not his. That's a cousin's." When we did get to the pharmacy there was a security monitoring company called Zeyadi. This of course was her dad's cousins. I was beginning to suspect a new definition to my understanding of what cousin meant.

Later in the mall, Lynn introduced me to three young ladies we just happened to bump into. They were her cousins. At home that evening I looked through her high school yearbook. There were a total of 14 Zeyadis in her school of 1400. In the Dallas phone book there are exactly ZERO Zeyadis. Of course she says, "They are my cousins."

The next day's Easter feast was held in the spacious back yard of the ranch-style home with a giant old oak providing shade. It seemed to me there were about 100 guests – all family. Surveying the crowd, I noticed one person with blond hair, obviously he married someone. The rest of the crowd – nice tans and dark hair. Well, and Lynn's mom whose family was French.

The food was a spread I had never had before for Easter or any other occasion. It was new then and now is familiar. I can say what the dishes are; I just have no idea how to spell them. Later I would learn about the preparation. Rolling grape leaves is a time consuming art. Among the desserts was a pastry the Greeks called baklava, and here I was told it was baklava with the accent on the first syllable.

Early the next year Lynn and I are back in Florida for a weekend of wedding parties and showers. I meet Fred out in the yard raking furiously on a Saturday morning. "I'm all upset. Two of my cousin's sons are missing. We don't know if they've been captured or killed." I hadn't noticed any stories about U.S. soldiers being taken prisoner.

Later in the day Fred tells me, "Now I understand about the Civil War. Family fighting family." Now I understand what he is talking about. I'm in the U.S. Army and his cousin's sons are in the Iraqi army. A month later, Fred learns the two young men are safely back home. They had been prisoners and released.

After months of preparation and bickering between Lynn and her mother, the big day arrives. Lynn's mom was doing her best to make sure the party was going to meet the social standards and norms with all the exact protocol. Her parents had just been accepted to the most excusive country club in town, and her mom was nervous something would go socially wrong.

Now knowing that Lynn's family is quite large, please understand there is a budget for the wedding. Our guest list was to be limited to 300. Lynn says I can invite 50. I can't think of fifty people to invite. She's happy, "Less family to insult." And it was a big wedding, half dozen bridesmaids, with matching set of guys in tuxedos, plus a group of Army friends decked in formal Blues carry sabers. More on that later.

Since the day of the wedding was on the same day as the Florida State – Florida football game, we held the wedding at night. For my friends and I, we just enjoyed the day at the sports bar. For Lynn, this just added to the nervousness since two of the bridesmaids were going to the game in Gainesville – three hours away.

Well they made it back and the wedding went off without a hitch. The reception had its moments too as Lynn had no idea of the military tradition of being swatted by a saber with the words, "Welcome to the Army, Mrs. Smith." And one of my less-bashful friends had organized a rendition of the song Tom Cruise sang in Top Gun, "You've Lost that Loving Feeling."

In the end Lynn had the last laugh, as the only line that made the social papers was that the Ice Sculpture was not a swan or something appropriate to the occasion, but was a penguin.

-Anonymous 4

Chapter Six
The Events

Some events over the past year and a half have commanded a lot of headline space and much has been written about them. Some of the contributors of this book were involved in one way or another, and others were witnesses.

The Background

The Military action in Iraq did not start as a bleed-over from Afghanistan and the War on Terror. The issues with Iraq started much earlier than 9/11. The conflict also did not start because Saddam Hussein has weapons of mass destruction (WMD). Lots of nations have WMD and just the existence is not cause for U.S. led invasion. The problem with Iraq started because of Saddam Hussein and years of learning that he could not be contained by peaceful means.

In 1980, Iraq invaded Iran because Saddam Hussein thought he could take advantage of Iran, in the aftermath of its recent revolution, by capturing a portion of their country and stealing their oil. The war dragged on for many years in a deadly stalemate. Finally Iran quit after Saddam Hussein began using chemical weapons on the troops and also bombing civilian population centers. His next plans were to actually begin dropping nerve gas on the cities. Saddam Hussein was the first to use chemical weapons since 1918 and the first to use a WMD since 1945.

During the war, Saddam Hussein had bankrupted his government and owed a few billion dollars to many nations including U.S., Kuwait, Russia, Germany and France. To raise the money, he thought he could just invade Kuwait and take their oil, gold and anything else he could cart off.

He put this plan into action in August 2, 1990, and within a few days he had most of the world condemning his actions. He proved that he was aggressive and had no bounds to his plans against others. Since taking over, he had attacked Kuwait and Iran, he had used chemical weapons, he was building a nuclear weapons program, he was building a super cannon, and he had build long-range missiles. In addition, he was threatening Saudi Arabia and the ability to dominate the world's oil market. Within a few months, he would launch missile strikes against Israel. It was easy for the world to stand up and say no.

Within about six months, a coalition of countries forced Saddam Hussein out of Kuwait. These countries agreed to not press the attack if Hussein would dismantle his programs to build chemical and nuclear weapons. To encourage a rapid enforcement the United Nations sanctioned a trade embargo against Iraq from selling oil. The thought was that he would comply within the next 60 days.

There was also some hope that the Iraqi people would rise up and overthrow Saddam, and install a new government. The Shiites in southern Iraq and the Kurds in northern Iraq did rise up. They were defeated and brutally slaughtered. Saddam's very loyal Republican Guards were left intact after Desert Storm and they were able to squash the unorganized rebellion.

Soon it became very evident that Hussein was just as ruthless as ever. He was not cooperating with the United Nations to allow for inspections to see if he was complying. He had no care of the effects of the oil embargo. He let his people slowing starve and was able to further his personal wealth by smuggling out oil and keeping all the profits for himself.

Back in the United States it was frustrating. The glorious victory lost luster. Saddam Hussein was worse than ever. Weapons Inspectors were led on wild goose chases and could only watch as trucks would leave with military escorts out the back gate when they knocked on the front gate.

It was also the time of a new administration that recognized the problem and worked on solving it while placing the issue behind other international issues. The thought was that Iraq was basically contained and situations in Somalia, Bosnia, Haiti and Kosovo were more immediate.

There was an effort in 1996 for the CIA to assist in a coup d'état and this failed. In 1997, there was a bombing campaign to get rid of the WMD programs. This was not successful. In February 1998, British Prime Minister said of him and President Clinton, "We've been discussing issues like Iraq, where we are considering if diplomatic solutions fail taking military actions."[18]

Secretary of State Albright led a town hall meeting in 1998 to test American resolve on dealing with Saddam and the result was an overwhelming no.

Later in 1998, America forced a showdown with Hussein on inspecting a palace and he kicked the weapons inspectors out of Iraq. This gave the U.S. an excuse to begin another bombing campaign. This failed, too. The issue wasn't going away; it wasn't getting any better.

Over the years, Saddam was working on his PR campaign and was winning more people over to him with sympathy. He would show how the U.N. sanctions were starving his people. He would show pictures of death and destruction from the U.S. bombing, because he would place military targets in and around schools, hospitals and other civilian areas. He also embarked on a new image creation plan by claiming he was a leader of the Muslim world, so to win over Muslim allies to his side. In 1991, he added the words, "God is great" to the Iraqi flag. He played up the notion of his crusade against the evil Zionists and their backers, the U.S.

Then on September 11, 2001, the world became suddenly very interested in the Middle East again. The U.S. was successful in tracking down terrorists in Afghanistan. There grew speculation that terrorists may have fled across the border. Iraq has had a history of harboring terrorists; the most notorious was Abu Nidal. Did Saddam Hussein support al-Qaeda and its plans to bomb the U.S.? So far the evidence is inconclusive. We know of meetings between the group and Iraq officials. We have not found any written contract or document.

One argument is that nothing justifies going to war. We should set the example of a peaceful nation and work toward solutions without violence. We as the world leader need to work our efforts toward peace. How can we convince others of the advantages of peace if we are attacking other nations? The underlying assumption is that people are basically good. People or nations may have grievances and if these are understood, then a workable negotiation is possible. Or, if he refuses to cooperate, then he can be persuaded by denying him something that he needs. This was the argument of the U.N. sanctions against Saddam Hussein. Since these particular sanctions were not achieving the desired goals, then there exists another possible peaceful solution. The argument is: Why didn't we try this instead of just attacking Iraq with violence? This is a valid question held by a large minority.

The majority of our elected officials chose instead to initiate a violent action to unseat Saddam Hussein. Their reasoning is that we tried twelve years with sanctions and these had no desired effect. He continued his crimes and he did not change his ways. This is likened to the criminal on the loose. Can you be effective at reforming him when he is free on his crime spree? Would it be better to try to bring him in and then reform him? Secondly, are innocent victims safer and more secure if the criminal is brought in? In the case of Saddam Hussein, the majority of our elected officials felt that it was better to capture Saddam and protect the innocents rather than working to find another peaceful solution. So is the U.S.-led invasion wrong for violating peace, or is it justified in the effort to save the people? This is a valid debate for future issues as we have the choice to vote.

Other folks argue that the U.S. should not have gotten involved without the rest of the world behind it. Having other nations support your actions is a good sanity check. In this case, thirty other nations joined in with the U.S. This is an indication that the idea to free Iraq has merit. If no one supported the U.S., then this is an indication that the proposed action needs to be fully scrutinized. The fact that France, Germany and Russia did not approve causes concern for some. The reason for why these did not is worth investigating.

Each of these countries has leaders elected by the people. If they want to get re-elected then they may not want to risk an unpopular decision. Because of the history of two World Wars fought in Europe, going to war again is difficult to justify. The U.S. has no memory of how devastating a war can be. Europeans still remember; they still see the effects. Support for any war for any reason will meet resistance.

Another reason why France and Germany are not supportive is the currency issue. In November 2000, Saddam also drove a wedge into the western countries. He switched the basis of his reserve currency from the U.S. dollar to the Euro. His intent was to win the support of Europe in any future confrontation with America. The value of the Euro would rise, helping the economies of Europe. Once this currency reserve was changed, then any future switch back would devalue the Euro. This would make any future move to support a U.S. led effort in Iraq very unpopular in any country using the Euro as currency. Elected leaders would have a hard time explaining to their voters why they tanked their economy to support the U.S. After all, the individuals who were concerned about the human rights violations would be satisfied because the U.S. was going to free the Iraqi people regardless of the support of France and Germany. The decision not to join in is very common for some elected officials, whose foremost priority is to protect their careers.

Because the United Kingdom does not use the Euro as currency, the financial pressure was taken off the decision for Prime Minister Tony Blair to support President Bush. Mr. Blair was able to weigh in based upon the same factors as President Bush. He actually had a more difficult decision as he had to go against his own Labour party in supporting the U.S. The Labour party was weighing in on the side to support peace. Whatever the reasons for Mr. Blair to join in against Saddam Hussein, they must have been very significant.

With the history of Winston Churchill, one factor that might have played into the decision is the memory of dealing with Hitler. All during the 1930's, Europe watched the activities of Adolph Hitler in Germany closely. He violently gained power internally and began taking freedoms away from the citizens. Soon he began massive captures of innocent people and throwing them into concentration camps. Rumors circulated that he was systemically killing off those he did not like, especially the Jews of Germany. Then he started peacefully annexing outside land into Germany, like Austria and parts of Czechoslovakia. The prevailing thought was that if you don't do anything to make him mad then Hitler would keep his activities within his borders. Up through 1938 everything was a German issue. Winston Churchill was furiously sounding the warning bell: Hitler is a rogue and needs to be stopped. There was no peaceful resolution that would solve the problem. By the time the rest of the world woke up, Hitler had attacked Poland, Norway, Belgium, The Netherlands and France. What we will never know is how the world would have turned out if Hitler was seized in 1938. The millions who died in World War II would still be alive. The seven million murdered would instead be set free. How could anyone have known in 1938 what was about to happen to the world? If we knew, then the answer on what to do is obvious.

Is 2003 like 1938? Does stopping Hussein now prevent a far worse future catastrophe? In 1938 there was no precedence to go by. Sir Winston Churchill had only his instinct on the nature of Hitler. In 2003, we had Hitler as a model of what can happen. What we will never know is what would have happened if we had let Saddam Hussein continue in power. We can't know the answer though we can speculate. Is the chance worth taking of repeating a World War II scenario? What if Hussein was able to gain control over all the oil fields of Iran and Saudi Arabia? What if he neutralized Israel with chemical missiles? What if he used oil as a weapon to keep Europe and Japan on his side? What if he used his wealth to buy off all the other Arab and Muslim countries? Could the U.S. stop him without oil, without staging locations to launch an offensive, and with a rapidly devaluing dollar? What would stop him from launching terrorist attacks against us?

Attack from Within

Before the conflict really began, the U.S. had suffered a serious blow from within. A U.S. Army Non-Commissioned Officer attacked the leadership of his unit with grenades and rifle fire. Two officers died and fourteen were wounded.

About 1:00 A.M. on March 23, 2003, just hours before the brigade was to rise and start movement into Iraq, the assailant tossed two grenades into the brigade headquarters tent. The commander, Colonel Hodges, was injured. The assailant then went to the next tent and tossed in another grenade. Major Gregory Stone, the Air Force Liaison officer, died from this attack. The assailant calmly tossed a grenade into a third tent. Two officers were seriously wounded. In the midst of flaming tents and obscuring dust, the survivors rushed out. The assailant shot two men, killing one, Captain Chris Seifert, the brigade intelligence officer. [19] Losing him in the final hours before war affected the S2 section so deeply that it literally took most of the war for the section to recover. [20]

In the attack on the brigade, the senior leadership officers were the wounded. To supervise the medical evacuation and secure a perimeter, junior leaders were needed to step up and take charge. Captains Townlee Hendrick and Tony Jones did just this and also organized a search for the assailant. Both captains were wounded and refused medical attention until the situation was under control. [21]

Later that night a suspect was apprehended. Sergeant Asan Akbar was quoted as saying, "You guys are coming into our countries and you're going to rape our women and kill our children." [22]

Tony Jones returned to the brigade two days later dressed in boots and a hospital gown. Colonel Hodges felt he had no right to order him back to medical care since he also had refused to have his shrapnel removed until after the war. [23]

[Allison Rowe]

20 March 2003

The Air War began today. Saddam started to fire his SCUD missiles today and we've had four SCUD alerts today already. It is now 10:00PM and we're expecting more through the night. Lying in body armor, Kevlar, and protective mask for long periods can actually be very relaxing...cause you tend to drift off into a nice sleep [smiley face]. The mask is ripping my hair and I'm not always certain that I have a good seal. Good night! G-Day begins on Sunday.

26 March 2003

Serial # 4 and 5 have been delayed as for departure time goes. I've had a difficult time keeping track of the days. If it weren't for my watch it would be worse.

We were supposed to leave on the 23rd but the events of the other morning as well as bad weather delayed our SP time.

All was well as we lay down to sleep on the eve of 22 March. I lay on my cot and woke up because my bladder was full. I was trying to decide if I wanted to put my clothes & gear on just to go to the latrine. I looked at the time on my watch (which is set 10 minutes fast) and noticed it was 0110 local time. The previous nights, the SCUD alerts were usually occurring around 0100 or 0130 local. The early morning of the 23rd of March was different though.

No sooner had I gathered my clothes and bent over to tie my boots did a loud boom sound. I heard aircraft overhead and then another boom. But no SCUD alarm had sounded. I couldn't figure out what as happening, but every one in the tent was up and putting their masks on.

Were people (the "Bad" people) invading our camp? Had they infiltrated the gates and the berm or were they flying overhead? No one knew. Voices began to come over the radio at the front of the tent. Still, no one in the back could really hear.

As for me, I still had to pee pretty badly so I began to cut a plastic H2O bottle with my Gerber. The tent was silent except for my cutting. SFC Burdin, got annoyed with it and instructed whoever was cutting to stop...of course he didn't know it was me or why I was doing it since then lights were out. I stopped and continued to hold my bladder.

To make a long story short, the attack came from within. A SGT Akbar (which means Great or Best in Arabic) had taken it upon himself to delay our convoys that were to leave that morning. His ultimate goal though was (and he said this to one of the MI interrogators) "I want to stop the pillage and plunder of Iraq." I hope they execute him right away. He deserves no mercy.

He ran into 3 tents and threw frag and incendiary grenades. I believe 14 people were injured to include COL Hodges, the 1st BDE Commander. He shot CPT Chris Seifert in the back. The CPT died on the way to UDARI. Today I found out that the Air Force major, Major Stone, passed away. His nickname was Linus and he was always very kind and he would smile when I'd see him at the BDE TOC.

I had the opportunity to see the three tents and where the explosions went off; I have pictures. There was still blood on the walls & floor.

We leave tomorrow.

Praise God for the peace He's given me. I thank Him for waking me up several minutes prior to the grenade explosions, so that I was alert and could act without hesitation. Praise God for delaying our trip for whatever the reason might be.

-Allison Rowe

The Start of the Battle

It was certainly a newsworthy event the day the ground war started. For those on the ground, it was indeed a memorable event. For the Iraqi forces fighting for Saddam Hussein, it was a bit of surprise. In 1991, they were prepped many days with air strikes before any ground forces started moving. This time the ground forces began moving before the air strikes. For those Iraqis with the task of sabotaging the oil wells, they were either surprised or they openly disobeyed orders so as to protect their country's resources and economy for a new Iraq. Only seven wells out of a thousand in southern Iraq were set on fire. [24]

[Gordon Cimoli (his last letter before the invasion)]

Wednesday, March 19th, 2003

I am doing well. I am safe and I am well trained. I volunteered to do this and am ready for the challenge. I love you all.

-Gordon Cimoli

[Michael Hanes]

In the Marines, I was a member of a Force Recon Platoon. We were the elite and our platoon was one of the best. I was a member of the Dive Team though for any mission we were all crossed-trained. When the war started we were there.

Our very first mission was to fly across the border of Kuwait into Iraq and to establish control of the highest point in Iraq, Safwan Hill. This was crucial because it overlooked the border. The day before we were airlifted to the hill, some Iraqi soldiers were spotted. Air strikes hit the hilltop and damaged the two buildings. When we flew in early that morning, we cleared the rubble and found no resistance.

After establishing control of Safwan Hill, it was watching history in the making as the First Marine Division past by. I remember seeing crop fields all over and houses on the fields. Seeing people driving occasionally from home to home. They had white flags on their vehicles. There were burning oil rigs in the distance.

My first contact of the Iraqi people was very positive and heart warming. A day later when the British bird came to pick us up to take us back to Kuwait to prep for more missions, I remember taking off from that hill and flying very low to the ground, going right over Iraqi people. They were running out there with their hands in the air jumping up and down with smiles on their faces. It was plain to see that they were happy to see us. There were men, women and children. We went from field to field, circling them occasionally and waving. It was a very positive initial interaction.

The British pilots were amazing. They flew right over the top of the ground banking to the left and then to the right. It was awesome.

-Michael Hanes

[Paul Colbert]

The border between Kuwait and Iraq was a desolate no-man's-land, 10 kilometers wide, starting with triple-strand concertina wire at the 5-km point on both sides, followed by a 10-foot wide ditch about 100 feet away from the actual border, which was a double fence with barbed wire at the top and patrol roads on both sides. Engineers began to tear apart the concertina wire and fill in paths over the ditch in preparation for the launch of war. Nearby, at Camp Udairi, north of 35th by about 16 kilometers, all the preparations were on a grand scale. The entire Third Infantry Division was scattered across hundreds of acres of open desert, with their engineers at the tip of the spear, preparing the necessary measures to thrust its M1A2 Abrams Main Battle Tank across the border for the first full-out, land-based American invasion of another country since Nazi-controlled Germany in World War II.

I sat on Alpha South Ramp as the first few aircraft began to roll forward to Runway 36 and a chill ran throughout my body. I was going to fly into Iraq. We launched with no problem, right on time, and never had any issues all the way up and all the way back. Having never flown a Chinook at 30 feet above the ground at 140 knots, it was a steep learning curve, needless to say. We dropped the guys off and came back to 35th with no problems. I eventually earned an Air Medal for that mission.

-Paul Colbert

[Chris Gehler]

All during December through middle of March, we were expecting that we would jump in to start the action. This is what the 82nd Airborne Division lives for – the massive airborne insertion. I know the routine having been with the 82nd in Panama in 1989. Now I was the commander of an attack helicopter battalion and training for our part to get in quickly to protect the troops. Then at last minute the jump was changed to a drive. We had just thirty-six hours to change our plans.

We began around midday and drove through the night from our base in Kuwait to a position two kilometers short of the border. That night it was very dark and we drove in total blackout. Then suddenly, out of nowhere, a potato truck comes hauling across a side road in the night desert. The driver had no idea what was about to happen to him. He was coming directly perpendicular into a massive convoy and he never saw it. This poor Kuwaiti farmer broadsided the HMMWV right in front of me.

In all my training there was never a contingency as to what to do when hit by a potato truck in the middle of an invasion. I had a wrecked HMMWV, two injuries, and a schedule to meet. I took care of the wounded, towed the Hummer and moved on. As it turned, out there were accidents all up and down the convoy.

When I got to bivouac site, I had a strange feeling. This was almost the exact spot I bivouacked back in 1991. That time it was my furthest-most advance. This time it was Day One – just the beginning.

-Chris Gehler

[Fred Wellman]

We finally got the word on March 14th that D-day was the 20th and that we would go in on the 23rd. I got all of two hours of sleep the night before our departure. I had gotten called at 2200 because one of the Generals wanted an aircraft for a mission the next morning and it took until after midnight to figure out that they had already given the mission to someone else. Then I decided that it was my last chance to take a "porta-potty" break and shower for a while so I did. Then I had to pack my own stuff after focusing on pushing out the battalion the whole time we were in Kuwait.

So, I finally got to bed only to be awoken by two huge explosions at about 0200. We all jumped up and threw on our gas masks until we could find out what happened. Fortunately, it was not an attack on us; however, it had been two Patriot missiles going off, taking out an incoming missile and sadly a British jet. It crashed not three kilometers from our camp killing both crew-members. All of this left me a little tired the next day.

We got up at 0400 and finally mounted up at about 1200 and took off into Iraq to make our way to our first Assembly Area at Forward Area Refueling Point (FARP) Shell. We all had to put on our chemical protective suits. I think my NBC sergeant was being funny because he gave me a large suit. Now I am not normally a thin guy but these things were huge. I had to roll the pants up like 8 inches and wear a belt to keep them up. So, I looked pretty silly with that, body armor and my survival vest.

We arrived about an hour before sundown after several stops for fuel and the discovery that the planned location was under water. But, FARP Shell was really not too bad. It was well out in the middle of the desert near an ancient trading post. The ground was rolling and rocky. We landed and found that our Advance Party Convoy had not yet arrived. So, we had 18 UH-60's and crews, 24 Pathfinders, no vehicles and only man portable radios. For staff I had myself, the Intel officer, the Signal officer and my Tactical Operations Officer and no one else.

I tried to raise the Brigade headquarters on the aircraft radio for about half an hour with no luck. They were some 8 kilometers away and the way the aircraft were positioned the antenna was pointing the wrong way. So, I went to my commander and told him that I could probably put up a combat expedient long antenna on one of the Pathfinder's radios and get hold of Brigade. But, they would probably want me to then monitor the radio all night or I could say screw it...post guards at every aircraft and set Observation Posts manned by our infantry and get a decent night's sleep. He and I decided that a good night's sleep was the best option.

So, I posted the guards, rolled out my sleeping bag under the tail boom of my aircraft and bedded down for the night. I was not aware of it but at about 0200 a single truck rolled up to collect my boss and take him for a four-hour excursion to see the Brigade Commander. When all of the other commanders finally arrived the Brigade CO had already gone to bed so they all went back to their battalion Assembly Areas. The funny thing is that this huge Army truck had rolled not 10 feet from my head some four times through the night and I never heard it once! Good thing we had guards.

I awoke at about 0800 to the chirping of birds next to my head and a nice cool morning. It would only last a short time because the same truck pulled up to collect myself and my boss to head to Division Headquarters to find out how the 11th Attack Helicopter Regiment had gotten pummeled in Karbala the night before. It was going to be a long first week in "combat."

-Fred Wellman

Missing Convoys

The story of Private First Class Jessica Lynch is one we all know. This story touched us all. We are accustomed to our sons going off to fight and die for our country. Even though females make a strong presence in our military and have many dangerous jobs, we are still not accustomed to young girls from West Virginia, or anywhere else, being shot and taken prisoner. The story of her capture and her rescue made a lot of headlines, though the story is not just about her. The 507th Maintenance Company was ambushed and eleven were killed, many were wounded and six taken prisoner. It is a tragic story of the effects of a fast moving, non-linear battlefield. To those used to being able to see lines on a map and telling where each side stood, this story seems a bit preposterous. How can a convoy of trucks end up so far behind enemy "territory"? These are not front line fighting troops. These soldiers never really expected to ever fire a weapon.

In summary, the 507th Maintenance Company was moving forward following closely behind the front line troops. They left Kuwait at 2:00P.M. on March 20th with sixty-four soldiers and thirty-three vehicles. They drove almost nonstop until the early morning of March 23rd when the company commander missed his turn and went into enemy territory. After passing two Iraqi military check points without incident, he realized his mistake and turned around.

Now the Iraqis were awake and set up numerous ambushes. The convoy under fire split into three sections. Obstacles were placed in the road to block them; the soft sand off the road was impossible to drive through. Trying to speed up they missed more turns. One section made it back and Marines went to rescue the others. By the time they did, they found a badly mauled company. [25]

Mainly because of the compassion of a few Iraqis, word leaked out that a female American was in a hospital in Al-Nasiriyah. After midnight on April 2nd, a task force of special operations troops stormed the hospital and rescued Jessica Lynch. [26]

Miles away in Samarra on April 13th, the remaining captured soldiers of the 507th and two downed pilots were rescued by the Marines. [27] The next step was to get these soldiers back to medical care and loved ones as quickly as possible.

[Gordon Cimoli]

Sunday, April 13th

Found out that the U.S. POW's were found — 2 Apache pilots and 5 soldiers from the 507th Maintenance Company. I guess they were found north of Baghdad (Sammarah). The Marines heard that there were some Americans ahead and when they drove north, they found them. They put them in a helicopter and flew them to Baghdad International then put them on a flight to Kuwait International. We received a mission to fly escorts from their unit to the Armed Forces hospital to assist the freed POW's in the repatriation process. Their escorts will stay with the POW's all through the repatriation process and will actually go home also. What an awesome bit of news! Everyone is excited. We are supposed to arrive at Kuwait International at approximately the same time as the POW's arrive.

We rushed out to the aircraft to get ready to take off. It was close to nightfall but we had our NVGs all ready to go when it was time to transition to wearing them. We waited in the aircraft for our passengers to arrive. Across the desert assembly area we saw a Humvee driving up. It had a small flag waving on one of its radio antennas and it was kicking up a dust tail behind it. We had 9 passengers in all--7 escorts, LTC Ball (1-227th Bn Commander) and the company commander (Viper 06). The escorts' sole function is to remain with the POW's as they go through their repatriation process. They will leave the theater with them and remain by their side as a familiar face until the process is complete. They do this to make the POW's as comfortable as possible and to have a friend with them.

We took off for Tallil airfield (An Nasariayah) at 14:05 zulu. We arrived there at sunset and refueled and saw lightning in the direction of our flight route. I called weather to update and it wasn't looking good but they said we may be able to make it around the thunderstorms. We took off and tried. It was getting harder to see because the sun was down so we eventually put our goggles on. It was just about the same as having them off but it was getting darker so we would need them anyhow. We could see the flashes still happening and tried to continue on. We wanted to get them to their people. We saw a huge streak that covered the sky to our front and all decided to turn around. We went back to Tallil and shutdown. I spent a few minutes on the radio with the weather forecaster trying to figure out when the storm would pass but after a bit of frustration, I asked them to send a vehicle out to our location to bring us in. We got a ride into Brigade by CW2 Sobel from Big Windy.

We talked to weather and looked at the radar loops and it didn't seem like it was getting better but weather thought it would clear in a few hours. We waited on the weather but it only got worse. A huge thunderstorm passed overhead and dumped large amounts of rain on us. Meanwhile, out at the aircraft, Javier said the lightning was causing static electricity to dance on the blades of the aircraft. The lines of electricity were a few inches long. They kept away from the aircraft but could feel their hair standing up.

We decided that we would not be able to make it there tonight so Brigade gave us a Humvee to take back to the aircraft. We went back to the aircraft and all 18 of us slept in or around the two aircraft. It was a rough night for sleeping but it wasn't too bad. I slept in my MOPP suit and we also broke into our survival kits and opened the sleeping bags.

Monday, April 14th

Woke up at 3:00 zulu and got in the Humvee to drive back to Brigade Headquarters. It was clear and beautiful outside. Got the weather and call sign information that we would need to fly today.

Took off at 4:20 Zulu and headed to Kuwait. While inbound to the hospital, we were cleared to fly directly over downtown Kuwait City. We had to remain below 300 feet so we were able to see quite a view that most people do not get to see. We flew low and at a moderate speed over the city. It was beautiful to see all the tall towers and ornate buildings. We passed one building that had some patriot batteries around it so we assume that it was something special.

We approached the Kuwaiti Armed Forces Hospital and surveyed the area to figure out how to land on the pad. Once we got around to the other side of the area, it was very apparent that we would land to the east as the landing pad had a nice cleared area for the approach. There was only room enough for one aircraft to land at a time so one landed while the other stayed in the air. Once everyone unloaded all their gear and cleared the pad, we both slid far left and right and made room to shutdown on the pad. Of course this was not the best idea because it blocked any other aircraft from landing there but we had nowhere else to go.

The escorts disappeared into the hospital where we were quite certain that a very happy reunion was occurring. We waited outside and found a beautiful, thick, lush grass field to roll around in. After a few hours, a couple of our passengers returned (LTC Ball and the Company Commander) and we took them back to Rams. The rest of the escorts remained with the released POW's.

-Gordon Cimoli

What happened to the 507th is a tragic story of how things can go wrong so quickly. With the speed of the coalition advance racing to the heart of the enemy forces, not everything went perfect. The plan was based on speed to dismantle the Iraqi forces. Protecting the supply lines at times became a risk.

[Kristen Lewis]

We crossed the berm the morning of 21 March 03. We were in a mass Battalion Convoy (703d MSB), broken down into march units (by company). I, 1LT Lewis, was just riding along in an empty seat in the company 1SGs HMMWV. The second full day across the berm, the 1SG went to ride in a different HMMWV because the radios in ours kept going out. Some time around the fourth day across the berm in Iraq, we started to lose vehicles. Some vehicles were breaking down due to mechanical failures. Some vehicles were just going at a snail's pace because they kept getting stuck in the sand.

We are a support unit; therefore, we have the Heavy Equipment Transporter (M1070/M1000 HETs) and Semi-trailers (M1088/M871 S&Ps) to haul equipment and supplies. These were the two types of vehicles primarily getting stuck in the sand. The S&Ps were heavy-laden with pallets of MREs and water, our unit basic load.

Around midday on day four, MAJ Musgrave, our Battalion S-3, drove up to my vehicle (a M998 HMMWV) and asked if I had a radio and a PLGR (GPS). I had both (I had one of our communication specialists fix the radios in the HMMWV the day prior), but no map. He told me to go back along the route we had just driven as a unit and pick up three HETs that were bogged down in the sand. He gave me a grid location to link back up with the battalion after I picked up the vehicles because they were going to continue north. I went back along the route and actually found four stuck HETs. Our company Truck Master, SFC Bargaineer, was already back with the HETs trying to dig them out. Anytime they made any progress, the next set of axles to touch the ground would dig in.

After an hour of digging, the Battalion Command Sergeant Major, CSM Brooks, drove back to our location to check on the progress. He also informed me that there were a couple S&Ps up the road from us that were now stuck. He asked us to pull them out too as we rode by on our way to link back up with the Battalion. CSM Brooks drove back up the route to join the rest of the Battalion. We finally had all four HETs moving and un-stuck and found the S&Ps that were a little farther up the road. We spent several hours pulling the trucks out of the sand. Anytime we made any progress, the trucks waiting to continue moving would sink into the sand and we would have to start all over again. We were able to move a few kilometers before another vehicle would dig itself into the sand.

Around nightfall, while digging out one of the vehicles, we noticed a couple of HMMWVs and Cargo Trucks about 200 yards away. Upon closer inspection, we discovered the vehicles and personnel belonged to companies in our Battalion. They needed our assistance (the pulling power of the HETs) to get their vehicles out of the sand also. In total, we recovered 14 vehicles carrying 34 people. Everyone starting moving forward and we made it a few kilometers before vehicles started digging into the sand again. Around 0300, we called it quits and slept in place that night.

We started moving out the next morning and eventually made it to the grid location MAJ Musgrave gave me. No one was there. I picked up the radio and started calling to any unit in the area to try and locate our battalion. There was no answer. I rummaged around in the HMMVVE and finally found a map. The only problem with the map was that it was an aerial map with no definitive grids or distinguishing features (i.e., Roads, rivers, etc). I started to get nervous when it sank in that the unit had moved on without us. Then, all of a sudden I heard the company 1SG, 1SG Seabrook, on the radio. I broke into the conversation and explained that I had the vehicles that had dropped behind and we needed a good link-up grid. The 1SG gave me a grid to their location and told me they would wait on us there.

Once again, when we made it to the link up point, the unit had already moved on. I tried repeatedly to get a response on the radio but all I heard was static. I did not know any follow-on grids to where the Battalion was going or to any fuel points. Several drivers informed me they were getting low on fuel. Now fuel was quickly becoming a priority along with finding our unit. CW4 Olinger, one of the warrant officers from my Battalion who was riding in a HMMWV we picked up earlier remembered the location of a maintenance collection point some kilometers back and volunteered to drive all the way back with the 5 gallon fuel cans from each truck and fill them. I knew it would take several hours but was a necessity.

About five or six hours after he had left, CW4 Olinger came rolling up to our area with full fuel cans. Because of CW4 Olinger, we were able to continue moving. We spent the night in place because everyone had only a couple hours of sleep in the last three days. I did not know any follow-on grids to where the Battalion was going and really was at a loss as to what to do next. I kind of sat back in my HMMWV, looked at the map, looked at the PLGR, looked at the sky, then looked at the vast amount of sand. I remembered hearing someone say during one of the night meetings that once the sand path runs into a hard road to take a right onto the road. I could see the tire marks of vehicles that had already been through the area in the sand. I looked up at the sun and thought to myself, "Well, we're supposed to be taking over Baghdad. Baghdad is definitely north of here, so if the sun is there..." I looked at my PLGR, set it to go north, and tried to follow the tracks in the sand northward as best as I could. We eventually hit what I thought was the hard road.

Unbeknownst to me, it was not the road I was trying to find. I took a right onto the road, thinking we were catching up to the Battalion. About three or four miles down the road, I had an uneasy feeling about the direction we were going. The PLGR was reading wrong and my sixth sense told me it just was not the direction we wanted to be going. So, I turned the convoy 180 degrees and went back towards the left. The drivers were starting to get a little disgruntled at this point due to the slow pace, wrong turns and nerves being on end. By this point, a couple of the soldiers had finagled an AM/FM radio to pick up the BBC news broadcast and heard that some Marines were captured and drug through the streets and some maintenance soldiers (Jessica Lynch's convoy) were being held as POWs. And once again, we were running low on fuel. Five gallons does not go a long way when the trucks are pulling heavy loads. Just when I thought we were going to have to stop in place and pull security for days until someone came back for us, I see a random unit set up in the middle of nowhere.

We go flying by, then turn around and link up with a HMMWV the unit sent out to see what we were doing. The SGT in the HMMWV led us into the unit area where a couple of CPTs who were very interested in our water and MREs on the back of our trucks greeted me. I asked one of the CPTs if he could show me a map and tell me some grid points, such as fuel points and unit locations. The CPT took me to see their battalion commander. I had ended up running into 5-52 ADA out of Fort Bliss, Texas. The battalion commander wanted to know why we were out roaming the desert with no security (I had only picked up supply trucks with the intention of linking back up with my battalion that day, therefore no need for any gun trucks to stay with me originally).

I explained that our unit had moved on without us and that I did not have the follow-on grid. After some more questions and answers, the ADA Battalion Commander told me I could fill up my trucks from his fuel tankers and stay inside their perimeter that night for security. I ended up giving them a pallet of MREs and water for helping us out so much. Later that night, the ADA Battalion Executive Officer came to my HMMWV and asked me what my plan for the next day was. I explained that, since seeing the map and getting a rough idea of where the support units from the 3ID were setting up, I could make my way there pretty easy. She asked what type of security we had and I told her we had our individual weapons with four or five magazines each. The ADA unit had heard about the attack on the maintenance convoy earlier that day also (the same one my soldiers heard about on the AM/FM radio) and the XO did not feel comfortable with letting us go out on our own. We talked about it for a minute, then decided the best alternative would be to stay with the ADA unit, continue north with them until we could get in touch with our unit through satellite phones. The ADA unit sent our names up to V Corps as found (since we'd been away from our unit for a few days now).

A couple days after joining the ADA unit at one of the nightly meetings, the Battalion Commander put out that the maintenance soldiers taken prisoners by the Iraqis were their maintenance soldiers attached to the 3ID. It was ironic to me that I (from the 3ID) wound up being "saved" by this unit while their soldiers were left by my (parent) unit. The impressive part of this story starts now. This ADA unit took me and my trucks in under their wing. It was as if we had belonged to them from day one. Any time they stopped, we were inside their perimeter protected by their firepower. Any time they fueled up, they fueled us up. Their Battalion XO would stop by at night and check on my soldiers. Any time my vehicles were stuck or broke down, they waited on us.

And what impressed me most, when one of their Batterys lost a radar due to enemy fire, they did not forget about us. The Battalion had to split into two and send one of the Batterys traveling with us out to replace the damaged radar. A lot of movement and confusion was going on at this point. It was the middle of the night on a crowded MSR with sandstorms blowing. At one point, I was cut off from the battalion and lost sight of them. When they realized they lost us, they stopped, waited, and walked me back into their area over the radio. They could have dropped us from day one because we were slow and only added more onto their load, but they took us in as their own and with that, I will never forget what true leadership is about, taking care of people.

To wrap it up, we spent six days apart from our unit. The ADA unit took us north to the general vicinity of where the 3ID and everyone else was set up waiting to attack Baghdad. The Battalion Commander took me to meet their Brigade commander and we talked about my situation. The Brigade Commander showed me on a map where the 3ID support units were supposedly located. The next day, I drove out with my trucks towards the grid we had looked at on the map the night before. When I was close to where the support units should have set up, I started calling on the radio for anyone to answer.

After about 45 minutes of trying, our Battalion answered.

-Kristen Lewis

The Airborne Drop

In battle, one of the most glorified and romantic military operations is the airborne drop. We all remember the movies, The Longest Day and The Bridge Too Far. Those devils in the baggy pants are real life heroes. In my earlier career, the big jump was the one the Rangers did in Grenada. This may be the old-time most famous jump – with the final pass of the planes just feet above the ocean waves and the jump made at only 500 feet with no reserve chutes used. I am fortunate to have been trained by some of those NCOs and officers when it was still fresh in memory. I listened intently to every first hand account I could.

Today the new officers and recruits will be told of the heroics of the jump into Bashur, Iraq. The 173rd Airborne Brigade, stationed in Italy, jumped in on the night of 26th of March 2003. The original plan to send the 4th Infantry Division overland across Turkey had to be scrapped at the last minute. Now to ensure a presence in northern Iraq and keep Saddam's forces bottled up, the U.S. needed to send in an airborne force to seize an airfield and allow for rapid deployment of forces from Europe.

Getting the team on the ground to set up the drop zone was an adventure. They had to be there early and there were many risks. One plane had flown in from Jordan and received fifteen holes from air defense fire. The Brigade S-1 was the officer in charge of setting up the drop zone. He described the night he arrived, the night before the jump as completely dark with pouring rain blowing in sideways. He sank up to his knees in mud. The next day, two hours before the jump it was cloudy and the ceiling was not high enough. Finally the clouds broke and one thousand paratroopers made the jump onto an airfield located in a bowl in the mountains. [28]

LTC Dom Caraccilo, commander one of the battalions in the 173rd Brigade, and author of a book about Desert Storm, sent me the following account.

[Dom Caraccilo]

I'm sure my story is about the same as everyone else's. We had some incredibly brave soldiers who had an extraordinary ability to display the restraint and discipline one would hope for in a diverse, ethnically-mixed environment that we saw in Kirkuk. My battalion was responsible for the city limits, so we had the full spectrum of conflict (combat ops to civil requirements).

We stood the battalion up from scratch. Our battalion 2-503 ABN was activated in Jan 02 and less than a year later deployed on back-to-back operational deployments (Kosovo for Rapid Guardian 3-01 and the jump into Iraq less than 30 days later). In fact, the last company stood up from scratch on 11 Dec 01 - just 3 months prior to the jump.

Didn't have a piece of equipment or a place to call our HQ. Gradually and by overcoming some challenges, we eventually got barracks space, weapons, etc., but we often had to borrow things like Mortars to train our paratroopers. I remember deploying back from Afghanistan with the Rangers in OCT 01 and then going TDY to Italy to take what existed of my unit to one of its first rotations in Graf and asking people like HR McMaster, then the 1/4 CAV commander, to use whatever he had - ranges, barracks, equipment, etc. In the year preceding the jump, we deployed the battalion, or bits and pieces to various places (Czech, Hungary, Poland, Germany, Botswana, France, and of course, training areas in Italy). In fact, on 25 March 02, one year and a day before the jump into Bashur Iraq, we jumped no notice into Beychne, the Czech Republic.

So it was a mad dash to say the least...remarkably, it forced us to focus on the fundamentals with an eye on individual soldiers skills (my intent was to train to a T on individual tasks) and small unit collective tasks (battle drills that mastered squad attack, react to contact, and enter a building and clear a room). Really didn't have any time to do anymore actually, but in the end I submit that that is about what is needed to succeed in Iraq - so in a counter-intuitive approach we did what we actually needed to do.

The jump was an incredible experience for our paratroopers. Introducing a force like this has habitually been risky in the history of airborne operations and this mission was no different. As we leapt from the aircraft on that pitch black dark night we, no doubt, knew we were entering somewhat of an abyss - just knowing once those feet left the platform that our lives would change for an extended period of time.

After about 2 weeks in Bashur, we attacked south into Kirkuk. My battalion was separated from the rest of the 173rd as they swung west towards Irbil to attack from the west. We went straight south with the intent to position ourselves to support the 173rd from the west. We had no combat multipliers so we were an airborne battalion pure - as we got to a place called Tag Tag we noticed that the city was indeed imploding - I had difficulties contacting my commander who told me in no uncertain terms to not become decisively engaged, but we knew the time to attack south was upon us and kept going, eventually getting permission from the commander through a series of radio relays. The plan to attack Kirkuk was done in 15 minutes on the hood of a Hummvee. Basically it went like this, "Battle Company leads, Able breaks left, Chosen breaks left." And that's how we attacked. We seized a series of objectives that night to include the K1 Military airfield, GOSP 1 and 2, and the commercial airfield. At this point we hunkered down for our year stay in the city, which could take volumes to define how we operated. New tactical missions like Civil R&S became part of our lexicon. We did hundreds of raids in the city and in places like Hilabjah (on the Iranian Border where we captured HVT #79).

Of note is the finding of the last downed American Pilot of the War - CPT Eric Dus USAF F15E pilot. One day, some informant came to the airfield saying he could show us a downed aircraft - we had gotten dozens of these types of leads daily and most were inaccurate but our modus was to follow all leads for even if it's a 1 in 10 chance that one time it is accurate is worth it. He brought us to a small installation with a tarmac out front. We saw the aircraft parts laid out as if they were on display. We realized that it wasn't a crash site but in fact a place where the aircraft was displaced - later we learned it came from Tikrit where it was indeed shot down. On the hill behind the aircraft parts was reported a burial site for the pilot. We went on a hunch that it was true, and searched. Finding a freshly dug spot, my Command Sergeant Major, CSM Earl Rice, got on his hands and knees and dug with his hands. We exhumed part of CPT Eric Dus' body - a note in Arabic with it stated as such. I remember CPT Eugene Martin, my S1 saying a prayer before extracting him and then resting the remains on his lap as he sat in the backseat of my HMMWV as we drove my vehicle back to the airbase.

Another interesting story is a story of the heroism displayed by SPC Christopher Holbrook and SGT Dan Pilo. Escorting about 60 miles south one day with the TM RIO folks (Return of Iraqi Oil), they were ambushed. Holbrook shot and killed a number of the assailants and recovered his wounded in his truck before getting shot thru the hip himself - the bullet entered his hip and exited his belly. Pilo was shot in the foot. Both soldiers, clearly in pain, drove from the ambush site and were ambushed again. Holbrook again engaged and killed his foe even with a belly wound. He then drove his wounded, as did Pilo, 60 km's to the airbase before collapsing. Both recovered. Holbroook was selected by the Sergeant Major of the Army (SMA) as the Hero of the U.S. Army and will be presented such honors at the USO Gala in DC in October. Okay, I'm rambling now but I could talk about my guys forever. In the end I lost 3 KIA and had 70 WIA - all my personal heroes.

-Dom Caraccilo

A Thanksgiving Visit

For those few fortunate enough to be at that particular mess hall in Baghdad for Thanksgiving in 2003, it was a great thrill. Actually it was a great thrill for all. Other dignitaries had been making their way over for visits and investigations. Celebrities were beginning to come over with USO tours. Even though it had been months since officially hostilities ceased, it was still a very hostile area. Those coming over were taking a risk.

Still no one really thought the President of the United States would venture over. This trip sent a big message to all. To the troops it was a show of support, to those still fighting, it showed the confidence of the United States, and to the rest of the world it was a statement of success. If the President can make a safe trip then the loyalists were truly defeated.

It was no easy feat. The security was tight. The secrecy of the visit was kept at the highest levels. Few people beyond Paul Bremer actually knew of the plan. Michael Parkhouse, Deputy Chief of Protocol for the CPA, usually was involved in all dignitary visits. He worked closely with security to ensure any VIP was protected and treated nicely.

Just prior to the visit he had been working on the details for Senator Hillary Clinton's visit. Since she was the former First Lady, Michael expected to work with the Secret Service. Still, he thought the number around Baghdad was a bit excessive. He still had no idea.

[John Galt]

November 23, 2003.

The President visited with the troops in Iraq for Thanksgiving. The troops loved it and it did the President good too. There was absolutely no advance notice except to a select handful of people in Iraq. The Thanksgiving visit by POTUS was the right thing to do.

December 3, 2003

An Email from a Captain in Iraq

"We knew there was a dinner planned with ambassador Bremer and LTG Sanchez. There were 600 seats available and all the units in the division were tasked with filling a few tables. Naturally, the 501st MI battalion got our table. Soldiers were grumbling about having to sit through another dog-and-pony show, so we had to pick soldiers to attend. I chose not to go.

"But, about 1500 the G2 came up to me and with a smile, asked me to come to dinner with him, to meet him in his office at 1600 and bring a camera. I didn't really care about getting a picture with Sanchez or Bremer, but when the division's senior intelligence officer asks you to go, you go. We were seated in the chow hall, fully decorated for thanksgiving when all kinds of secret service guys showed up.

"That was my first clue, because Bremer's been here before and his personal security detachment is not that big. Then BG Dempsey got up to speak, and he welcomed ambassador Bremer and LTG Sanchez. Bremer thanked us all and pulled out a piece of paper as if to give a speech. He mentioned that the President had given him this thanksgiving speech to give to the troops. He then paused and said that the senior man present should be the one to give it. He then looked at Sanchez, who just smiled.

"Bremer then said that we should probably get someone more senior to read the speech. Then, from behind the camouflage netting, the President of the United States came around. The mess hall actually erupted with hollering. Troops bounded to their feet with shocked smiles and just began cheering with all their hearts. The building actually shook. It was just unreal. I was absolutely stunned. Not only for the obvious, but also because I was only two tables away from the podium. There he stood, less than thirty feet away from me! The cheering went on and on and on.

"Soldiers were hollering, cheering, and a lot of them were crying. There was not a dry eye at my table. When he stepped up to the cheering, I could clearly see tears running down his cheeks. It was the most surreal moment I've had in years. Not since my wedding and Aaron being born. Here was this man, our President, came all the way around the world, spending 17 hours on an airplane and landing in the most dangerous airport in the world, where a plane was shot out of the sky not six days before.

"Just to spend two hours with his troops. Only to get on a plane and spend another 17 hours flying back. It was a great moment, and I will never forget it. He delivered his speech, which we all loved, when he looked right at me and held his eyes on me. Then he stepped down and was just mobbed by the soldiers. He slowly worked his way all the way around the chow hall and shook every last hand extended. Every soldier who wanted a photo with the President got one. I made my way through the line, got dinner, then wolfed it down as he was still working the room.

"You could tell he was really enjoying himself. It wasn't just a photo opportunity. This man was actually enjoying himself! He worked his way over the course of about 90 minutes towards my side of the room. Meanwhile, I took the opportunity to shake a few hands. I got a picture with Ambassador Bremer, Talabani (acting Iraqi president) and Achmed Chalabi (another member of the ruling council) and Condaleeza Rice, who was there with him.

"I felt like I was drunk. He was getting closer to my table so I went back over to my seat. As he passed and posed for photos, he looked my in the eye and 'How you doin', captain?' I smiled and said 'God bless you, sir.' To which he responded 'I'm proud of what you do, captain.' Then moved on."

-John Galt

[Matt Gapinski]

We made it through all the Holidays. The mess hall actually did a pretty good job with all the holiday meals; although I think all three meals (Thanksgiving, Christmas and New Year's) were the same (turkey with all the trimmings). Even though most of us didn't get to see him, the President's visit on Thanksgiving was a big morale booster for the troops. Saddam's capture was a nice early Christmas present, too!

-Matt Gapinski

[Scott Travis]

Thanksgiving was a fun and relaxing day. We played an Officer/Enlisted game of football in the morning on the front yard of Saddam's Al-Salam Palace, and started eating dinner at about 4 in the afternoon. The food provided was great. Our food is now contracted out, and they really went overboard for us. We ate shrimp, steak, stuffing, potatoes, cranberry sauce, and of course, lots of turkey. Actually, this Thanksgiving was much nicer than last year's, which we spent covered in frozen mud in the woods of Bavaria while training for this deployment.

The news that President Bush visited the Airport was an incredible morale boost, at least for me. That's the kind of leadership that truly inspires, and it meant a lot to see our commander in chief make the trip for us. Unfortunately, since we don't live at the airport, we watched it on TV like everyone else, but even so it was a thrill.

-Scott Travis

Saddam's Capture

One of the most memorable events over in Iraq was the capture of Saddam Hussein. Early on, someone came up with a deck of cards of the fifty-five most wanted criminals. The goal is to catch them all and bring them to justice. Psychologically, there was one that stood out above all others; that of course was the dictator and source of all the problems. With Saddam Hussein on the loose and his billion dollars in cash he was carrying around, he was always a risk to reappear with some new menace. Even the number two villain on the list who was captured in September 2004 pales in comparison to the Ace of Spades.

The most amazing thing is most of us never knew or could comprehend how evil Saddam Hussein is. His capture is a very reassuring for Iraq because with him on the loose, the people could not feel comfortable. He has had such an influence for so many years.

In 1979, Saddam Hussein forced the president of Iraq to "retire," then he appointed himself dictator and for the next twenty-four years he ruled with an iron hand, crushing all free thought and expression. Volumes could be written and need to be written on his atrocities: how he murdered, tortured and stole from his people. There were no rights – no free press, no free speech, no trials, no justice system, no dissent allowed (his spies were everywhere), and no way to fight back. Information was blocked and the people could not communicate with the outside world. There was one political party, which all government employees had to join, and to resign was against the law under penalty of death. There is no way in this book to begin to chronicle the misery and destruction brought upon Iraq by Saddam Hussein.

Immediately after becoming President, Saddam Hussein addressed the Revolutionary Ruling Council and had the Secretary General read a "confession," along with a list of fifty-four other party members in the room. Each one of these was led out of the room by armed guards. Then those who remained were ordered to pull the triggers on their comrades' executions. Things went downhill from there.

Sometimes I think you can stare at facts and not comprehend their magnitude. Fifty mass graves have recently been discovered where hundreds of thousands may be buried. [31] For Iraq, it was the total domination and intimidation – the callousness toward human suffering.

Secret informers were everywhere, ready to report anyone. People were taken from homes without any notification to relatives; sometimes parents were taken and children were left without even a note to say what happened. People were beaten, raped, starved, electrocuted, burned, and maybe finally executed. Families would wonder for years the fate of missing relatives. If one tried to run away, the remaining family would be tortured. Parents would be forced to watch their children beaten and raped.

To make sure his orders were carried out many tortures and executions were video taped. In a book just published, Richard Engel describes seeing what was for sale in the shops of the new Iraq. These were gruesome actual film coverage of barbarous acts such as putting dynamite in shirt pockets of victims and watching the tops of their bodies rip apart. [32]

Saddam Hussein had no regard for anyone except himself. During the 1990's, 15,000 people died each year due to malnutrition and lack of health care. This was his plan for outside sympathy to blame the U.N. and U.S. During this time he spent ten billion dollars building hundreds of palaces for himself. He controlled smuggling of oil and everything else.

He robbed Kuwait of everything his men could cart off. He murdered his son-in-law after swearing on the Qu'ran that he would not. He jailed his son. He jailed his personal physician for a life sentence because the man refused to run for Parliament. He jailed the doctor's wife for two years and the son for ten. [33] He cheated on his wife. He killed her dog by chaining it up just out of reach of a swimming pool and then denying it water. [34]

Saddam thought nothing of the rest of the world. He killed and stole from anyone whom he could. He attacked Iran in 1980 just to steal their oil when he thought he could. The war went on for eight long years. Three percent of his entire population became casualties – three percent of America is eight million. The war ended after he repeatedly bombed civilian population areas. He used nerve gas at will. In one village in the Kurdish area of Iraq, he killed

5,000 in one gas attack. After he bankrupted Iraq, he attacked Kuwait. His Special Forces were actually able to rob four million dollars of gold bars from Kuwaiti banks. In March 2003, he made a personal withdrawal from Iraq's Central Bank of almost a billion dollars in cash. This was an unusual amount since his impending ouster was forthcoming. Normally his pilferage of the country's coffers was in smaller amounts, like five million dollars. [35]

He also had little regard for the environment. He dumped millions of gallons of Kuwaiti oil in the Gulf, setting off one the worst natural disasters in recent history. He set over seven hundred oil wells on fire, which belched black smoke into the atmosphere for over nine months until they were extinguished. In Iraq he destroyed 8,000 square miles of wetlands for the purpose of starving the people who lived off the food and game from the marshes. [36]

Growing up, Saddam was beaten as a child and taught to steal by his stepfather. As a young boy Saddam had an iron rod that he would heat up until it glowed white and then poke it at dogs and cats. At ten he moved in with his uncle, a pro-Nazi who had written a book, *Three of Whom God Should Never Had Created: Persians, Jews and Flies*. [37] He failed admission to military officer training. He joined the Ba'ath party, carried a gun and became a muscle man for them. In 1959, he was on the assassination team that tried to kill the Iraqi president. The Ba'ath party tried another coup d'état in 1963 and this lasted just a few months. After that, Saddam organized a group of thugs much like Hitler's Brown Shirts, and created secret cells to inform on people. By 1969, his intimidation policies were well enough in place that the Ba'ath coup in 1969 was successful. He built a military arm within the party to rival the military just as the Soviets had. By 1979, he was able to take over completely.

When Saddam took over, Iraq had a growing economy with a billion dollar surplus. Health care, education, literacy and women's rights were all leading the pan-Arab world. Cities were growing, the middle class was well established, and religious toleration prevailed. By 2000, Iraq's economy was shrinking at a rate of 5.7 % per year. It was a socialist state and he just stopped spending any money. Salaries were cut, education spending stopped, nothing was spent to improve or even maintain healthcare, and he even refused to pay the workers building his palaces. People existed by slowly selling everything they owned. People moved back to the farms were they could at least grow their own food. The new shiny cars of the 1970's limped along. Factories closed when spare parts could not be purchased. Water treatment facilities slowly closed. Raw sewage was dumped into the rivers.

On December 13, 2003 at 8:30 P. M. local time in a small village near Tikrit, soldiers of the 4th Infantry Division found Saddam Hussein in a spider hole next to a small hut on a poor sheep farm. A pistol, two AK-47s and $750,000 cash were found in the house.

[Paul Colbert]

Operation Red Dawn

On the 13th of December, my conversation with Mandi was cut a bit short. It began when unnamed people like Mr. Smith and Mr. Jones with social security numbers of 111-11-1111 and 222-22-2222 began showing up at my desk wanting a flight to Tikrit. We eventually planned to launch the Operational Reserve Chinooks (2 CH-47s on standby, releasable only by MG Miller himself, whose sole purpose in life was to pick up HVT #1 – Saddam Hussein). The crews of Hooker 45 and 51 from A/5-159 got alerted and I then began to put the pieces of the puzzle together. The final picture looked like an Ace of Spades.

Around 8 p.m. on the night of the 13th, a patrol of 4th Infantry Division soldiers, part of Operation Red Dawn, found a hole in the ground in between two farm houses northwest of Objectives Wolverine I and II. Originally, they had gotten intelligence from an enemy source on the U.S.S. Higgins as part of Operation Eel. This source led them to Tikrit, Saddam's hometown. The Ironhorse Soldiers picked two houses as their targets, but initially found nothing. Their cordon moved northward to more houses and small neighborhoods. Still nothing...Afternoon turned into evening and evening into night. Soon, though, as they continued northward, they eventually came to a small two-house complex. Inside, they still found nothing, but an out-of-place piece of corrugated metal exposed what held the man himself.

On two previous occasions, we had "spooled up" the Operational Reserve Chinooks to do this type of mission. Several days before the actual launch, however, we sent two DLQ (Deck-landing Qualified) aircraft and crews to Basrah to retrieve an intelligence source that had been previously taken to the Higgins. They went to get the source, brought him to Basrah, sent him to Baghdad on a British C-130, and the operation went from there. We never knew what the source was going to reveal, but it was the biggest piece of intelligence anyone could have ever expected. The Chinooks brought the "spooks" up, along with CID (Criminal Investigation Division, a part of the Military Police that heads up interrogations, forensics, and crime scene investigations) to the capture site to retrieve Saddam. Unfortunately for those Chinooks, though, because of the restrictions placed on CH47s for daytime flight (CJTF-7 FRAGO [FRAGmentary Order] 1038 restricted passenger movement by Chinook to night, only), we launched two Blackhawks to go retrieve the spooks, CID, two Iraqi bodyguards, and, yes, Saddam Hussein himself.

The following morning as we sat in amazement watching the television broadcasts of medical personnel looking over the toppled dictator, the catch phrase from L. Paul Bremer ticked across the bottom numerous times: "We got him." It was a huge day in the justification of our presence in Iraq. Many believed it was impossible to find the man, much less take him into custody, but we did. I'm proud to say that I was a direct part, although small, in the capture of Saddam Hussein.

-Paul Colbert

[John Galt]

Sunday, December 14, 2003

A New Day. We Got Him!

Got the SOB! Saddam reported in Coalition military control. News spread through CPA like wildfire. Smiles all around to a bunch on a hard working people--Iraqi, American, British, Spanish, Italian, everyone!

Celebratory weapons fire around city in celebration. Some quick duck and cover by guards but the word has spread. In the new day, our Coalition and Iraqi guards now stand together and watch the tracers.

It's a New Day, as of 1:30PM, Baghdad time.

-John Galt

[Fayrouz Hancock]

Today is a nice day. I won't sit and talk about someone who stole the best years of our lives. I'm glad the new Iraqi generations won't have to live under his tyranny. I'm glad they can look forward to their future. I'm going to enjoy my day in the sunlight.

-Fayrouz Hancock

New Hands

The story of the new hands is the one story of people helping Iraqi victims of

Saddam Hussein's atrocities that did get a lot of publicity. There were stories in the Houston Chronicle and Washington Post as well as in military news publications. The President held a press conference and highlighted the recipients of the aid. He mentioned the story again during his acceptance speech for the Republican Party nomination in September 2004.

Seven Iraqi gold exchangers had their right hands amputated for conducting transactions in U.S. dollars. In the Iraqi justice system this was viewed as stealing from Saddam Hussein. So Muslim law was used as an excuse to cut their hands off.

One man's left hand was injured in the Iranian war and was useless. He begged that they amputated that one. He was told, "You gave your left hand to Saddam Hussein and you stole from Saddam Hussein with your right hand. Your right hand is to be amputated."

Their operations were videotaped and it was this tape that led to their eventually having new prosthetic hands attached in Houston, Texas. Amnesty International estimates that hundreds had their hands amputated by Saddam Hussein's cruelty. While sedated for the surgery the victims also had x's tattooed on their foreheads to forever brand them as criminals.

Donald North, in Iraq did produce a movie, came across this torture video and started the process to help these men. In this particular case, there were originally nine men. One died, one fled to Europe and seven remained in Baghdad.

North contacted a Houston TV newsman, Marvin Zindler, who in turn enlisted the services of Joe Agris, a plastic surgeon who had previously volunteered his services in performing reconstructive surgery on children in Vietnam and Nicaragua. [40]

The Air Force transported the men to Germany and Continental Airlines supplied the trip to Houston. The Methodist Hospital donated the hospital stay and operating room, Marriott and Warwick donated hotel rooms, and the German prosthetics company, Otto Bock, provided the artificial hands.
[41]

These hands are the latest in technology. Carefully matched to the skin tones and arm size of each man, these $25,000 artificial hands are as close to real hands as current medical technology can provide. Electrical pulses control small motors to open and close the thumb and two fingers. Special sensors in the thumb and fingers detect when an object is slipping and automatically increase pressure on the grip. [42]

After the surgery, the seven flew to Washington and met the President.

"When I first walked into the White House, it was like I was surrounded by a halo," said Qassim Kadhim. "Then suddenly we were with the president, and he made us feel we were with a friend, that he understood us. For the most powerful man in the world to be so warm, it was the apex of my life." [43]

Al Fadhly, said, "Having lived my whole life in Iraq, I can tell you America is not getting the real picture. There are good things happening every day and no one is seeing them." [44]

Anne Trenolone worked as the Public Affairs Officer for the Ministry of Health in the CPA starting in September 2003. She explains her part in bringing these seven men to America.

[Anne Trenolone]

On May 25, 2004, a group of Iraqi men, all right-hand amputees, met with the President of the United States. I was proud to see these men welcomed to the Oval Office. Theirs is a courageous story but also a story of useless violence, waste and tyranny like so many that occurred under the regime of Saddam Hussein.

The last time I had seen this group of men was on a helipad near one of the former dictator's palaces in Baghdad. It was a warm, dark night in April when they boarded the helicopters that would take them on the first leg of their journey to the states.

These seven Iraqi men—who all had their right hands amputated by the former regime as punishment for dealing in foreign currency, a forbidden practice in Ba'ath-Party Iraq—left for the United States and my home state of Texas on Palm Sunday. I remember it was Palm Sunday because I especially wanted to attended services (the first I had ever been to that were BYOP: Bring Your Own Palm).

However, if I attended services, I missed my ride to a news conference scheduled prior to these men's departure. I couldn't remember the last time I missed a Palm Sunday service, but I had come to Iraq to serve as a CPA public affairs officer assigned to the Ministry of Health and attending this press conference was my job. Trying to rectify the two events, I weighed my options as to the quickest way to get myself the few miles I needed to travel across the fortified Green Zone to make the media event.

Having been only a passenger since I had arrived six months before, I signed-out a vehicle from our office motor pool. At 5:30 p.m. (1730 for the military types) directly after the services, I drove Land Cruiser IV across the Green Zone. This seemingly uneventful occurrence was complicated by the fact that the only vehicles available were standard transmission. Now driving a standard is something I have done on occasion and that I understand in theory. In practice, I am just really, really bad.

I received a few stares as I rode the clutch and suffered through the gear changes. But I made it to the news conference on time and it went very well. Although a bit camera shy at the onset, the men grew more comfortable with the attention and shared their story with Arabic and English language media outlets.

After the news conference, the seven amputees, an Iraqi man who had been working to get them out of the country for treatment, a U.S. Navy doctor, and I all went to dinner at the chow hall in the Al Rasheed hotel where we awaited word of the helicopter departure time. I told these men about Texas and I hoped they would like it. Their final destination, after military bases and commercial flights would be Houston, where they would receive medical treatment and new prosthetic hands. They were excited about the treatment and the trip and their young Iraqi friend was anxious to see the months of planning among the Ministry of Health, medical specialists, the U.S. military, and the U.S. government culminate in their imminent departure.

During the meal, the men discussed losing their hands; how losing their hands had affected their lives and the lives of their families. How they endured constant physical pain in their right arms because of nerve endings left unattended, too, after the amputations. They discussed the shame they felt in interacting with others, even with their own children. Besides losing their hands, many also had their foreheads marked with an X, which only added to this shame. They were forbidden from seeking follow-up treatment for their wounds and from acquiring prosthetics.

I learned so much in listening to their stories and I, too, was excited and proud to be playing even a small part in their journey, a journey which would begin after a short drive across the Green Zone. A journey I realized that would require my driving them in the standard-transmission Land Cruiser.

It would be a ride I will always remember and treasure. I was in the driver's seat, accompanied by three Iraqi gentlemen who speak only limited English and none with right hands. As I was backing out of the parking space the car stalled and I prepared to start it up again. The three men looked very nervous and the gentleman in the passenger's seat said: "I will drive, I can drive." I was confident his driving had to be better than mine, so we did a little swap. He took the driver's seat and I took the passenger's seat.

So reaching across the wheel to shift with his left hand—the same hand he used to steer, this Iraqi man drove the four of us across the Green Zone. I talked about how my standard driving was a big "mushkala" or problem. They all agreed.

As he drove, he told me that under the former regime, he was never allowed to drive the streets we were now traversing. I was even happier he was driving. I believe the other two passengers were as well. The group visited the Republican Palace (another place they would have never ventured under Saddam Hussein) on the banks of the Tigris and was then taken to the helipad for their departure. I wished them luck.

Although I was not surprised, I was humbled by the fact that a man with no right hand drove standard better than I could. I had learned early on during my time in Iraq that its people are intelligent and resourceful. I saw the evening's events as another step toward progress in Iraq, a blending of resources and talents to accomplish a common goal. But more importantly, I saw an Iraqi, overcoming the scars left by years of tyranny, taking the driver's seat toward his own destiny.

-Anne Trenolone

Prison Scandal

It may be hard to fathom for those of us used to living in the comfort of a Western democracy, the extremes of the tortures under Saddam Hussein. We define police brutality when a policeman hits a suspect with a stick during an arrest. We expect nothing other than every suspect is read his rights, he is not unduly searched, he is treated humanely and given chance to call his family or lawyer. We expect the suspect to be quickly arraigned and given a fair and speedy trial. He has the right to an attorney, to cross-examine witnesses and to not be forced to take the stand. If sentenced, he can expect a punishment to be consistent with his crime. If the guilty is still not satisfied, he can appeal and appeal again. He can apply for clemency. He can ask to be pardoned. While in jail, he will be taken care of with more living space than a sailor on a ship. He'll have the opportunity to learn an new trade, consult a library and receive counseling.

All of these things are so much a part of our society that we hardly imagine what brutality is. Sometimes we see the words or actions and it all seems so far away and made up. For the Iraqis living under Saddam Hussein, it was a nightmare.

Some of the types of torture include: nursing babies starved to death while being held at arm's length from their mothers, eyes gouged out, limbs cut off, hands and feet smashed with hammers, and people dunked in vats of acid. [45]

One man tried to defend his young female cousin from being taken for Uday Hussein's personal pleasure. Guards tied him to a tree, beat him and left him there for two days. He then was injected with a rat poison that slowly kills through internal bleeding. [46]

Much of these tortures were video taped so the torturers could have evidence that they did their job. After the collapse, many of these tapes have been put on sale. One man told me of watching a movie where people were thrown from a third-story window. If the victim survived, he was drug back upstairs and thrown out the window again. This interrogation office was a few blocks away from the residential area and parks where the interrogators lived. The children could very easily have watched their dads throw victims out the window.

Men accused of deserting the army had an ear cut off. One man accidentally had the wrong ear cut off. So they cut the other one off also. [47] It became a stigma to be an amputee, with some many having appendages cut off. Amputees became social outcasts.

Jean Sasson wrote a sad story of a group of women and their lives in jail in her book, *Mayada: Daughter of Iraq*. One woman, traveling with her brother and three-year-old daughter, was accused or traveling with a stolen passport. Her brother was beaten and poked with a cattle prod. They spent the next three weeks left alone in jail. Then the beatings started and her daughter was forced to watch and later she too was beaten. The worst part of her ordeal was being moved to a jail in her hometown and no one in her family even knew. Another woman was thrown into their cell one day with blood oozing from her head from a power drill, three of her fingernails ripped out, and many cigarettes burns on her legs. [48]

In another account in the same book, a man tells of his finger nails being extracted one each day for ten days. Then his toenails were removed in similar fashion. After that a man pulled out each of his teeth one by one. Then he was placed in an oven just long enough to burn his skin and melt his hair. [49]

One fifty-year-old woman was taken by police without a chance to tell her husband or sons. She was thrown in jail and told her sentence was to twenty-five years for undermining the economy. [50]

Another woman had her two fourteen-year-old twins taken away because they were staring at some members of the secret police. They woman was never told what happened, to her they just disappeared. With some inside help the mother was finally told where she might find her boys. She baked a cake to take it to them in jail. She was led to a room filled in stench where she found her sons bound together in a room full of others tortured to death. She describes the room. "I saw one young man whose chest bore the searing print of an electric iron, I saw a second young man whose chest spilled open, having been dissected from his neck to his stomach. I saw a third young man whose legs had been hacked away. I saw a forth young man whose eyeballs lay on his slack face." [51]

In another book, *A Fist in the Hornet's Nest*, the author Richard Engel tells a story of a man's jail cell, which had been infested so thoroughly with roaches that they would climb into the prisoner's nose at night. [52] The man's crime? The man, who had once been Saddam Hussein's personal physician, was sentenced to life in prison for refusing to run for parliament. For this crime, his son had to serve ten years and his wife only two. [53]

These stories go on endlessly. To keep their sanity, Iraqis would pretend not to notice. As long as it was not your immediate family, one could close an eye to it. One could justify it in one's mind by saying that these arrested were guilty of a crime. As long as one kept one's mouth shut, minded one's own business and outwardly pledged loyalty to Saddam Hussein, one could convince oneself that one was safe.

Most of these stories are not well known to the general public in America. They are not discussed on the nightly news, nor have they been discussed in the public debate about going to help Iraq. What sells in America news is wrongs of Americans. Sadly, a handful of U.S. soldiers provided months of worldwide coverage by sexually abusing and humiliating a group of Iraqi detainees. Even though this story shocked us all, we can be glad that we live under a fair justice system where the accused have rights, and can expect a fair trial.

Mike Sheridan, a reserve officer from Long Island, New York, is a staff officer of the battalion responsible for the Abu Graib prison. He sent me this email.

[Mike Sheridan]

Sorry to vent in this way, but sometimes you just gotta let it go, and you're the one who happened to mash the pressure bleed valve....

So, did we (800th MP Brigade and subordinate units) torture people on behalf of the nation or in pursuit of some grand intelligence plan? Absolutely not. Never. Wouldn't do it for anybody. And you can't make me.

Detainees were abused at Abu Ghraib in the isolation wing on the night shift sometime in late October or early November. None of the parties involved reported it to their chain of command. As you can imagine there is a lot more to this story.

I left active duty after ten years as a tanker and cavalryman and joined the reserve MP Brigade on Long Island (800th MP Brigade). They worked me on staff in operations (all combat arms go to ops) and intel slots, and I became branch qualified in the Military Police.

The only mission for my MP Brigade is the theater level Enemy Prisoner of War (EPW) mission. We are the experts in EPW; if anyone in the military (all branches) wanted an answer on how to do EPW operations correctly, we were the source. Even Non-Governmental Agencies came to consult with us and attend our planning conferences and symposiums.

We had the attorneys, we had the staff planners, everything else necessary for doing things according to doctrine and international law. We ran EPW exercises (FTX) every other year, and we always included Geneva Status problems, Article 5 Tribunals, and Law of Land Warfare situations. Our special expertise is so rare that it was tough to find evaluators with a background that could evaluate our annual exercises.

I became the Executive Officer (XO) of the MP EPW battalion. I did that for four years, and I know that the battalions were training exclusively for the EPW mission. We hammered home Geneva III. That training also has ancillary application to their alternate mission of taking care of refugees and displaced persons (Geneva IV). But that's it, we did nothing else. We trained for our mission and never worked on other MP operations and duties such as convoy support, law and order, writing tickets at the front gate, or breaking up a fight at the NCO club. We're not that kind of MP. We have a very specialized mission.

From long past experience with this Brigade, we were generally the red headed stepchild wherever we went. EPW ops (and exercises) cost big money, HUGE logistic burdens, and nobody understands our requirements. Everybody else thinks they're an expert on what we do for a living because of some basic familiarity, while we knew how demanding all the requirements are. Our mission is often misunderstood, frequently even within the MP community, and little appreciated anywhere else but within the MP community. Until they need us to come take this problem off their hands.

We (800th MP Brigade) are a Theater asset, designed, manned, and equipped to hold EPWs way in the rear out of SCUD range. Instead we found ourselves deployed forward into the divisional maneuver space.

Incarceration? That's nowhere in our skill set. One detachment of one battalion that worked for us in peacetime had the mission for "Joint U.S. Confinement," but that would be for holding U.S. military who were awaiting trial in theater (think in terms of who is now holding the idiots who did the deed in Tier 1A, that would be a guard mission for one of our detachments).

I'm not sure what international law would apply for incarceration, but a loose construct interpretation (which is what the ICRC would apply) would be that an occupying power would be responsible for ensuring Geneva IV standards are used for any non-combatants being held in occupied territory, whether held in occupation military custody or in civil custody by an Iraqi agency (because they, too, answer to the occupying power). Geneva IV is really more applicable to internment of civilians (think west coast Japanese heritage during WW II), but that would probably be the closest fit, and ICRC would (and did) invoke that convention.

By around May 2003, V Corps PMO and V Corps MP Brigade (18th) (and to some extent the maneuver divisions) couldn't handle and were overwhelmed by the prison mission. This even with the additional assets they had received. These assigned missions included police station detention cells (doctrinal mission for Corps MPs), and post trial incarceration (maneuver units responsible for all civil administration functions within their boundaries during an occupation). CFLCC gave the tasking to us, right around the time we were changing command, and coincidentally paroling (under provisions of Geneva III) the tail end of the EPWs (what we came to the war to do) from Camp Bucca, down south, where we did the majority of the EPW mission.

So, after telling them that we aren't in the incarceration business - aren't equipped or staffed for it, never have been; we go north anyway.

Because CJTF-7 withdrew logistical support, and declared they weren't responsible for site security around our (their) sites. They told us if we had a problem, we could go call CFLCC for help. You can't run a prison when half your force has to be looking out from the perimeter instead of in where the prisoners are. Oh, by the way, it was 16 prisons!

The 800th MP Brigade gets the place called Abu Ghraib and the one company that was running it. It was looted and burnt out, but had been picked by the 18th MP Brigade (V Corps) as a collection point, and they had put a company there.

The place was not built for long-term, because that's not what Corps MPs build. It was a cesspool, and the ICRC was breathing on CJTF-7 to fix it. Our recommended solution was to transfer them all down south to Camp Bucca. Recommendation denied, build something new, build it quick and cheap, and it has to be near Baghdad, so the Corps and Division MP wouldn't have to escort them all the way down south. Also in the thought process, so the MI can centralize their interrogation operations near the HQ.

We at the 800th pulled a Bn (320th, reservists, EPW MPs) from Camp Bucca up to Abu Ghraib, and we give them the company that had been doing the collection point mission (on behalf of 18th MP Brigade). So now we (800th MP Brigade) have to build a replacement Corps Holding Area to relieve Camp Cropper, renovate a prison complex for post trail incarceration (CPA Prisons Department didn't have anybody to do it), and guard the people inside, all the while defending a forward location. Simultaneously, prisoners are constantly inbound to us.

Remember that we have nobody with military corrections background. Our unit was EPW, so who do you use? Any reservist who had a civilian corrections background.

Then the maneuver units started ramping up the size and frequency of raids to capture insurgents and find Saddam. They planned a big one and needed a place to put them. Hey, here's a good idea, they've got a tent compound at Abu that holds 600, let's put them there! And MI said, great idea, we'll interrogate them right there instead of horsing all the way down south to Camp

Bucca. We said no, send them to Bucca, MI said yes, that's what we're doing. And now you know how "security detainees" (not a Geneva term) came to Abu. Then population continued to climb. Built quick and dirty version of a 4K set of compounds on only a third of the required acreage. We blew that capacity by early November. We kept saying "Bucca", MI kept saying "right here". CJTF-7 response was "put up more tents".

Meanwhile, the MI didn't like the fact that tent compounds house people in groups, not individually. "We need some isolated away from the rest." So, they convinced CPA Prisons to give up the first two wings of the prison that had been renovated for them to isolate people. This has a nominal capacity for roughly 220 criminals, and now used to isolate less than 25 "detainees". Still it requires an MP shift of 6 or 7 soldiers to guard it; I'm just guarding fewer people with the same amount of my people.

So what happened? What went wrong at Abu Ghraib? Not saying the kids who did it aren't guilty, but that company had been on ground at Abu working under the 320th MP Bn and 800th MP Brigade for less than three weeks when they pulled detainees out of their cells in the middle of the night and stripped and photographed and everything else. Not saying one or two or even all of the MPs that night might not have had a bit of a perverse streak themselves (a couple had a rather extensive personal video collection of themselves), or even a sadistic streak. But for them to develop in less than three weeks an idea to photograph detainees in ways that cut to the core of Arab sensitivities (dog leash, homosexuality) is pretty far fetched.

As far as I can tell, the photography session happened in one or more instances during the night shift in October or November. Six or seven soldiers were on duty supervised by one NCO.

The kid who is being hailed as a hero for reporting it may well have known about it himself since November, and only reported it on January 13th, a few days before he was due to rotate out as an individual. He got conscience and went straight to CID, leaving them a CD with the photo files and an anonymous note.

The night that CID got the CD and saw what was on it, they came to my room next as a courtesy (we had a good working relationship with CID) and showed it to me. I immediately notified LTC Phillabaum (Bn Cdr), and together we made the commo arrangements and notified BG Karpinski (Brigade Commander).

Since the first stop was CID and not the chain of command, it was a criminal investigation from the beginning. All materials were immediately evidence, and no amount of chain of command involvement was permitted (or attempted) in order to forestall any appearance of "undue command influence" that could potentially be used as a matter in defense at trial

The kid who took the Special Court Martial and turned evidence against the others in exchange for it, made a statement in which he said (words to the effect of), "Hell, no, my chain of command never knew about this, they would have slammed us."

A criminal investigation was begun in mid January. No one in the chain knew about it until after CID knew. And yet this was a criminal investigation, and somehow materials (evidence) were released to the media. MP chain of command didn't have copies of these materials. At the Bn level, we only saw what CID had as a courtesy. At the Brigade level, the CID commander briefed the Brigade commander, but didn't show copies or originals. HOW DID EVIDENCE GET RELEASED TO MEDIA??? If I was a Trial Defense Attorney, I know I would be attacking evidentiary chain of custody on any photographs presented at trial....

These guilty rat bastards are entitled to a fair trial, and I will defend to the death their Constitutional rights to due process under UCMJ. And I can reconcile myself to whatever outcome the trials may have, because I am confident the military justice system will operate. Wheels of Justice grind slowly, but they do grind.

We all completely discount the American media's response, who wouldn't have expected that? But to have the Army destroy so many professionals was amazing...

How does an Army Reserve unit chain of command at Bn and higher completely prevent and preclude anything bad from ever happening somewhere under them? You can expect the Army Reserve system and the peacetime RRCs to produce trained and capable units. You can expect the mobilization station to provide the proper equipment and some limited orientation training. You can expect the company level chain of command to have provided all the mandatory annually required training. But the bottom line is this: whoever gets off the plane in theater is who you are stuck with, whether they were trained or not. So you do a quick assessment, pull people off of the line if necessary to provide the new company with some orientation, and get them to work as quick as possible to give the rest of the units under you some relief. But even with all the mandatory training every soldier has ever gotten, did anyone ever really think we needed to have a class on "Don't stomp on people's hands when you have them buck naked with a dog leash and panties on their head"? I know I never scheduled that topic in my old battalion training calendar. And the Army Reserve insists on tying all training classes to our wartime training guidance, and I know Third Army and CENTCOM never told our Brigade that was a mandatory training topic either.

My old answer was always "Commander always and at all times responsible for all that happens or fails to happen under his command." I still feel that way, but my old sense of watching someone fall on his sword being a somewhat honorable conclusion to any unfortunate set of circumstances has turned to a bitter sadness. LTC (P) Jerry Phillabaum, USMA '76, the battalion commander of the 320th MP Bn, fell on his sword for this whole deal, and it is a loss. It's a loss because his soldiers trusted him, and because he as a person was humane. He did things and led Soldiers in a way that you knew that his expectation was that anyone in our custody was a human being, not some "mutt" or "perp" or "hajji" or any of the other terms bandied about. That was the loss.

What went right?

So we did what we knew how to do the best we could, and for what we didn't know how to do, we came as close as we could (while keeping Geneva in our thoughts).

We established contracts for food service so they would have culturally appropriate meals instead of MREs or HDRs (nasty vile). We ran competitive bids among three vendors to see who could provide the highest quality, freshest, and varied menu, while meeting caloric content for people living in tents in an open field in the winter (Geneva requirements).

We brought in a ROWPU unit for fresh water supplies, and established contracts for clothing, blankets, footwear (all oriented towards meeting Geneva requirements).

We took money out of pocket for some hardship case EPWs to have bus fare home once we dropped them as far north as possible when paroled.

We had a Major buy kid-size sleeping bags from Cabela catalog for a family that we took in at Camp Bucca when their home was destroyed by insurgents. Gave the father a job working with the food service contractor there.

-Mike Sheridan

Since the above note was written, the soldier who admitted his wrongs has been sentenced to one year in jail. A second, of the six remaining, was charged for on four counts of indecent acts totally unrelated to the incidents in Iraq. The trial is in process and investigations continue to find more in the chain of command at fault. It's a tradition in the military that if something dire happens then someone in command must pay even if that someone had no way of controlling the situation. The person in charge pays for all the crimes of the troops.

The old prisons in Iraq are now being converted into housing to alleviate the urgent housing shortage. Human Rights groups are working to identify the bodies in the mass graves. It's time to heal and create a new government that protects human rights and respects life.

Michael Parkhouse worked for the CPA for many months and had a chance to meet many Iraqis in his daily duties. Some of these had their own stories of prisons.

[Michael Parkhouse]

One of these persons I had a privilege to meet was a former colonel in the Iraqi Army. He had just been released from prison a few years earlier. His job in the Army was as a strategic planning officer for the general staff. He was highly educated and extremely well spoken. He was a graduate of the Military College of Iraq, Iraq's version of West Point. In the early 1960's, he was invited to study abroad in England. He is a student of History, Language and Culture. He taught me a thing or two about my own deficiencies with the proper application of English grammar rules. He would sometimes correct my spoken word, when not in public. He was very refreshing to be around. He told me several stories about his family and invited me to visit his village in the Al-Anbar Province, which is west of Baghdad. One such story was the time when he had finally come to the conclusion that he must confront the "madman." He had been trained to protect and defend Iraq. He never thought he would have to defend the country against itself, against its leadership. He struggled for years on how to approach this matter. He had witnessed several colleagues perish in several failed coup attempts. He had watched as family members were imprisoned and tortured.

One morning while in a self-reflecting moment, he announced to himself, "NO MORE"!!! He immediately went to his wife and announced his intentions. He laid out his plan and asked for her blessing. He went to his family

193

and received their blessing also. There was a huge risk in this matter. He could be exposed even before he could begin his plan. He had to trust them. Years earlier his nephew had been involved in a coup attempt. His nephew was an Iraqi Air Force pilot who had conspired with two other pilots to bomb Saddam Hussein in his palace or his convoy while he was in en route somewhere. He took off to bomb one of the palaces where Saddam was staying, not knowing he had been betrayed. His plan failed. He was publicly tried and executed. Family members were tortured and their property confiscated. The betrayers were executed along with immediate family members in private.

The colonel shared that Saddam said, "that he admired bravery even in his enemies and that cowards deserve a coward's reward." The colonel dressed himself in his uniform and his driver drove him to the Republican Palace where he demanded an audience with the President. He left the house that morning not knowing his fate or the fate of his family. Because of his position in the Army he had access to many places even Ba'ath Party had no access to. He was not a Ba'ath Party member. Because he had not joined the party, he was denied any further promotion to the General Staff. He was becoming a thorn in the flesh to the political apparatus now running the Army.

He handed the Appointment Secretary a note that was handwritten with a personal message for the President. He waited all day in the reception area. He was told to come back the next day and the President Hussein would see him. Around 2 o'clock the next afternoon, he was summoned back to the Palace. He walked into the Throne Room area. This area has a mural behind his chair that depicts nuclear missiles in flight to destroy the United States. Several chairs were placed in a semi-circle in front of throne chair. He was led into the room and told where to sit. One by one the other gentleman came into the room. They all seemed curious as to why they were being summoned. Saddam would routinely call a meeting and the participants had no idea of location or subject of the meeting. Saddam showed up within minutes of the last participant's arrival. He was very warm and cordial. He began the by saying that "one of you has issues and problems with the way Iraqi is handled." Everyone in the room began to look around, and the colonel just stood up and said, "I am he." The room seemed to shrink in size. The air became stale. He new his time had come. One way or the other he life was over as he knew it, maybe his family's life also.

The colonel began by praising the Republic and the history of the Iraqi people. He praised the early vision and courage of Saddam Hussein. Then came the pivotal moment in the conversation when he started to talk of his days in England; where he had studied history and government. He talked of the goodness and ingenuity of the American people who had been a colony of England. They had rights, which were insured by a constitution. These basic human rights were supported by a rule of law and enforced by the government. He talked about the freedom of speech and the freedom to dissent. He said that the President and the nation could be served by the exchange of ideas to help formulate a national policy instead of arbitrary dictates. It was time for Iraqi to grow up and lead the Arab world into the family of nations. His ideals were lofty but he tried nonetheless to lay a groundwork in hopes that Saddam would listen.

The colonel talked about Hyde Park in London and the mall in Washington where large groups of people could assemble peacefully and speak of their differences with the government. The men in the room began to mock him but Saddam surprisingly remained silent. He spoke for more than six hours. Saddam made two comments and asked one question. After the colonel had rested in his presentation, Saddam stood up and thanked him for his duty to his country and his courage to speak his heart.

He praised him for being a brave man. He told the colonel to go home and he would have his answer in the next few days. The colonel felt that Saddam did not punish him right then because he wanted to expose the greater conspiracy. There was no conspiracy. Just one man who made up his mind that he was going to do what was right no matter the cost. The colonel went home that night to his wife and family. They were eagerly awaiting his return home.

A few days passed and two men came to his door. These men were from the Intelligence Service. They wore plain clothes and drove a black sedan. They were very polite and respectful. They told him that he was being summoned by the President. He turned to his wife and told her goodbye. His wife gave him a small bag of clothes and belongings. The agents told him that he would not need those things where he was going. He was put into the back seat of the car and blindfolded. He was driven around for what seemed like a long time. He found himself in a room with a desk and a couple of chairs. A man came into the room and removed his blindfold.

The man proceeded to read from a transcript of the colonel's conversation with Saddam a couple of days before in the Palace. After reading some of the comments the man began to make a list of criminal charges against the colonel. He was going to be charged, tried, judged, sentenced and convicted right there in that room. He was ordered to die by firing squad at the earliest possible convenience to director of the Abu Gharib prison. He was blindfolded once again and driven to the prison. Every chance the guards were given they would beat him. He was thrown in a dark cell with no blanket, no food or water. The next thing he knew he was being dragged out to an open area and put up against a wall. There were obviously other men there. He could hear them sobbing and begging. He thought of his wife and family. How were they doing? Did they make it out of the city? He had made arrangements for them to flee to their ancestral village in hopes of escaping to Jordan and a new life. His wife would have none of that that; she ended up staying in Baghdad. He could hear the guards talking and laughing.

An officer of the prison came to him and removed the blindfold. For the first time in couple of days he could see the horror around him that earlier he could only hear. The firing squad was given orders to come to attention and ready to fire. The order was given to fire. The machine guns blazed and men fell to the ground dead. Their bodies were mangled and torn by the bullets of the firing squads AK-47's. He and another man were left standing. He did not know what to think of it. Over the next months he was taken out of cell, beaten, dragged outside to stand against the wall. The execution scene was played out over and over again. He would later find out that his colleagues in the military had heard through the official channels of what he had done. Those who were sympathetic to his cause made it a commitment to keep him alive. They were responsible for keeping him alive and not enforcing the judgment of the Ba'ath Party had against him. He would walk out of the prison stripped of his rank and his career. His reputation was demolished except for the clapping of the silent majority. His day of fulfillment would come when he heard about the Coalition's liberation invasion. His prayers have been answered. Now the struggle must continue to rehabilitate and educate his people to the common dream of a stable, secure, responsible and free Iraq.

Another person I was to meet was a man who had been Saddam's Intelligence Chief in the Western Province of Al-Anbar for over twenty years. His entire family was killed in front of his eyes because he was suspected of treason. He was suspected of providing information to the Jordanians. He would later find out that this information was provided to Saddam's son, Qusay, who was in charge of intelligence by a man who was envious and wanted his job. Here was a man who was loyal to Saddam and his life was turned upside and destroyed by a rumor. The paranoia of this regime was extreme. This man is now dedicated to driving the foreign members of the insurgency against the CPA from his land. He does not agree totally with the new provisional government but he does agree that Iraq has seen too much violence and needs the hope of a new tomorrow.

-Michael Parkhouse

A Weapon of Mass Destruction?

There is a popular debate today that since we have not found a bona fide WMD then the operation in Iraq was not justified. Other nations have WMD. We are not worried about most of these because the posture of these countries has always been defensive in nature and the leaders are stable mentally. Under control of Saddam Hussein, a WMD is a real threat.

Today many people are worried that we haven't yet found any large stockpiles of WMD. Some argue that since we have not found a WMD then they do not exist. There is an interesting logical flaw here. If we find one, then they exist. If we find none, then this does not mean that they do not exist. We may search a dozen years and never find a WMD. This does not prove they do not exist; this only proves that we didn't find them. We do know that they did exist and their destruction was not entirely documented as ordered by the United Nations.

The topic of WMD is a major concern for two reasons. One is he had the weapons and two is he has a history of using them. Since now we are in Iraq, we have better access to try to find any remaining WMD, and more importantly what happened to them. This June, we discovered what could be a WMD or it could be something innocent. We don't know what would have happened. We are sleeping better that this item was discovered.

Imagine yourself a project manager, working for the CPA and living in the Green Zone. You are in charge of 2700 separate projects, which employ 65,000 Iraqis. This is Rick Clay. The following is his story as he is called upon to expand his job description to help with a classified mission.

[Rick Clay]

It is Friday [April 2, 2004] and I had every intention of sleeping in late today. I was fast asleep this morning when my phone rang and it was Bernie Hite, the new guy now in charge of special projects. Bernie knew I was sleeping in today and hated to wake me up but this was important. "Rick, you need to get up and come into the office and get your gear on and go meet a Lieutenant

Colonel (LTC) Parish at the parking lot to go out to Camp Slayer for a briefing on a mission tomorrow." Now, this is new. Usually I have a day or two's notice about any mission but to wake me up with no warning is very unusual. I stick my head under the showerhead and soak my head and get dressed as fast as I can and rush to the office to get my body armor. After grabbing my armor, I head to the parking lot, trying to figure out what is going on. As I approach the parking lot, I pass Bennie and he tells me they are waiting on me at the bus stop. Man, I have no idea what is going on.

As I approach the parking lot I can see two men in full "battle rattle," all the combat gear a solder needs to fight. I do not recognize either of them. As I draw closer, I introduce myself and they tell me it is good to meet you and the Chief Warrant Officer talks into his com mike (Microphone) and informs someone, "We have the primary and we are on our way to the unite house." The LTC introduces himself as Doctor Parrish, a neurosurgeon, but he has a PSYOP patch on his uniform and the Chief Warrant Officer has an Intelligence insignia badge on his. The Lt. Col. tells me to get in and he will brief me on the way to Camp Slayer. I have never been to Camp Slayer, but I knew what it was and what it is now used for.

Camp Slayer was build by Saddam around a manmade lake he built out by the Baghdad Airport (BIAP). He then built a huge Palace that sat out in the middle of the lake with lakefront villas all around the lake shore. The Palace has a boat dock built into the Front of the Palace. Each lake front villa sites right on the shore and you can step out your door into the lake itself. When the WMD (Weapons of Mass Destruction) solders were looking for WMD they stayed at Camp Slayer and a good portion of them still do. LTC Parish starts his briefing as we speed out of the "Green Zone" on our way to Camp Slayer. Now for the rest of this story you are not going to believe what I am about to do.

LTC Parish begins to brief me on this mission that came out of nowhere. This mission is very important; that will become very evident as you read this. Back in 1993 Saddam opened a Neurosurgery Center, built around his WMD labs. Wonder why? Then he bought what is called a "Gamma Knife." This is a 20-ton piece of medical equipment, which is used for the elimination of tumors in the brain. There are only 201 of these machines in the world. It has 201 focal points that radiate radiation onto a singular point. Now this radiation is produced by Cobalt 60 isotope. They call the isotope a "seed" which is no bigger than the point of a ballpoint pen.

This seed is so "HOT" (radioactive) that if you took one "seed" and put it in a room as big as a gym and filled it with people they would all be dead within 15 minutes. This Cobalt 60 isotope has a half-life of 5 years. Saddam purchased 15 years worth of "seeds" and he made his last payment two weeks before the war started. The coalition only found out about this machine a month ago when LTC Parish received a phone call from an Iraqi doctor who also was a Neurosurgeon. The day of the war he had the doors of the facilities welded shut. Makes you wonder just how many more welded doors are out there? This area has already been searched by this team I am going with. They found "Yellow Cake," cesium and uranium.

Now we have many fears about this facility and the "seeds." First is going to be getting there safely. It is in the "Sunni Triangle" (Fallujah). Then there is the problem of not knowing which building it is in, within this huge Medical Complex. Then the even bigger problem is this place "Hot" (radioactive)? Then the even bigger problem: are the "seeds" still in the machine and the replacement stored safely? If they are not, then God help us. This stuff would make one great Dirty Bomb, nuclear material wrapped around an explosive; this stuff could kill a lot of people. If it is not there, then where?

Now LTC Parish tells me that our mission is going to be to enter this complex and ascertain whether the "seeds" are still there and if the Machine is working at all. My job is to evaluate the building and its civil, electrical, mechanical integrity as well as the condition of the shielding around the Machine. I will be one of only three men allowed to enter the building. He tells me we are on our way to link up with MCT-3, the unit that is in charge of escorting these types of movements in and around Iraq. We will be receiving an Operations Order from LTC Kane and a US Marine. Then we will undergo several rehearsals drills for convoy support. In short, we will be practicing what we need to do in case we are ambushed. We will do two live fire simulations.

We pull into Camp Slayer and into the MCT-3 Villa - what a place. I step out of my vehicle and it is a great day - sunny but not too hot. A slight wind is blowing across the lake and the water ripples as the wind blows gently over its surface. The sand stone villas look great, as does the Huge Palace in the middle of the lake. I did not bring my camera because I had no idea what this was about. I will bring it later. Then a tall, slender but muscular, red-headed Marine LTC walks out carrying a cup of coffee and introduces himself to everyone. You can tell this man is a hard charger and knows what he is doing. He escorts us into the Villa and into a large room with a glass wall facing out towards the Lake - what a view. Inside the room are 20 young and old soldiers who make up this unit. For this mission we will be called "Long Star." I sit down into one of the empty chairs. On the wall, I can see large maps of Baghdad and blown-up pictures of the Medical Complex that have possible location sites for this "Gamma Knife." Then there is a large sheet of white paper with the Operations Order written all over it. An Operations Order is a plan that covers many areas. It starts out with an explanation of the Situation, Weather, and then the Enemy and Friendly forces are addressed. Next, then the Mission is described. After that is an explanation of the Execution of the plan. The schedule is laid out as well as coordination measures and what to do if we have Enemy Contact. Command is clarified. My vehicle in the convoy is 350.

LTC Kane gives one of the most impressive Operations Order presentations I have heard in a long time. He knows what he is doing.

After LTC Kane finishes the presentation, we go outside to receive a demonstration as to the proper procedures when one finds himself under fire in a convoy and there are casualties. There is one woman assigned to this team and she is one of two medics. I have been assigned to the third vehicle in the rear right seat. It is my job to pull the driver over the seat if he is wounded or killed so that someone can drive the vehicle. You do not stop when under fire unless immobilized. I also have a sector of fire from the 3 o'clock position to the 6 o'clock position. Our vehicle is also designated at the CCP or "Casualty Collection Point." This means all wounded and dead are brought to our vehicle so the Doctor (LTC Parish) and the two Medics can render aid. I must dismount the vehicle and protect the wounded. When the SGT is finished giving the brief, we leave for a training area to practice two live fire exercises to simulate an attack on the convoy. We end up drilling for most of the day.

We return to the villa and do an "After Action Report." This is a review of what happened and what went wrong and right. This is where we can learn from our mistakes and reinforce what we did right. Now yesterday we had an ambush in Fallujah, so I looked around the room to assess the others. I felt that I am the weak link and I hope I can perform as well as these guys did in training. We shall see.

I return back to the Green Zone with my aerial photos and Operations Order, and begin putting together my equipment for this convoy. I make sure my weapon and gear are in top condition. I will be carrying a MP-5 with 7 magazines as well as my .45 caliber with three mags of ammo. For some reason, this does not feel like enough. It hits home when they ask you your blood type. I feel comfortable and safe with these men and one woman. I hope I don't let them down.

It is very cold when I awake. I did not sleep much because of my excitement and anticipation of the coming mission. I called my family the other day to tell them I would not be able to contact them for a few days because of the nature of this mission. I get out of bed with plenty of time to shower, get my gear on and have some breakfast. I usually do not eat breakfast but I don't want to find myself in a fight and have no energy. I put on my body armor and strap on my .45 and hang my MP-5 from my D-Ring on my shoulder so I will have it connected to me no matter what happens. I borrowed a few things from my neighbors, Mike and Marv, and feel real happy about the rig I now have on. I have room for all my magazines, water, and other equipment such as radiation detection devices. It takes me about 15 min to hook everything on to my gear and I walk out into the cold morning. It is unusually cold today. I walk to my office and find Mike, Burney and Chief Byars sitting behind their desks. They are surprised to see me today. I pick a few things from my desk to take with me and bid them good day.

I catch up to LTC Parish at the CPA parking lot. We are waiting on an Iraqi doctor to join us because she knows the way to where we might find the "Gamma Knife." The strong wind makes it seem colder than it was. I should have worn long sleeves. LTC Parish is excited about this mission, as am I. If this equipment is intact then we might be able to use it to help a lot of people with brain cancer or tumors. If it is not intact then we are in trouble. This is a high priority mission.

We have one of the best convoy commanders in the business, Colonel Kane, USMC, and a great convoy crew, all U.S. Army. We will have air support by two AH-64 Longbow Apache Helicopters backed up by Blackhawk medivacs. The Iraqi doctor arrives and she insists on driving her own car. This is okay with us but she will have to follow the convoy because LTC Kane will not let her join our convoy. Several of my friends pass me by as we wait on the convoy to arrive. It is a few minutes late. Finally it shows up and it is impressive. The first two vehicles are HumVee's loaded with .50 cal machine guns on top. The two rear vehicles have 50's as well. There is an antitank missile slung over each top hatch of the vehicles for use on hardened structures. LTC Parish and myself are assigned to 350, a white 250 Ford pickup truck, extended cab. This truck is white and is armored. It has been designated by LTC Kane as the CCP (Casualty Collection Point); it is my responsibility to protect it. LTC

Parish and I climb in after clipping on the radiation badges that are given to us by the WMD guys. We climb into the truck and load our weapons.

The convoy pulls out of the "Green Zone" through Gate Two and we head in the direction of BIAP (Baghdad International Airport). We take the interstate and head towards our objective, a Medical Facility that is located next to the University. This was the scene of heavy fighting in the first days of the war as our troops went into Baghdad. The events of the past few days are fresh in our mind. Seven U.S. troops were killed last night and we expect more fighting today from ambushes. The Marines have walled off Fallujah and they have started to enter the city to get those bastards that mutilated those Blackwater boys. Ambassador Bremer has declared the Shia cleric that was responsible for the fighting the last few days an "outlaw," and he is now wanted for arrest and we will get him. All of this is on our minds as we plow down this four-lane road in staggered formation. We pull behind another convoy headed in the same direction we are going. They have 4 vehicles in their formation with the middle vehicle being a SUV. We slowed down to let them move ahead of us. We drop back about a mile behind them. I am watching out the window covering my sector of fire and watching every car we pass as well as the roadside for any signs of ambush.

Then a pressure wave hits our convoy and I look ahead of our vehicle as the radio starts to chirp with load chatter. "CONTACT FRONT, CONTACT FRONT!!!" The convoy that took our lead has just been hit by a RPG "Rocket Propelled Grenade" and the SUV is in flames. A civilian small bus is also hit by collateral damage. We pull up and dismount from our vehicles and provide perimeter security. I hop out and run to the guardrail and as I run I pull the collapsible stock out so I can aim for long shots because there is a big field on the other side. I look left and right to make sure I locate the shooters on both my sides. They are there. I can hear screams and loud Iraqi and American voices. I take a fast look backwards at 350 and the CCP is being set up with the doctor, LTC Parish, and our two medics. I return my attention to my sector of fire and you can hear some shooting going on from the convoy ahead, then it goes silent. "Target neutralized, MP's OUT!!!" What this means is the attacker is down and the MP's who are a part of every convoy get out and do a "box search." Two men on each side of the convoy run out 50 meters and then turn 90 degrees and search up the side of the convoy then head back in making a box. This is so any of the enemy can be flushed out. We find none.

I hear "Lifesaver 1, Lifesaver 1 inbound." The Medivac is inbound and we have to expand the perimeter so that we can cover "Lifesaver" as the wounded are loaded. The civilians are being treated by our convoy's medics. We push out 100 meters to the edge of the field near the housing area. I find an old cart that provides some cover. Again I check my 9 and 3 o'clock position to see were the others are and they are there. Very glad we rehearsed this. "Lifesaver 1 On Station." I feel the rotor wash on my back and dust begins to rise, making seeing very hard. A few seconds later "Lifesaver 1" is off and headed for the Combat Area Support Hospital (CASH).

Then the order comes over the com system, "Remount, Remount." I rush back to 350 while watching my sector of fire. We are on the road again and moving very fast. We pass the SUV as it burns and the bus is surrounded by broken glass. LTC Kane comes over the com system and asks for a body check. All vehicles report all persons accounted for. We are headed for our objective. Man what a rush! Adrenaline is pumping through my body like never before. The funny thing is when I look out the window as we drive by, the rest of Baghdad is acting like nothing has happened. Life goes on. We finally pull up to the University and I can see the Medical Center coming up fast.

To our surprise this is not a Medical Center that is abandoned and unguarded. This is a hospital that is under reconstruction and there are guards. We pull up to the gate and the guards open it. People pour out of the buildings of this sprawling complex to catch a look at our convoy. It is like being on parade. LTC Kane positions the vehicles around the drive port as we dismount the vehicle. LTC Parish; Craig, a technician from Raytheon; and myself have been chosen to enter the building to look for the "Gamma Knife."

We are met by an Iraqi doctor who is the head of this facility. LTC Parish introduces each of us to the doctor and then asks if he can take us to see the "Gamma Knife." A gleeful expression comes over his face and we are escorted into this huge complex that is neither destroyed, burned nor looted. I walk into this hospital and it is like any hospital I have seen in the states. I grew up around Charleston Area Medical Center (CAMC) and I know hospitals. This is part of the reason I was chosen for this mission. This hospital could accept patients now but it is empty. It only needs a little work to become operational, and this could be one of the best equipped.

We follow the doctor down a long hall that is very familiar to me. It looks like many hallways I have seen at CAMC. At the end of it, we are pointed to move into a room that has several 4-inch lead doors with danger signs painted on it in Arabic. They welded the door shut so that looters could not get to the expensive imaging equipment. Craig pulls out a Geiger counter and begins to monitor the radiation and it is only a little hot - within safety ranges. We go inside this heavily shielded room and, man, what a machine! Craig goes to work to see if the "seeds" have been tampered with. They have not. All the equipment is there and so are the "Cobalt 60 seeds." Thank God! The good doctor is proud of his hospital and the fact they were able to protect the "Cobalt 60 Seeds" and Machine. I immediately go to work, walking all over the building checking the civil, mechanical, and electrical systems. This hospital is one great building. It has its own power source, water source, sewage system and oxygen plant - all brand new. It will only take me 4 months to get this whole complex up and running ready to accept patients.

I spend about 3 hours going through this complex. Craig picks through every inch of the "Gamma Knife" looking for leaks and any missing "seeds." All check out. LTC Parish spends his time interviewing the staff and forming relationships. It has become very apparent that we have stumbled on a great medical gift. We can get this 250-bed hospital open in a few months and the Iraqi people will have a hospital that has 5 new operating rooms, a CAT Scan, modern X-ray machines and one of only 200 "Gamma Knifes."

LTC Kane and the rest of Lone Star are manning the vehicles and guarding the building. We decide to have the military start patrolling this site because of the "Cobalt 60 seeds." They agree to place guards around the building and expand a nearby FOB (Forward Operating Base) to cover the hospital. We bid farewell to our new friends, and we load up into the vehicles to head back to the CPA Compound. We go back the way we came. We drive by the University, which is swarming with students in school uniforms, thousands of them. They all wave as we go by. These kids are moving forward, not backward like the ones who fought us last night or on the road today.

Then the radio cracks, "MP 1 is disabled!" I look for MP 1, which is in front of the column expecting to see combat, but instead I see nothing. Then over the radio it comes "MP 1 disabled. Throttle broke." We pull up into defensive positions so we can protect MP 1. We dismount and push out 50 meters to provide security. Then "MP's Out" and the MP's start their "box search." It only takes 15 minutes to fix MP 1, but it feels like a month. I watch the brush. We are in a very fertile area and it reminds me of home with all the green grass and trees. I scan my sector of fire and see the MP doing his "box search" then the command comes from LTC Kane, "MP's In!" We fall back onto the convoy as I watch the MP run through the field under cover from the .50 cal's. We load up and head back to the CPA Green Zone.

We pull into the parking lot and we all fall out and wonder what happened to the men that were loaded on to "Life Saver 1." I walk back and run into some of the same people I passed when I was leaving; they are glad to see me. They were all worried about me going out and I am touched. I have only known these people for a few months, some even less, but we all have a bond. Now I have an additional bond with the men and woman of Lone Star.

-Rick Clay

This story of the potential hazard was reported by Fox News on July 7, 2004. Many of the details are classified. Also announced by the Department of Energy was the discovery of 1.95 tons of low-enriched uranium. In the effort to make the world safe, two soldiers died that day in the convoy. The search continues.

Soccer

Soccer has been a magic healing remedy for Iraq. They have used it to build up a sense of national unity. Throughout all the hardships and miseries, they keep playing. Everywhere Americans have gone, they have seen kids on a dusty field kicking a worn-out ball. One man told me a story of watching three lonely soldiers guarding a gas station in an almost hostile neighborhood; they had every right to be scared and tense. One starts kicking a ball with some little kids, right there in his full battle gear and weapon slung over his back. The tension in the air breaks.

This year was a big year for Iraq. They were allowed to play their national sport in the Olympics for the first time since Iraq invaded Kuwait in 1990. What a turn-around! They had a good run and just missed getting a bronze medal. Just a little over a year ago, soccer players were living a nightmare. Since Uday Hussein took over the Olympic Training Facility in 1986, soccer is not a sport. Soccer is torture. If you lose, you are tortured; if you win, your earnings are stolen by Uday. Why did children even keep playing? Yet, they did and within a year after the death of Uday the soccer team is re-born and does very well.

In 1996, soccer player Raed Ahmed defected to the United States. He was sentenced to death in absentia, his wife was forced to divorce him, and all of his family was subjected to intense questioning, including his nine-year-old daughter. [54]

Another soccer player relates his story of what happened to him when he got tired of the abuse. He knew he couldn't quit, so he tells Uday he has a stomach ulcer and would be unable to play. He was taken to the Olympic Training Center and his feet beaten twenty times a day for three days with nothing to eat but a slice of bread and water. Next he was drug on the ground until his back was bloody, then forced to jump into a pit of sewage. [55]

One of Michael Parkhouse's interpreters was a man in his thirties. He had two brothers who were stars on the Iraqi National Soccer Team.

[Michael Parkhouse]

When the Iraqi National Soccer failed to win a game in the World Cup, all the members of the team and their families were publicly humiliated. Some members of the team were jailed, beaten and tortured. One of his brothers was jailed and beaten. The family was subjected to their heads being shaven and a zero painted on their foreheads. Every member of his immediate family, including the women and children, were subjected to this humiliation. His wife became so distraught the she abandoned her husband and children and fled to Germany. She would later denounce her husband and children in order to obtain a divorce.

-Michael Parkhouse

In America kids play sports for the dream of some future day playing before thousands and collecting a large salary to do so. In Iraq, there was some other reason to play soccer. And they did, no matter how dismal the game looked. Somehow they kept it alive and showed the world they are a nation.

One eight-year-old in Texas sees a photo of his Iraqi peers playing soccer with a wad of rags. He is so moved he sends three of his own balls along with a pump he buys with his own allowance money. The boy, living in the luxury of the U.S., where he gets a new soccer ball for each season he plays, cannot bear to think of playing with such meager equipment. No one asked him, he just saw the photo and reached out.

Another American on duty in Mosul decides to take matters into his own hands after seeing children playing in the dust. Captain Alex Fyfe decided to help and through his efforts was noticed by the media. He wrote me the following email.

[Alex Fyfe]

Yes, this soccer program has gotten a really healthy response from everyone back home. I guess I'll try to explain to you how the idea began.

As the Civil affairs officer for my battalion, I get to visit all of Mosul's outlying villages and meet with the mayors and town councilmen from those villages. Together, we discuss how to improve the village's infrastructure and their standard of life. After years of neglect, most of the villages appreciate our attempt to help them out as best we can. My unit, 1-37 Field Artillery, 3rd Brigade, 2nd Infantry Division (Stryker Brigade) has been in Iraq since November and specifically Mosul since early January.

I've contacted many schools back in the states about sending school supplies over and have had a great response. However, after speaking with teachers at the schools here, they also expressed a need for soccer equipment. Since I was getting a lot of help from schools at home with school supplies, I tried contacting a few sporting goods companies to ask for help. After getting no response, I decided to ask my former high school coach, Al Ellis from Rocky Point, if he could help me and gather some soccer balls to send over. As usual, my coach wrote back right away and said he would help me as best he could. I knew if I asked him to send one ball, he'd find a way to send 500.

At the monthly town council meetings, we ask the mayors to give us a list of three priorities that they'd like us to help them with. The mayor of the village Bartallah (30 miles NE of Mosul) listed his priorities as #1 building a police station, #2 the need for medical equipment for their health clinic, and #3 soccer equipment.

This town has electricity 12 hours a day, no running water, and no sewage system. None of us expected to hear #3. However, once he mentioned soccer, I knew I would be able to help out somehow.

We have discovered that the way into a village's heart is not by force but by friendship. If giving a few soccer balls to these kids gives them something to do after school and keeps them from roaming the streets looking for trouble, then that makes our job much easier. And right now, because of security issues, my soldiers and I cannot play with the kids...yet. I am working with a village 30km east of Mosul called Qara Qosh and I will be supplying them with some jerseys, cleats, and soccer balls later this week. Hopefully I'll be able to get out on their dirt field and kick the ball around a little with them.

The kids here see a soccer ball and immediately recognize the connection with us. They kick an "American" soccer ball the same way they kick an "Iraqi" soccer ball. Although our governments might disagree over certain issues and our people do not fully understand each other, we can at least enjoy soccer together.

The Iraqi kids do not know what it is like to live in a society that promotes education and athletics. What they need are the resources and, more importantly, the opportunity to try new things and better themselves. The game of soccer opened a few doors for me and I'm hoping by helping these kids out, soccer might do the same for them.

What is really amazing to me is how much support from home I am getting. It seems that everyone wants to contribute and has wanted to; it's just that they didn't know how. So, I am glad that I can help everyone from back home help these kids in Iraq. The New York Times published a story about the project and I interviewed with "Fox and Friends" morning show to promote the project. So the word has gotten out. And just last week I received over 70 boxes of equipment from people all over the U.S. (even Japan).

-Alex Fyfe

Soccer is not just a game; it is a vehicle to bring hope for the young and to also gauge the progress of the new stability in the country. What a relief when you can focus on the nation's pastime as a sport again.

Terrorists

As a justification for entering Iraq, going after those responsible for the attacks on 9-11 was a major factor. Now the direct hostilities are over, some people are clamoring for hard evidence of a connection between Al-Qaeda and Saddam Hussein. So far no direct documents have been found, or made known, though it is common knowledge of Saddam Hussein's support of terrorists like Abdul Nidal and for his financial payments to families of Palestinian suicide bombers. It is also suspicious that leaders of the Mukhabarat met with three of the four 9-11 pilots a few months prior to the suicide attacks. [56]

Another cause for concern is the specialized terrorist group Saddam Hussein started called al-Qare'a. These were highly-trained commandoes who were taught how to hijack planes, among other things. These men trained under extreme conditions with many live fire exercises. For those that did not pass the course, they became the targets in future exercises. Each member was given a new identity and a forged passport from a different country. They were sent out from Iraq in small groups and their whereabouts are not known. [57]

Saddam Hussein is known to be not religious and his motivations have always been devious. He doesn't like Israel so he supports Palestinian terrorists. He doesn't like Iran so he fights against the Shi'ite terrorists. He doesn't like the U.S. and he may have supported Al-Qaeda. His world view is based on his own power rise and security and not any extreme religious fanaticism. In Iraq, he murdered religious leaders who became too popular.

Regardless of any Saddam Hussein and Al-Qaeda links, right now the coalition is battling a terrorist war. At least four factions are creating anarchy with the hopes the U.S. will grow tired and pull out so the respective groups can take power in Iraq. They are terrorists, killing American military, government contractors, humanitarian relief workers, and innocent Iraqi civilians. Maybe these aren't the exact ones who planned 9-11, still they are dangerous and killing Americans.

The most notable is Muqtada Al-Sadr whose goal is to rise to power. His base is the mass of uneducated Shia living in the slums of Sadr City in Baghdad. To further his chances of success, he has accepted hundreds of millions of dollars from Iran to build up a base in southern Iraq. $70 million of this is believed to have gone directly to arms build-up. [58] Muqtada Al-Sadr uses truces to re-fit and re-arm as the Vietnamese did with the U.S. years back.

Another group is what the military call FREs – Former Regime Extremists. These are those who had gained considerable power and prestige being loyal to Saddam Hussein and they see their future as bleak with those they tortured and oppressed now in power. Like Nazis, their hope is a return to the old ways where they lived the good life.

Another faction is the foreigners. These are mercenary fanatics coming from Jordan, Syria and Iran. They are sent by those who resent democratic ideas – the ones who have most to lose if democracy and freedom take a hold in the Middle East. Many of the Syrians believe in a Pan-Arab world that will rise up and take its rightful place as the rulers of the world. The most notorious of the foreign terrorists is Abu Musab al-Zarqawi from Jordan.

The final faction adding to the violence is the Wahabis. This Moslem sect has been around since the 18th century. Their missionaries started most of the schools across the Islamic world, especially in Afghanistan and Pakistan. For decades, many had no education if not for the school system the Wahabis established. Along with teaching reading, writing and arithmetic, this group taught religion and its fundamentalist view extolling violence against everyone except other Wahabis, to include non-Wahabi Muslims. This went against the traditionalist view that people "of the book" are not infidels, only unconverted Muslims. The Wahabis are intolerant of anyone not being other Wahabis. Al-Qaeda is an extreme version of Wahabis. The Taliban is Wahabi. The House of Saud is technically Wahabi and this sect is the official religion of Saudi Arabia. Though as a large royal family and a large country, there is a mix of feelings between being more open and being strict.

With all these groups now converging in Iraq, life for the coalition is becoming dangerous. There is a lot of money, weapons, hatred and power at stake. Most Iraqis don't want any part of the violence. They would rather build a new country based on the opportunities that freedom allows. The Information Age is changing the landscape. No longer are people easily kept ignorant.

In listening to public debate, Zeyad, the blogging dentist from Iraq, cautions to know the background of who is speaking. The Association of Muslim Scholars is an official sounding name. Recently they have been defending actions of violence and terrorism. He cautions.

[Zeyad]

The Association of Muslim Scholars is a self-appointed body that was formed a few months after the war by Sunni clerics who lost their governmental positions with the fall of the former regime.

Sunni Imams and clerics had to be approved by the Ministry of Religious Affairs if they ever intended to preach in mosques. They had to use sermons that were provided beforehand by the government...or the Mukhabarat. Muthanna Harith Al-Dhari, the son of the general secretary of the association is actually rumored to be a former Mukhabarat employee. His great grandfather Dhari Al-Mahmoud was the Sheikh of the Zoba' tribe in the Fallujah and Abu Ghraib areas and was a major player in the 1920 Iraqi insurrection against the British occupation.

Unlike Shia clerics, Sunni clerics do not study for decades in religious seminaries. All it takes to be a Sunni Imam is to graduate from a 4-years Sharia college. For centuries, it has been the traditional role of Sunni clerics to support the rulers and to provide them legitimacy. Shia clerics, on the other hand, have always been known to be dissidents and distrustful toward rulers.

Ideologically, the Shia believe that there will never be a 'just' ruler until the reappearance of the Mahdi, which is the reason Shi'ite clerics keep out of politics as much as possible and turn to religious and spiritual matters, with a few notable exceptions. The Sunni position is that an 'unjust' ruler is preferred over chaos or disunity, or 'an unjust Muslim is better than a just infidel'.

However, the Shia doctrine of Wilayyet Al-Faqih (rule of the jurisprudent), adopted by the Islamic Revolution in Iran, basically contends that the Marji'iya should rule on behalf of the absent Imam (Al-Mahdi) until the day he appears again; challenging their rule would be akin to disobeying Imam Al-Mahdi. This ideology was (ab)used by clerics at the time of Al-Mahdi's disappearance around the ninth century; it was clearly a clever invention by the clerics for them to assume power themselves. It was dropped eventually until Khomeini came to the scene.

Similarly, Sunni clerics over the centuries have defended the 'divine rights' of the successive Muslim Caliphs, Sultans and rulers, especially under the Ottoman Caliphate. They would declare Jihad whenever they had a chance. This continued until Mustafa Kamal abolished the Caliphate in the early twenties of the last century. Afterwards, Sunni clerics were divided over the rulers that came to rule the now independent parts of the empire, and since then there has been no distinct Sunni Marji'iya that can claim to speak for all Sunnis. Some follow the Mufti of the Azhar in Cairo, some follow the Mufti of Mecca, and so on.

In Iraq, the former regime used Sunni clerics in whatever way it saw fit. They were paid governmental employees and would readily issue a fatwa for Saddam Hussein to bomb Mecca if he wanted. When he wrote the Quran in his own blood there were scores of clerics who said it was 'okay', although Islam clearly states that blood is najis. If there was ever a dissident cleric they would at least be 'removed'. Some chose to leave Iraq (such as Sheikh Ahmed Al-Kubaisi). They had to mention his name as the 'leader of the Islamic umma' at least once during Friday prayers. When the late Ayatollah Mohammed Mohammed Sadiq Al-Sadr (Muqtada's father) refused to pray for him at Friday prayers in Kufa, he was conveniently assassinated in 1999, and Friday prayers for the Shia were prohibited afterwards. There were smaller Shi'ite clerics that would support the regime but they were scorned by the mass of Shia, and since Shi'ite clerics depend on their followers for their livelihood and not on the government, it has always been that way.

The Association of Muslim Scholars and a handful of other similar Sunni groups were formed from the remnants of the mentioned clerics and Imams who preached for the government. They have limited support from Iraqi Sunnis even though they claim otherwise. Like Al-Sadr, most of these groups have refused to join the political process unless the occupation ends, most of them support armed resistance and some even went far as to justify beheadings, the assassinations of Iraqi figures and other barbaric acts. It is obvious that they have lost dearly from the fall of the dictatorship and they are aware that they have no place in a democratic system since they have no true support. [59]

-Zeyad

On September 5th, I spoke with Major Joel Hagy, who was sitting on the roof of his building on the edge of Sadr City. Joel is a member of a six-man Civil Affairs team. While we talked, a 120mm mortar round was shot by one of the terrorist groups. He says sometimes as many as sixty mortar rounds will be lobbed at the Americans. A few minutes later, the main gun of an Abrams tank was responding. Through it all, Joel was unfazed.

Joel sees the terrorists as losing. They are being augmented by foreigners coming through the open borders. They have an abundance of new weapons. Still they have lost 1200 in the last three months. Joel's observation is that they are untrained and fire wildly without aiming. They stick their barrels of their weapons around corners and squeeze off rounds. They never hit anything. Joel thinks here and Najaf, the other place with a terrorist threat, is safer than some places in Iraq where they have IEDs and car bombs.

The main concern of Joel's is the danger they pose to Iraqis who help the Americans, like the translators or the city council members. Many of these have been stalked and killed. The influx of Wahabis and Syrians is a concern. They are taking advantage of the chaos to further their agendas. They tend to hide amongst the local terrorists.

Overall, the general population likes the humanitarian help of the coalition. The projects are achieving great success except recently as Al-Sadr's group is acting up again. People are seeing sewage lines cleared, trash dumps cleaned up, schools re-opened, medical clinics opened and people treated.

The lack of clean water and waste removal have caused a rise in diseases. These programs are helping. At one point, the U.S. was delivering five million liters of water a day. The people appreciate the help. They see the true issues. The terrorists do not help, only intimidate. Now most everyone has satellite TVs. People are learning the truth.

Many are impatient. After living in a world where the state took care of their needs, the people are slow to learn responsibility for themselves. Despite Al-Sadr, despite the foreign terrorist, progress is being made. It might be slower in Sadr City. Joel estimates ten years until this place is brought up to civilized standards for cleanliness, economic viability, self-government, healthcare and education. Sadr City is a large slum with the violence problems that other parts of Iraq don't have. In the long term, it is inevitable. The people will choose peace. [60]

[Bob Ohl]

I hope everything is going well for everyone at home. Our time is flying by here in Iraq. It really is an experience seeing how other nations other than the U.S. live. There is such a drastic change in how Saddam and the chosen elite lived and how they forced the rest of the population to live. The majority of the population lives like we did in the U.S. in the 1950s and 1960s. There is very little electricity and/or running water. Because city power is so limited, generators are the most reliable source of power. The majority of homes do not have cable TV, traditional telephone service, or even a town sewage system. For the TV, satellite has replaced the need for phone lines, cell phones have replaced the need for telephone lines and as for sewage you can't transmit lines through the air to take care of that issue so it usually just runs into the back yard or streets. When we were working in Sadr City, it was not uncommon to drive through puddles of human waste in the streets and the streets were lined with trash (there is no formal trash system). At times when we had to get out of our vehicles to get through a busy traffic section, I felt like I was walking through a public landfill. If you had ever been to a landfill, the trash gets compacted into the ground and debris is everywhere. There was always a constant stench in the air of either sewage or burning trash in the distance.

A classmate of mine works for the Corps of Engineers and the Coalition has plans in place to provide the city with infrastructure such as sewage treatment facilities and power plants.

We also had quite a learning experience from talking every day with our interpreters, Qusay and Muhammed are two of our best. They are both currently taking classes at the local college so that they can be English professors. Qusay was raised in Great Britain because his parents feared for him growing up in Iraq. When the war started last year, the Iraqi government went door to door to take sons and husbands to fight. Qusay's mother lied and said that he was already south waiting to fight the Americans when he was really hiding downstairs. No wonder that their Army didn't put up a fight, no one felt in their hearts the will to go and win. Qusay tells me now that he knew that the Americans were going to take Baghdad and apprehend Saddam. Qusay's uncle, a Colonel in the Iraqi Army, fled Iraq five years ago and now lives in Germany. He was fearful that Saddam would kill him or his family at any given time. Saddam was able to stay in power by killing those around him who were a threat to him and his regime. One police station commander from Sadr City, LTC Sadoon, was imprisoned for 5 years during Saddam's regime and feared for his life every day. The coalition forces gave him back his badge, a police station and police officers last October. His station is in one of the roughest areas in Sadr City and I wish him and his policemen well.

By the way, interpreters work 26-27 days a month and work in a very hazardous job. Qusay told me that he earns more than he will after he becomes a college professor. The pay for interpreters is $450 in American dollars. Police officers make around $330 a month (which I read before coming here that it is six times what they use to make). The cost of living is much cheaper and you can buy a lot for an American dollar. DVDs are $5, haircuts are $2, a uniform cleaned and pressed is $2 and those are the rates to Americans because they know that we'll pay them.

From 01 March until 17 April our main area of operation was in Sadr City. We were working closely with the Iraqi police force and trying to equip them in order to secure the streets of Sadr City. Sadr City is mostly of Shi'a Muslims. Most of the Shi'a population is farmers and found further south, but those in the north are mostly found in Sadr City. Saddam Hussein restricted the Shiites and did not allow them to endure politically or economically. The majority of Arab Muslims in Iraq are Shiites, but with Saddam, a Sunni, in power, all of the prominent positions in government were held by Sunnis. So for years, Sadr City did not receive any attention or basic upgrades. Add the

Kurds up north to the mix and you have a very challenging society. I'm going to do great social science projects with my kids in the future.

Little more history, Muqtada Sadr that you may have heard about on the news is just rising to power. His father, the lead Shi'a Cleric, was murdered by Saddam in 1998, and Muqtada's uncle was murdered in the late 1980s. Both of these men were considered to be great leaders and were well thought of by the Shi'a community. Sadr City is actually named after both of them. Sistani is the lead Shi'a cleric now and welcomes the democratic move and the coalition support. Muqtada Sadr is gaining the Shi'a support that his father and uncle's name have created. I feel that we must take care of him now or he'll always be threat to the Iraqi democracy. Unfortunately there will be a lot of revolts against his capture or his death.

Sadr City when we started our tour was very quiet and respectful of the Coalition Forces. One police station commander told me that, "They didn't even think God could remove Saddam." After the legislation was signed for the Interim Constitution, all of Baghdad had a holiday the next day. The professors gave our interpreters off the day from school and many businesses were closed. I asked Qusay if they took the day off after we had captured Saddam. He said, "No, everyone wanted to be joyous and be outside." There was massive celebration in the streets of the city.

Sadr City was pretty quiet, the police stations did not have any major issues (at least that the Iraqi Police told us about), the mosques were quiet and the streets appeared to be quiet as we would travel through them. The constant threat of improvised explosive devices (IEDs) and small arms attacks were random all over Baghdad but Sadr City was quiet. I actually felt more confident driving through the streets in the city because at the time, no one would set up an explosion to hurt innocent civilians. When Muqtada Sadr started his uprising in Najaf and Fallujah, we saw a slight turn in the attitude in Sadr City. The police stations have a lot of Shiites working in them and some of the policemen may even be showing a sign of loyalty to Muqtada Sadr. Many would not defend the police stations and many lost AK-47s in their arms' room to the demonstrators. Sadr is also hiding weapons in mosques because he knows that places of worship are off limits during wartime. The Iraqi government will eventually get the right police officers together and target the mosques in question. This has to be done by the Iraqis or the coalition forces will be viewed by the Muslim world as total aggressors.

215

This makes the situation very complex. On 04 April 2004 at approximately 2000 hours, the military police started to get alerts that large demonstrations had been gathering around police stations and bureau buildings. Sadr's intent is to attack the areas of Iraqi security such as the police stations and government headquarters to show a greater instability in the entire government building process. Battery B 1-109 FA was able to move out quickly and assist the Iraqi policemen in defending their police stations from these demonstrations. We worked closely with the 2-5 Cavalry Regiment from Fort Hood, Texas. For the next 96 hours, our guys worked closely with the armor and the infantry active duty soldiers and we earned their respect as field artillery guardsmen who could defend a sector. A few of our guys even made the Stars and Stripes Newspaper on their extraordinary efforts. This was at the same time that the aggressive assault heated up in Fallujah and down south.

There will be another aggressive assault soon with the intent to take Coalition control over cities such as Fallujah.

Even though Battery B 1-109 FA is out of the center of harm's way, there is still significant risk involved and our leaders are continuing to enforce controls to lower those risks. As always, continue to take the time to think about the soldiers who are getting ready to start this aggressive assault in Fallujah and other key anti-coalition cities. As things heat up there, so will the activity in and around Baghdad. Remember the news is often exaggerated and one sided but the soldiers need our support as we cross the last major obstacle to a free democratic state in Iraq.

God Bless the U.S.A.

- Bob Ohl

Chapter Seven
The Folks at Home

The outpouring of love and support for efforts to support the military in Iraq and to support the Iraqi people build a new beginning is mind-boggling. Everywhere people are donating money, time, and resources to established charities. Some are starting new charities and some are just doing charitable work on their own. There are so many stories of individual contributions, it is an almost impossible task just to discover all the individual stories. Every rock I turn over reveals so many more examples.

Some get a lot of publicity and some get very little. Some don't even want to be known. One particular organization is a multi-million dollar charitable effort with workers in Iraq being attacked and killed and still they're more comfortable being quiet.

Here I'm taking a stab at just trying to do a small amount of justice to honor the efforts of so many. If there are any efforts I have failed to mention I apologize, and I'll add to new editions of this book. The intent is to honor those helping free Iraq from oppression. It's not a military operation; it's thousands of individual contributions.

Fallen Patriot Fund

The Fallen Patriot Fund helps families of military who were killed or seriously wounded by providing financial assistance. The Mark Cuban Foundation is involved in deciding who recipients will be, and it matches charitable donations dollar for dollar. So far the Fund has awarded almost three quarters of a million dollars to thirty-five families. [61]

http://www.FallenPatriotFund.org

Fisher House

The Fisher House is a program that augments benefits provided by the government with additional humanitarian assistance. When someone in uniform is injured, Fisher House will provide lodging for family members to be with their loved ones during time of need.

Fisher House is building homes on military bases and where they haven't yet built a home will provide lodging nearby. Currently they have built thirty-two homes on all the major installations. This allows family members to get involved in the care of their loved ones who have been wounded in Operation Iraqi Freedom or other operations.

Fisher House also partners with several airlines to provide donors' frequent flyer miles to help the families be with their wounded in times of crisis. So far, OIF families have received over 450 plane tickets. [62]

http://www.FisherHouse.org

Freedom Alliance

This organization provides scholarships to children of military who were killed fighting terrorism. For the second year in a row, Six Flags Great Adventure in New Jersey has hosted a Freedom Concert. Those buying a ticket to the show get into the park also. This latest concert on July 8th raised 2.5 million dollars. Martina McBride was the headlining act. Sean Hannity, a nationally syndicated radio talk show host, is the spokesman and his daily radio program generated most of the publicity. [63]

http://www.FreedomAlliance.org

Operation Iraqi Children

Actor Gary Sinise and author Laura Hillenbrand have organized an effort to get school supplies to the children of Iraq. This organization creates structure to the generosity of Americans wanted to help. They have a standardized kit for each child and a method to pack these. They have organized a VFW warehouse in Kansas City for collection and they are receiving free shipping from Kansas City to Iraq via Federal Express. Their organization also works with the troops on the ground so the school supplies can be more quickly distributed. They also assist in getting local collection campaigns started.[64]

http://www.OperationIraqiChildren.org

Spirit of America

Spirit of America is based in Los Angeles. They raise money and goods to supply the requests in re-building Iraq. Its website is filled with dozens of stories of its charitable giving. They also work closely with many Marines. A Marine in Iraq will see a need and send a request to Spirit of America. In many instances, Federal Express provides for free shipping. Some examples of what this organization has provided include:

• 10,000 school supply kits, 3 tons of medical supplies and 2 tons of Frisbees printed with "Friendship" in English and Arabic.
• $4500 worth of pianos and violins.
• 1,500 book bags filled with school supplies.
• Yo-yos.
• A cow.
• 480 red, white and blue soccer jerseys and a greeting "A gift of friendship from the people of the United States to the people of Iraq."
• Equipment for Iraqi-owned and operated television stations.
• 2,000 dental care kits (toothbrushes and toothpaste) with an insert of images of the American and Iraqi flags.
• 250 water barrels.
• Sandals for Iraqi children.
• 50 sewing machines for a new women's sewing center. [65]

Lieutenant Colonel Dave Couvillion of the United States Marine Corps Reserves brought his battalion to Iraq in 2003 and to his surprise he was appointed the Military Governor of Wasit. Everything in the province was his responsibly. He had to fix all the infrastructure, create local governments, get the economy going, and provide security and rule of law. One of the things he realized was to win over the people so that they would view the Americans as liberators and not conquers. Dave had an idea to allow the children to be children by encouraging sports. He promoted the national sport of soccer and asked Jim Hake, the founder of Spirit of America for soccer jerseys. The Spirit of America responded with 480 red, white and blue jerseys. Now he could outfit many teams.

Another thing Dave noticed was that the people were fond of displaying America flags on their vehicles and putting American flag stickers everywhere in show of their support. This was the reason for the color of soccer jerseys. The people were wanting to show their loyalty so as not to be branded as insurgents of Saddam loyalists.

http://www.SpiritofAmerica.net

TAPS

The Tragedy Assistance Program for Survivors, Inc. (TAPS) is there to provide comfort, support and care to the surviving loved ones of military personnel. Bonnie Carroll started TAPS in 1994 after her husband, Brigadier General Tom Carroll, was killed along with seven other soldiers in an Army National Guard aircraft crash. Mrs. Carroll found strength and support from others and now her organization provides that same support and more to military survivors, including family and friends.

Since the start of Operation Iraqi Freedom, TAPS has been sadly too active. When a casualty occurs, the family is referred to TAPS for long-term emotional support and care. So far over one thousand have died, and many more have died while serving at home and around the world. TAPS' network of hundreds of "peer mentors" has been very busy. Grieving is a tough process and the sudden death of a loved one can be devastating. But the families need to pick up and continue living. TAPS provides emotional support in many ways. TAPS also provides welcome assistance for commanders and chaplains so they can better support the survivors in their unit. [66]

Mrs. Carroll, who has provided a source of encouragement for this book, sent me a couple of emails explaining more about what TAPS does.

[Bonnie Carroll]

"The Department of Defense announced today the death of three Marines who were supporting Operation Iraqi Freedom..."

These words scrolled across the screen of our television more often than we care to remember. We read them, and then we focused elsewhere. It was too difficult, too painful, to imagine that somewhere in America, a family who had sent its son or daughter, husband or wife, brother or sister, mom or dad off to serve our country in a far-off land was now going to get a fateful knock on the door telling the family members that they would never see that precious loved one again.

Statistically, over the past 20 years, there have been six deaths per day in the armed forces. Sixty percent are classified as "accidents" and the average age of those killed is 24. The families left behind include young wives, often with infants or expecting a baby, and young parents in their forties. In some cases, these families must turn in their ID cards, move immediately away from their friends and support systems, and rebuild a life that was once devoted to service but is now focused on just surviving. These young Americans deserve the very best care we can give them.

TAPS' staffing is primarily based on volunteer efforts and outreach. The donations we receive go directly into programs that help those affected by the death of a service member, including the crisis hotline answered 24 hours a day, 7 days a week; TAPS' SurvivorLINK and peer support network within the U.S. and overseas; extensive materials on coping with grief and trauma, including the website at www.taps.org; the annual Memorial Day Weekend National Military Survivor Seminar and Good Grief Camp for Young Survivors; a quarterly magazine offering hope and comfort; long-term case work assistance that complements the immediate help from casualty staffs; grief counseling referral; and so much more. Everything TAPS provides is free of charge for the families, and is made possible by the generosity of those who honor the lives of those who have served.

The following is a personal story, one of thousands, of a connection made by TAPS between an OIF "survivor" and a peer mentor. It tells of a love honored and a life remembered, and shares insight not only into the help provided by the next of kin, but also to the many "disenfranchised grievers" TAPS reaches out to, those not normally recognized by other organizations, such as siblings and significant others and parents.

Rebecca saw her precious soldier, a military policeman with the Alabama National Guard, head out for Iraq along with their hopes, dreams and plans for their future. He promised her he'd be safe, she knew he'd be home. She spent her days working in her flower shop in Alabama, writing letters daily, and sending weekly care packages. She kept busy, especially around the holidays. Two days after her busiest day of the year, Valentine's Day, when thoughts were still on roses and love, her world stopped turning. Her worst fear had been realized, when on February 16, 2004, Chris was killed in Baghdad, Iraq. The story was an all-too-familiar one, he had been hit by shrapnel after an improvised explosive device detonated alongside the road. This is the rest of the story, of a life back home in America forever changed by that single event, that solitary headline.

There were immediate responses, including a commemoration by Congressman Jo Bonner of Alabama, who said that Chris "set a standard of excellence and displayed the qualities of discipline, devotion, and dedication to country that are hallmarks of men and women throughout the long and distinguished history of the American military. As a result of his hard work, Christopher was advanced to the rank of Specialist, and he was posthumously awarded the Bronze Star and the Purple Heart."

Rebecca wrote in tribute to her beloved, "Chris Taylor was an amazing man and the love of my life. He was only 25 when he was killed. He was driving in a convoy in Baghdad when an explosive device struck his convoy on February 16, 2004. He understood that freedom was not free and mentioned that in letters he wrote home. He was always very patriotic and so proud to be doing what he was doing, which was serving his country. He rarely complained and remained quite positive even under those conditions. He made the most of everything and always looked to the brighter side of life. I learned a lot about sacrifice through him. If there was one thing that meant the world to him, it was his family and friends. He sacrificed time away from his family and the people he cared about in order to better someone else's life. He felt honored to do so and wouldn't have had it any other way. I could go on and on about Chris...He was such a giving person and he gave right to the end. He made the ultimate sacrifice for something he truly believed in. He told me not long before he was killed, it was for the greater good of our country and for the people of Iraq, that he was over there, and he truly believed that.

My life has been forever changed, not just by the tragic events that have taken place, but also just by knowing him. He taught me a lot about love, about life, and about sacrifice. I will forever be proud of him and what he did. He was proud to wear the uniform of the United States Army, and I will remain forever proud for him."

But where was Rebecca, not a "next of kin" according to the Defense Department or someone officially recognized as a beneficiary of financial benefits from the Department of Veterans Affairs, to turn for support and help? In addition to peer support groups for spouses and parents, the Tragedy Assistance Program for Survivors, Inc. (TAPS) also offers loving care for siblings, significant others, children, extended family and friends of those who have died while serving. This pledge to honor and care for the loved ones of those who have died while serving in the armed forces means open arms and a loving response to all who reach out for help. Rebecca's father found TAPS on the internet and encouraged her to check it out. It was there she discovered a peer support network with "significant others" from around the nation also grieving the death of a loved one.

When she logged onto the TAPS Chat one Tuesday night, she met Ellen. Ellen's fiancé, David, a Navy instructor pilot, had died in an aviation accident on Valentine's Day in 1995. Today, Ellen facilitates the Chat online for TAPS, and lovingly offers a national support group to all who enter. Talking to someone who has been there, who has lived and survived a similar experience, gives a "moral authority" that only a shared tragedy can provide. Their friendship has helped offer a kind of empathy no one else could offer.

Through referral from TAPS, Rebecca also was able to participate in grief counseling at her local Vet Center. The VA Vet Centers, like TAPS, are peer-based. Many of their grief and trauma counselors are also combat veterans. They understand from a very personal perspective the trauma that accompanies the grief of losing a loved one serving in a far off land. Vet Center counselors have been described by TAPS survivors as being therapists who really "get the military," who "understand what it means to be posthumously promoted or awarded the Bronze Star for Valor," and who "have been on the receiving end of those care packages and letters, and know how much a mom's love means to a soldier in a foxhole." They offer not only professional therapy, but personal connection and loving care, and have been a strong professional partner to TAPS peer support network.

Rebecca described her counselor as someone who had "tremendous insight and a great way of explaining things," and the Vet Center as a "great place to work through this pain." And she said of TAPS, "The loss of a loved one in the military is not just any loss, especially when the loss is due to combat situations. Most people do not have to experience losing a loved one to war, so do not completely understand what it entails both emotionally and mentally. There is a comfort in knowing that you can journey through the grieving and healing processes with people who have gone through similar situations. TAPS provides the loving support, and the caring understanding that is impossible to find elsewhere."

TAPS offers support and loving care in many ways for thousands of those grieving the death of a loved one, and for Rebecca, TAPS became a home where she could find others who understood.

-Bonnie Carroll

http://www.TAPS.org

Wounded Warrior Project

The Wounded Warrior Project is dedicated to assisting the wounded to adjust to a new life with their wounds. Many of the military are seriously wounded, some are paralyzed, some missing limbs, some permanently crippled, and some with disfiguring burns.

These troops will need to adjust to a new life in the civilian world with their injuries.

The Wounded Warrior Project works closely with Walter Reed and other major medical centers where these troops are being treated.

The website has a very emotional photo essay by Nina Berman. Additionally they have delivered twelve hundred "warrior packs" in the first of 2004 alone, consisting of personal CD players, calling cards, magazines and other health and comfort items. [67]

http://www.WounderWarriorProject.org

Individual Efforts

There must be hundreds of individuals creating their own drives whether totally by themselves or through other groups like Rotary, Lions Club and local churches. Everybody has probably been touched in some way by someone collecting for a drive for either the Iraqi people or the military supporting them. How many school children have written letters of encouragement or sent a care box for our troops? How many radio stations have run drives? How much free long distance service have phone companies provided? How many fire trucks have been purchased by fire fighters passing the boot on street corners? How many yellow ribbons have you seen? How many "Support our Troops" signs are in your neighborhood?

What follows is a small, a very small, sample of some of the efforts people here on the home front are making. I can make no attempt at completeness; I attempt only to point out just a few, knowing that for each one here there are so many more below the surface. Every one of these folks is thanked. If you haven't done so, please let them know how much you appreciate their support.

Mike Bradle

Mike Bradle from Lampasas, Texas is working to help bring scouting to Iraq. Mike, himself an Eagle Scout, is raising $4 million to build a scout camp on the banks of the Tigris River in northern Baghdad. At this camp, the children of Iraq will learn Scouting values of good citizenship, trustworthiness and responsibility, as well as camping skills.

The coalition in Iraq has donated 40 acres of what was once an intelligence compound for a proposed Scout camp. This compound is bomb damaged and will need repairs.

William "Chip" Beck, is promoting the program in Iraq, working with American troops and Iraqi scout leaders to organize a vibrant, new, scouting program.

The Boy Scouts of America has opened two funds to collect donations for Iraqi Scouting. [68]

Busy Bees

You command a National Guard unit and you get activated to deploy overseas. How do you communicate to your troops' families? How to you provide them with emotional support and a hand in time of need when the head of the household is gone for a complete year? How do you keep up the spirits of those left wondering? How can you help the families that are now run by one parent?

Some units are fortunate to have a family support network. Some are fortunate to have a very active and outgoing network. One such organization calls themselves the Busy Bees supporting B Battery, 1-109 Field Artillery from Nanticoke, Pennsylvania. Just one of their monthly newsletters indicates all of the projects in which they are involved. The Commander, Bob Ohls, tells me that Jennifer S. is the driving force for the Busy Bees. He sent the following e-mail:

[Jennifer S.]

I would like to start this month's newsletter by thanking everyone that came out to support our soldiers at the March meeting. We had over 110 people in attendance. If the soldiers could have seen the amount of support that I felt that night they would have been very proud.

Our next Busy B's meeting will be held Tuesday, April 6, 2004. The meeting will again take place on the Nanticoke Armory drill floor at 6:30 pm. The Red Cross will be in attendance to give us a briefing on some of the services they provide.

Nancy E. is working very hard on organizing a recipe book for the support group and requests that anyone with a favorite recipe please bring it to April's FRG meeting.

If anyone has a picture of their soldier that they would like to display at the armory, feel free to bring it in.

The care packages have all been packaged and are ready to ship. Thank you to everyone that helped separate, weigh, package, and ship these items. The Dallas School district also did an excellent job having the children package items for the soldiers.

The Busy B's are right now selling a few different items. The yellow bows and red, white, and blue bows are our main fundraiser right now and the other items such as the pins, and t-shirts are nice to be able to buy to not only support the Busy B's but to also show our support for our soldiers to the public by displaying these items. Anyone interested in ordering any pins or t-shirts can call Joy Adams at 570-xxx-xxxx or see her at the next meeting. Bows will also be available at the armory for purchase.

I received a request from the soldiers to collect some items to make their lives in Iraq a little more enjoyable. Some items they had requested are coffee, stirrers, creamer, microwaveable popcorn, horseshoes, darts, volleyballs, basketballs, etc. Rich B. is working on getting these items together for the soldiers. If anyone has any ideas or companies that they think might help out in this area, please get in touch w/Rich at the next meeting.

Our Annual Easter Egg Hunt will be held Saturday, March 27, 2004. The Hunt will be at the Nanticoke Armory at 2pm. Anyone that is interested in helping w/food or setting up for the hunt is asked to contact Carol B. Carol's number is 570-xxx-xxxx.

The Times Leader is going to be putting together a monthly publication for the local soldiers that are deployed overseas. If anyone has any ideas for them or anything they would like to include in the paper please let Jennifer S. know and she will get your information to the right people. Jennifer S. – 570-xxx-xxxx. Any info that you would like submitted in April's publication must be given to Jen S. by March 30.

The Wilkes-Barre YMCA will be holding a swim party for all families of the 109th. The party will be held Sunday April 18 from 1-3pm. This will be a great party I'm sure and I hope to see everyone there. Please RSVP to Jen S. by April 7 with the number of children and their ages.

-Jennifer S.

Sauna

Sauna started a project at Lutheran High School in Orange, California as a freshman. Now other students are involved sending letters to the troops. Their project is called Thanks a Million and their goal is to send a million letters of thanks. So far her web site indicates that they are way past the 900,000-letter mark. [69]

http://www.aMillionThanks.org

David Gifford

Dr. Gifford is a retired army colonel – retired from the army but not from anything else – who got a bright idea to fill a need. Dr. David Gifford's son, Lieutenant Colonel (then Major) Mark Gifford, on duty in Iraq told his father of the status of the hospital library in Tikrit. There was nothing in it except for a few photo-copied journals and some very old, out-of-date text books. The really sad news is that the hospital in Tikrit was the best equipped in all of Iraq. David's idea was to donate medical books to this library.

The task proved more difficult than he imagined as he at first was stone-walled by bureaucracy. Finally David called the publisher of Scientific American Medicine and within twenty minutes he received a call from Susan Yox, RN, EdD. She had earlier found a similar problem in Afghanistan and helped raise four thousand books to be donated there.

David says, "All I did was come up with idea, if it wasn't for others to get so actively involved it would not have been successful." Indeed others did. Besides Susan Yox, Dr. Alex Garza became actively involved. Dr. Garza, who did duty as an Army doctor in Tikrit in early 2004, was contacted to help by Mark Gifford. Dr. Garza was instrumental in making the project successful because of his relationship-building with the Medical College in Tikrit. With these core individuals, the idea became a reality as nearly 100,000 medical textbooks have now been delivered to hospitals and medical schools all over Baghdad. David says that these people really took the ball and made the idea a reality.

Dr. David Gifford had no idea how successful the drive would be. At first he just went to the local post office and paid for shipping. Before he knew it he had 17,000 pounds to ship. He received help at Dover Air Force Base who shipped these on space available on transport flights. Later, Elsevier, a medical publishing company, paid to ship two thousand books collected by the University of Tennessee Medical School. The project just kept growing.

David has received hundred of inquires and donations from Japan, Italy, New Zealand. The project has grown so large and now is shipping to four separate sites in Iraq, that David has lost the ability to keep track of all the donations. Many people just ask for the address and ship a box or two on their own.

The results of these efforts are going to pay huge long-term dividends in the healthcare in Iraq. The doctors there are dedicated and are committed to providing quality care. Their problem was being so far out of date and suffering from a lack of resources. These books will provide education that will go further than donations of band-aids and aspirin. Education today provides hope for the future. [70]

Ellen Harpin

Michael Sapp, a trainer for the New Iraqi Army, noticed a local family and also Ellen Harpin, who is doing her part to help the needy.

[Michael Sapp]

At the reconnaissance site was a local family. Actually, there were 3 families that were living together. They were obviously poor, living in an abandoned Army bunker complex left over from the 1980s/90s. Between the three families, they had 14 children, most of which were not wearing shoes even when it was around 40-45 degrees. They kept clear of the soldiers for the first several days, but after a while, the children became more courageous, as well as one of the fathers. We (1st BN and a few of the advisors) gave them some of the food we had when they came out. We also gave the children some knitted caps, which Dave Baer had received in the mail from an Ellen Harpin (her group, The Ships Project, ellens12@yahoo.com, is voluntarily making and sending knitted stockings and caps to soldiers in Iraq from their spot in Florida). It was really heartwarming and heartbreaking all at the same time. It was also good to put things in perspective, again. Sometimes it's too easy to think about Iraqi citizens based solely on the explosions and RPG attacks we read/hear about in the news every day.

-Michael Sapp

http://www.TheShipsProject.com

Fern Holland

To continue the work of Fern Holland to provide for human rights for all people everywhere, her family established the Fern L. Holland Charitable Foundation. Fern Holland, Bob Zangas and Salwa Ali Oushami were murdered March 9, 2004 in Iraq while working for freedom and democracy.

Fern began her crusade when she entered the Peace Corps. She helped build schools in Namibia and later she worked in Guinea for the American Refugee Committee where she worked to get rid of human rights abuses. She has been working in Iraq since July 2003 where she investigated human rights abuses by Saddam Hussein and helped write the new Iraqi constitution. She has also established several women's centers so the women in Iraq can learn to take a more active role in the future of Iraq. [71]

[Vi Holland]

I was asked to say a few words about my sister, it is hard to say a few words about Fern.

Fern had two passions in life: human rights and her nieces and nephews. She played a significant role in their lives, involved with: music, sports, academics, family vacations, and all things important to them – Her personal commitment to them both in life and death is proving fruitful; for they share with her, and because of her, respect and love for all people. They carry with them her hope.

Fern loved all children. It was through the eyes of children that Fern found the courage, determination, and the motivation to make change in the world. She had planned to study medicine and work as a child psychiatrist. After spending several months working with dying children in a Russian orphanage and with African children living in squatter camps (literally garbage dumps), she concluded that through law she could implement change that would protect the rights and provide hope to more children globally. Fern then made a decision to change the course of her life, and that decision did change the world.

"Baby steps," she called them, fundamental changes: Fern believed the only way to protect human rights, equality, and the freedoms of the individual is through democracy and the rule of law. She believed strong democracies are built through education of people. To Fern education was paramount. – Further, she knew to sustain a strong democracy, women must participate in their government.

You see, it is well understood that Women in government protect health care, women in government ensure the protection of human rights, equality, freedom, education, and most important to Fern, educated women in government protect children.

You ask? What can I do for Fern?

Women in Iraq and conflict situations all over the world continue to need the commitment and support that only we can provide -so they too, can help protect human rights. I encourage you to make contact with your director of the women's outreach program here on campus and I encourage you to become a good global partner so that we may create a safe world for our children's future.

Fern's influence around the world continues...

Before leaving for Iraq, Fern co-authored with Professor John Norton Moore, the concept of a Democracy Institute in Africa. She was seeking funding for this project in DC when offered the opportunity in Iraq. * The House Appropriation Committee recently voted to appropriate funds for the creation of a Fern L Holland Democracy Institute in Africa. This institute will serve to further educate and support individuals who share Fern's vision of equality, freedom, and the protection of human rights for all people.

The Fern Holland legal aid clinic for refugee women and children is now being implemented as a solution for the widespread problem of gender-based violence now occurring in Sudan, and other regions of Africa. (This project is up for a global award and too, was a project Fern was told would never work).

A book about Fern's life written for children has been commissioned.

The Bill of Rights Institute has requested permission to enter Fern's life into history texts books.

And the foundation, the creation of the foundation...

Fern had recently written in a very personal email to me "I would not want to live in a world without you...Now I, all of us, are forced to live in a world without our Fern. But we are committed to keeping her spirit alive and ensuring that her work continues thru her foundation. Fern was loved and adored by her family. We were, and continue to be, incredibly proud of her: she was a loving sister, aunt, and a remarkable human being who made a huge contribution to her family, country, and to the world. She planted her seeds deep and nourished them with love – they will continue to grow.

With the help of friends, we have created the Fern L Holland Charitable Foundation. Through Fern's foundation her projects will continue, and hope for today's children will always exist.

My sister would not want to be remembered because of her death and the brutal way she died. She would want to be remembered because of her life and the way she lived. Fern held two very core beliefs: that all people deserve basic human rights and that one person really can make a difference in the lives of others -- and, she did.

The last time I saw Fern was in January. I dropped her at the airport to catch her flight for Iraq. I recall, as I embraced her (for what would be the last time) that I whispered in her ear, "It is people like you, Fern, that make me proud to be an American".

On behalf of my family, I would like to thank those recognizing and honoring the work and life of our beloved sister, aunt, and my closest friend - Fern Holland.

-Vi Holland

www.FernHolland.com

Barbara Ivey

Barb Ivey, of Stonebriar Community Church in Frisco, Texas, went to women's retreat in March 2003. There was a prayer request to help families left behind at Fort Hood. At that retreat was a chaplain's wife, Michelle Duerksen, who said she needed things for deployed families.

Barb led a drive to at her church and raised $12,000 to buy books, tapes, t-shirts for families at Fort Hood, two hundred miles away.

The Cadence Ministries at Fort Hood was building a house at post for families to go and provide support for each other while their soldiers were deployed. Mrs. Ivey supplied the library: books, coloring books, prayer books, and devotional books. [72]

http://www.stonebriar.org

Frankie Mayo

Frankie Mayo, Delaware housewife, has created a program to send air conditioners to Iraq for American troops. Her son wrote and asked for help with the heat and she sent him an air conditioner. So others started requesting air conditioners. She started fund raising and has so far shipped 500 air conditioners. Home Depot has helped by providing her with a great bargain. To buy and ship the 500 units will cost about $130,000. After the air conditioners, her plan is to ship ceramic heaters. She also ships medical supplies to two hospitals. [73]

http://www.OperationAC.com.

David McCorkle

Specialist David McCorkle, a reserve soldier, was activated for duty with the 101st Airborne Division in northern Iraq. Here he noticed some of the children were not able to attend school because of family financial needs. Instead these children were on the streets selling candy and sodas to help their mothers make ends meet. David used his own money to file for a non-profit organization and begin collecting money to help these children in and around his area where he was assigned. His charity is called American Aid for Children of Ninevah, Iraq. This charity is specifically for helping orphans or fatherless children who would not have opportunity to go to school.

Does every soldier set up charities? It does take a special person. David was making a six-figure income when he watched the events on September 11th. He decided right then to make a difference. He lost 125 pounds and enlisted in the reserves at age 44. David is making a difference. [74]

http://www.IraqKids.org

John Ritchey

John Ritchey is a 68-year-old ophthalmologist with a successful practice in Fayetteville, N.C. In April he closed his office, turned his patients over and began readying for his deployment. Dr. Ritchey volunteered to serve his country and go back on active duty as an eye surgeon. Twenty-seven years earlier, Dr. Ritchey retired from the Army. In his original military career, Dr. Ritchey served in Vietnam where he was a flight surgeon with the 101st Airborne Division.

Since retiring from the Army Dr. Ritchey has traveled to Mongolia, Bulgaria, Nepal, Africa, El Salvador, Guiana and Peru to provide medical eye care in conjunction with Surgical Eye Expeditions (SEE). [75]

Tim

Tim, a retired military officer, is married to an active-duty army captain deployed in Iraq.

While his wife, Patti, was away, Tim spent many hours every day sourcing for news – good news. He did this for 427 days until she returned to their home in Germany. He then transposed those good stories on his blog – Captain Patti.

[Tim]

I would estimate I'd have to read the headlines of 80 to 120 stories in the search engine to find one that had a positive tone. More often than not, the positive stories came from local news outlets, rather than the major wire services, interviewing a soldier home on R&R.

The blog started out as news for the family. I didn't advertise it around...but so desperate were family members to find news of our soldiers, many folks stumbled into the blog via search engines. Over the course of the year, several hundred readers became daily readers. Not huge numbers for the internet... but tellingly...most of those readers I heard from were as deeply invested in the war (had a loved one there) as I was. And CPT Patti's blog became a mild antidote for the large doses of hatchet-job reporting.

I was able to capture the good-news type stuff...and frequently would provide it to Patti, who would share these stories with her soldiers during formations. It gave them a sense of purpose and a sense of being a part of history. Many soldiers, I'm told, had begun avoiding the news on TV due to the incessantly negative coverage.

Anyway, these stories and historical perspective (big picture stuff) were a boost for the morale of soldiers who were exposed to the possibility of danger every day. One couldn't blame the soldiers for feeling "what on earth am I doing here?" if the only feedback they received was from a cable news station - all negative, all the time.

Ultimately - an investment of a few hours of my time each day made a difference to an amazingly scattered network of moms, grandfathers, fathers, husbands, wives, girlfriends...from those based in Germany to Florida, Texas, Michigan - all over...not to mention helping my wife keep her troops' spirits up. For that reason the internet and blogging are amazing tools.

Anyway...as you know, the good news needs to be told - else, left to the media, this war becomes nothing but body counts and insurgents. And my darling wife and all of America's bravest can tell you it is far, far more than that.

-Tim

Fred Wellman

While in Iraq, Major Fred Wellman started his program his friends dubbed Operation Fred, which was just a way to start a collection for school supplies and over-the-counter medicines with volunteers helping raise the donations in his hometown. Through family, friends, Sunday school groups and civic groups he was able to collect, ship and distribute two tons worth of medical and school supplies as well as toys, clothes and household items.

His little project is now a fully functional charity called Warrior Relief Inc. This charity connects service members conducting charitable acts with organizations willing to help out. He says the charity all started when he couldn't get medical supplies for the people of Jeddalah near his base south of Mosul.

His unit was involved in trying to build a community of friendly villages around their base camp. "I'm just lucky to know some crazy people in Georgia who could help."

At first his brother Joe and his friends adopted Fred's battalion and shipped about 45 boxes of supplies for the soldiers. Then Carol Fritz, a former City Council member in Peachtree City, helped lead the local effort to collect and ship overseas.

- The children of the Peachtree City United Methodist Church collected 11 boxes of school supplies and then six boxes of athletic shoes.
- St. Matthew's church collected and shipped another eleven boxes.
- A YMCA swim team in Texas sent 100 backpacks filled with school supplies.
- A retired pharmacist in Alabama sent boxes of medicines that helped an Iraqi doctor open a clinic.

Eventually, thanks to publicity on CNN, the project brought in supplies from around the United States and even Canada. [76]

Chief Wiggles

Chief Wiggles is a National Guardsman from Utah who alternates between collecting toys for Iraqi children and serving time overseas as a soldier. Chief Wiggles speaks to civic organizations, organizes other charities to help, solicits corporate sponsors and even packs toys himself. The last time I checked his website, he had shipped over ten pallets of donated toys. Federal Express has provided free shipping for 1700 pounds.

Chief's philosophy is to have the soldiers, sailors, airmen and marines distribute directly to the children. This solidifies the bond between those there every day and the Iraqi children of whom they come in contact.

It's a battle out there - a battle for the understanding of clear minds. The hate-filled terrorists only seek to oppress and teach prejudice and violence. The path to success is to demonstrate kindness and offer hope for a safer tomorrow.

Operation Give, c/o Bridgepoint Systems, 542 Confluence Avenue, Salt Lake City, Utah 84123. [77]

Trey Yates

Specialist Trey Yates was serving with the 2nd Armored Cavalry Regiment in Sadr City when he noticed the situation of the schools. One particular school had been devastated by looters and the children were without school supplies. He wrote a letter to his mother who collected donations. Soon she was able to send her son five hundred pounds of school supplies. Trey is a soldier who just felt a need and did what he needed to do to help the children who otherwise would have little chance growing up in the crowded inner city. This is just one example of many more of people doing what they feel is right in their hearts without ever expecting any personal reward – a true random act of kindness. [78]

Chapter Eight
The Results

After World War II, the U.S. stayed five years in Japan and seven years in Germany making sure these countries got back on their feet. Every indication so far is that the timeline in Iraq is more advanced. (See Figure 1.) This is something for which we can feel pride. We are also fortunate that the Iraqi people are eager to get up and running and become fully independent.

All over the country, little projects are being enacted that are making a difference. Money as aid and as loans is flowing into Iraq. Investors are coming to Iraq to capitalize on the economy that will grow. Iraq is shedding some of its privatized industries. Military units once geared for combat are changing missions to build and re-build. It's hundreds of things all going on at once.

Milestones (Figure 1.)

	Iraq	Germany
Local Governments Installed	2 months	8 months
Independent Central Bank	2 months	36 months
Police Established	2 months	14 months
New Currency	3 months	36 months
Cabinet Seated	4 months	14 months
New Constitution	10 months	48 months
National Elections	20 months	48 months

If you look, you will find reports of major construction projects for new housing, re-building of the power plants, cleaning out clogged sewers, rebuilding water treatment facilities and expansion of phone and internet system. You will see schools built, libraries re-stocked, doctors being trained, and playgrounds re-stored. You will see new local governments, a new constitution, and new elections on the horizon. You will see oil flowing again, pipelines repaired, refineries moving back to capacity. You will see a new police force, a new military defensive in nature, and a new Coast Guard.

It's not just a wish list; it's real action. It's a real desire to get Iraq back to what it once was. Iraq was once the most advanced, liberated, growing, educated and free of all the Arab nations. Even though it's been years, people remember what it was like. They have something to grow from.

Below are just a few stories of all that is going on, grouped by healthcare, education, economy and government.

[Fred Wellman]

There is no kind of job satisfaction like that when a child hands you a bundle of flowers and thanks you freeing his country. Nothing I have done in my life outside of the Army can compare to having that kind of impact on someone's life. Not politics and not business. So, I guess it is worth the sacrifice and pain.

-Fred Wellman

Healthcare

It's sinful to think how a country could move so rapidly backward. A once-thriving medical community - with teaching hospitals, universities, plenty of doctors, nurses, technicians, and the latest in medical equipment - just collapsed. What progress can be made when a dictator stops the importation of information and bans books? Thousands of doctors left the country when they saw that it was only getting worse. Since then many of those who stayed have been kidnapped or killed. It is senseless.

The hospitals were left to rot and many had no way to expel sewage or some could not get clean water. Medicine was in short supply. Salaries dwindled so low that doctors were only getting $20 per month. Learning stopped. Like in a time warp, research closed down over ten years ago. The Ministry of

Health's 2004 budget is nearly $1 billion, which is nearly 6,000 percent more than what Saddam spent on health care. All 240 hospitals and more than 1,200 primary health clinics are now treating patients again. [79]

One indication of the state of health is the life expectancy for a country. The average life expectancy for Kuwait is 77, Saudi Arabia is 72, Jordan is 70, Syria is 70 and Iran is 65. [80] Another indication of a nation's health care status is the infant mortality rate. Over the last ten years in Iraq, this rate has doubled and is now among the lowest thirty countries in the world. [81]

Since March 2003, there has been a deluge of volunteers descending on Iraq to help. Dozens and dozens of stories have been written and not widely disseminated. Even more stories have never been told. The USAID reports the facts. A search of the multitude of government information web sites will reveal story after story. Most military units have a public affairs office and each one of these has written many stories about the volunteer efforts to save the healthcare in Iraq.

- A 3-year-old Iraqi girl with 3rd-degree burns on her hands, chin, cheeks, nose, forehead and left leg was helped by Samaritan Purse, a nonprofit organization based in North Carolina, who flew her to the Shriners Hospital in Galveston, Texas for treatment.[82]

- Iraqi and American doctors working side-by-side removed a large tumor from a boy's hip. The two American doctors were from the Second Armored Cavalry Regiment. While there, one also performed an appendectomy. [83]

- A ten-year-old Iraqi girl was born with a hole in her heart. After being treated for pneumonia in a Navy hospital, she will be flown to the U.S. for surgery. [84]

- 12th Cavalry Regiment (Task Force Lancer) delivered two large truckloads of medical equipment totaling $170,000 to the Habi Bija Obstetrics-Gynecology (OBGYN) and Pediatrics Hospital July 15. The new equipment will replace worn and outdated equipment in this busy hospital, which helps deliver an average of 40 babies every day. [85]

- A ten-year-old boy with glass shards in his eye is being flown to Japan for treatment. The Rotary Club is sponsoring the boy's treatment. [86]

- A Field Artillery Battery from the 101st Infantry Division rebuilt a clinic that had no bathrooms or electricity. This clinic is responsible for 60,000 people. [87]

- A young soldier from the 12th Cavalry Regiment of the 1st Cavalry Division noticed a twelve-year-old boy with a bullet wound to his head from celebratory gunfire. He encouraged the battalion surgeon to treat the boy and the surgeon then ensured the boy received the necessary therapy to work on his partial paralysis. [88]

- The Fourth Battalion, Fifth Air Defense Artillery Regiment has started an outreach program to travel around and follow up with Iraqi citizens who were not getting health care. They call this Community Health Outreach Program (CHOP). This is a traveling clinic complete with five exam stations with a doctor or physician's assistant for each station, and a dentist. [89]

- Iraq's new ministry of Health is offering free reconstructive surgery to anyone who had his ear cut off by order of Saddam Hussein. There is an estimated 3,500 that had this done to them. [90]

- The 411th Civil Affairs Battalion led an eight-day physicians' leadership workshop to teach health care management. [91]

- The Second Armored Cavalry Regiment taught a course in Advance Life Support in Obstetrics (ALSO) to teach how to handle abnormal birthing situations. The Regimental surgeon has also been involved in the creation of the Iraqi Family Physicians Society to promote primary care in Iraq, and the Physicians Leadership course (PLC) to teach hospital administrative skills to physicians. The American Academy of Family Physicians donated materials. The goal is to reduce infant mortality by 50%. [92]

- The 422nd Civil Affairs Battalion has re-opened the Spinal Injury Center in Baghdad. It had been used as a warehouse for military items. [93]

- The 1st Cavalry Division and Iraqi doctors trained local practitioners in neonatal resuscitation July 21, 2004 at the Baghdad Convention Center as the third in a three-part series to lower infant mortality rates. [94]

- The Overseas Disaster Humanitarian and Civil Assistance donated new equipment to the Elwiyah Maternity Teaching Hospital. The donation includes five ultrasound machines, five defibrillators, and an electrocardiograph machine. [95]

- 70 percent of Iraq's 4.3 million children under the age of five have been vaccinated against diseases including polio, tetanus, diphtheria, measles, and tuberculosis. [96]

- 8,000 Iraqi workers are being trained to screen and manage malnourished children. One-third of the children in southern Iraq suffer from malnutrition. [97]

- More than 25,000 tons of pharmaceuticals and supplies have been delivered. [98]

- The Polish Humanitarian Assistance Coordination Center working with the Polish Army and the Philippine Military have been distributing medicine to local communities in their areas of Iraq. [99]

- The British Military is training 24 Iraqi nurses in general nursing and critical care. Local Iraqi doctors and nurses will lead the instruction along with a liaison with the British Military. [100]

[Matt Gapinski]

In early January, the Humanitarian Operations Center (HOC) in conjunction with the Kuwaiti Ministry of Health sponsored a four-day Cardiology Conference. Yours truly was assigned the duty of flying to Baghdad, gathering up 40 Iraqi doctors, flying them to Kuwait, escorting them during the conference, and flying them back to Baghdad. Other than the use of military aircraft for transport, the entire conference (meals, hotel, etc.) was paid for by the Kuwaitis and private sponsors. They were quite an interesting bunch. Some had never flown before, let alone been outside of Iraq. Once we got airborne, it was like a circus with all of them looking out the only uncovered windows on the paratroop doors and taking pictures with the crew.

The conference was entirely in English, which apparently is the preferred language of medicine. The doctors warned us to be careful of any doctors that only spoke Arabic/didn't undergo their medical training in English. The content of the conference wasn't too technical (we sat in on most of the sessions). After a session on mitral heart valve replacement surgery (which my Mom had done several years ago), I asked one of the doctors if they only did replacements with mechanical valves or if it was acceptable (as Muslims) to use pig valves. It turns out the pig valve is OK because they're not eating it!

The doctors couldn't get enough time shopping (we brought them to the local mall) even though they did complain that the prices were expensive. After we taught them the expression "shop 'till you drop!" they came up with their own - "buy until you are dry!" We were worried that they would have too many shopping bags going back on the aircraft, but most of them bought extra suitcases and we were well within our weight limit.

We had to build in plenty of extra cushion whenever we had to meet a time schedule. Not sure if that was an Arabic cultural-thing, a doctor-thing or a little of both! We amazingly got them all to the airport on time, but of course our flight back to Baghdad was delayed for several hours due to bad weather. When we finally landed in Baghdad, there was all kinds of chanting and praying. No matter where you live, it is always good to get home!

-Matt Gapinski

In a small village near Mosul is a man, Dr. Mohammed, who had given up his medial practice to take over running his tribe as the sheik ten years ago when his father died. He has completely internalized his responsibility to take care of his village. It is a calling – a duty he has fully embraced.

Major Fred Wellman of the 101st Air Assault Division met Dr. Mohammad and could not say enough about his admiration for the Sheik. He said that soon after moving to an abandoned air base, an old man from a nearby village approached his unit with a note in English asking for help with the water supply.

When Fred met the man, Dr. Mohammed, all he asked for was help for his water supply, even though the villages were in serious need of more things to bring them out of a third-world condition.

During that hot summer of 2003, Fred spent weeks getting to know Dr. Mohammed. They would drive from village to village, assessing the needs of the people. Dr. Mohammed was always trying to help everyone. He shared his food with Fred. Dr. Mohammed served as a liaison and introduced Fred to thirty-five other villages.

Dr. Mohammed was selected to the Tigris River Council, which interacts with U.S. CENTCOM for cooperation and development. Dr. Mohammed is the point of contact and go to man for forty villages encompassing seven different tribes. Working with this council and his role as Sheik combine for more than a full-time job and pays nothing.

Working with his chain of command, Fred was able to surprise Dr. Mohammed with a new, three-room clinic for his village. Families back in the U.S. donated 4,000 pounds of medicine and medical equipment.

After his day work is done, Dr. Mohammed, so excited about his new clinic, now is back practicing medicine. At 4:00 P.M. each day, he starts taking care of patients until about 11:00 or twelve. It's an amazing feat that he manages every single day.

He sees patients that have never seen a doctor before – children who have never had a check-up. Sometimes a patient comes in with a minor aliment and he'll bring his whole family.

Dr. Mohammed treats all his patients, which can average sixty a day, for free. Right now his supplies and medicines have been donated by people back in the U.S. or have been purchased with U.S. dollars in the Iraqi market. Dr. Mohammed explained that he stopped his doctor practice because he felt it wasn't right, as Sheik, to charge for his services.

One evening a woman came into the clinic suffering respiratory arrest from a severe asthma attack. Dr. Mohammed opened the boxes of medicine he received through Operation Fred, gave her an injection and saved her life.

Dr. Mohammed is one of those rare individuals whose attitude can change a life and change the thinking of a new hopeful generation. Fred is convinced that Iraq will rebuild and thrive under the leadership of people like Dr. Mohammed. [101]

Colonel Bob Adams, MD, a family practice physician from Fort Bragg, North Carolina, assigned to the 82nd Airborne Division in Iraq, was reassigned to the Coalition Headquarters in Baghdad, to help organize a medical forum for Iraqi doctors. This was for physicians across all specialties, and included young doctors and residents. The result was the first Iraqi Medical Specialty Forum (IMSF) from February 14th to 17th 2004. It was funded in large part by a grant from the U.S. Agency for International Development, and by the Coalition forces.

Dr. Adams recognized that significant advancements in medicine have taken place over the last twenty-five years, and most of this has completely passed by the medical community in Iraq which has suffered from an information embargo imposed by the Hussein regime, and prevented doctors from leaving the country or receiving medical texts and journals.

Prior to the Ba'ath party, the quality of medical care in Iraq was the highest in the Middle East. After the Ba'ath party, the healthcare system was devastated, with 35 years of corruption and politicization. Professional organizations became pawns of the regime. Organizations were told whom they could elect as leaders. The Iraqi Society of Physicians IMSF conference in February 2004 was held to enable independent non-governmental professional medical societies, provide scientific updates, and jump-start a return of Iraq to the modern medical age. The IMSF Conference was a huge success with international press coverage, scientific updates, organizational medical specialty meetings and rave reviews by Iraqi medical leaders and individual physicians.

Part of the conference was for Iraqi doctors to present their own research. Dr. Adams was flabbergasted by the complete stoppage of research. All submitted papers were on research conducted ten or more years earlier. One doctor submitted a paper on the effects of calcium and pregnancy. In the past ten years, medical science has moved past this issue, though this Iraqi doctor had no idea. Dr. Adams, and his Iraqi Board of Physician Directors, allowed these types of presentations, because the workshop was to encourage research and share knowledge in a professional forum in medicine - something that had been suppressed. Doctors had not had a chance to share information or research before, and had never imagined that they might be able to form an independent professional organization separate from the government. The few freedoms enjoyed by the people of Iraq opened the door for physicians to join the international community as equals.

The Forum was almost a disaster as terrorists had plans to blow up the convention center where it was held. This would have been a catastrophic blow to healthcare in Iraq as the country's top physicians were all in one place. Just three days before the forum began, Dr Adams was tipped off about a bomb. He quickly made arrangements to move the forum to a safer location. In day two of the forum, dog teams found the bomb in the original site, where it was disarmed.

In the end, the forum was a huge success and a watershed event in the future of medicine in Iraq. It will serve as a catalyst for professional development and future professional exchanges.

Dr. Adams shares this email which was sent to him by Dr. Mohammed Nemat from Baghdad.

"Dear Dr. Adams,

Hello. Thanks for the picture. Dear Bob, you are the first American doctor to E-mail with, I am very happy with that, because I like to communicate with people from other nations and cultures especially with medical staff members. It is quite an opportunity for me to have a medical, cultural, ethical and social issues to be discussed with you. And on this occasion I would like to thank the people of United States for their big help in the liberation of my people from Saddam's criminal regime. Dear Bob, your nation gave my people a new birthday, you gave us the most valuable thing, you gave us freedom. Dear Bob, I owe my new life to you and to your people, thanks for every thing."

Education

Like so many things, education in Iraq was one of the best in the Middle East up through the 1970's. By 1980, Iraq schools had achieved almost 100% enrollment of primary-age children.

Before the rebuilding began, teachers were unpaid, textbooks when available were outdated, most curriculum was party indoctrination, students had no school supplies, enrollment was down, attendance was way down especially for girls and rural areas, and illiteracy was up. Education was not a priority for a dictator who wanted his people uneducated and brainwashed. Contact with the outside world was blocked. Even the infrastructure was crumbling. Many buildings were in need of structural repair and most everything was looted: desks, chairs, chalkboards, plumbing and electrical wiring.

Literacy in Iraq dropped to 60%. In Jordan it is 87%, Turkey 85%, Kuwait 78%, Saudi Arabia 78%, Iran 72% and Syria 71%.

Since May 2003, things are improving. Here is just a sample of some of the progress.

- Iraq has established a Supreme National De-Ba'athification Commission to stop the teaching of corrupt policies.

- 5,800 of the 15,000 teachers fired for political reasons under Saddam Hussein have been re-hired. [105]

- 33,000 secondary school teachers have been trained in modern teaching methods. [106]

- More than 5.5 million children are back in the classroom. Girls now outnumber boys and overall attendance during exam week was 97 percent. [107]

- The U.S. Agency for International Development (USAID) has granted $12.6 million to the United Nations Children's Fund (UNICEF) to continue to provide support to the Ministry of Education. The money will be used for training of 250,000 primary school teachers and ensure that schools have potable water and bathrooms. [108]
- The World Bank has granted $40 million to Iraq to print and distribute 72 million new textbooks. [109]

By trade, Major Fred Wellman is a helicopter pilot with the 101st Infantry Division. During Operation Iraqi Freedom, he served as Operations Officer and later Executive Officer for his battalion. After the hostilities of 2003, Fred's unit moved to an old Air Force Base in northern Iraq near Mosul.

Fred fell in love with the local people and never stopped trying to help. "They're amazing people. I never expected to be so impressed by a people. Good, hard-working country folk trying to eke out a life. Tears shed when I said goodbye," he told about the local community be became so close to.

Major Wellman, a veteran of Desert Storm, had gotten out of the active Army and was running for Mayor of Peachtree City, Georgia in 2001. After September 11th, his reserve unit was activated and Fred dropped out of the mayoral race. Fred's wife, Crystal, has been very supportive at home, raising their four kids and keeping active, volunteering for many activities.

When his battalion arrived at the abandoned air base, there was no security fence. Fred asked his commander if he could create an environment where the local villages would appreciate them and become loyal. They embarked on many community programs and Fred says, "I never felt threatened."

Things started when a local sheik handed a note to the checkpoint asking for help with the water supply. The village used to get its water from the air base and now the pipe was broken. The battalion brought in water bottles and a truckload of water until they could fix the pipe.

Then the battalion started building. His unit organized and helped pay for the locals to build 23 small schools, repair thirty-eight kilometers of roads, build and stock a medical clinic and improved the water and sewage capabilities. Fred says the leadership and passion of MG David Petraeus, 101st Division Commander, made the difference. The proof that the concept was working came when many local village Sheiks came to check on the unit the next morning after a rocket strike.

The summer was very busy and temperatures climbed to 120 degrees. The optimistic Fred described the climate as "comfortable and the best in Iraq."

In just six weeks the battalion was making great success. Most of the villages had never had a school. "If a child wanted to go to school from these farming villages, he would have to go live with relatives in the city to get that opportunity."

In another case the leaders of a small village of 800 asked for pipes for running water. They have not had running water in the village for many years. They only asked for some money to borrow for digging equipment and they did all the work themselves. Now every house has running water.

"I think - I firmly believe that what we're doing is building - it's about building relationships. Our commander has said early on that what we need to do is build a bond with the people we're living with, and that's what we're doing. We're not approaching as an occupying army, we're approaching it as good neighbors, and the people around our base are our neighbors."

The formula certainly paid off for Fred. Everywhere he went he was respected.

"The children in one village especially are trying to learn English and they have gone to great lengths to learn English. And as we were leaving about two weeks ago, a little boy, probably about 8, ran up to my vehicle when I was getting strapped in, and he said, 'Major Wellman, Major Wellman, I love you'. And, you know I'm a big softy. I've got four kids at home. And I just got out of that truck and gave that little boy a hug, because he -- it meant a lot. It meant a lot." [110]

Ben Wallen, an engineer officer, spent three months in Iraq and to him all his memories will be centered around three days. Three days making life better for some children.

Working side by side, Army engineers and local civilians completely cleaned up a hazardous dump and restored it to what it was originally intended – a park for children. Ben was most amazed by the energy and enthusiasm of the Iraqis as they became excited what could be possible with cooperation.

His unit spent three days (June 30th to July 2nd 2003) refurbishing a playground, soccer field, a school and hospital.

Before they began, the playground had trash everywhere, unserviceable, rusty and broken playground equipment, no swings, and power lines were being held up by the playground equipment.

The school's basketball court was missing backboards and painted lines on the court. The front of school was covered in graffiti.

Next to the playground was an open pit and a small lake filled with open sewage.

Working together they hauled off all the trash and fixed the playground equipment. They secured the power lines to a safer support.

At the school, they fixed backboards, painted the basketball court, painted over the graffiti, and placed a support beam to support a stress fracture in the school. The soldiers donated school supplies and a soccer ball.

For the hospital, they installed air conditioners, hooked up a new water tank, repaired the plumbing and installed a new generator.

Most importantly they build a culvert to redirect the flow of sewage and put fences around the pit and small lake. [111]

In June of this year, I was at a conference and heard Brigadier General Dan Kaufman, the Dean at the United States Military Academy; tell about his experience of going to Baghdad University and helping the faculty with education programs. He brought with him a dozen or more faculty from West Point and they worked with professors on modern teaching methods. This was the first occasion for U.S. troops to be working in the office-styled green uniform instead of the usual desert-camouflaged combat uniform.

[Scott Travis]

Most recently, we were paid a visit by two separate groups of visiting West Point professors. My task force commander is an old grad and arranged to host some department heads and professors, as well as the Dean. The professors gave lectures to Iraqi students at Baghdad University during the day, and in the afternoons were given tours of our sector and the green zone (where we live). They even went along for the ride during evening patrols.

-Scott Travis

I think the winning idea for "The Blinding Flash of the Obvious" goes to the 101st Infantry Division. In the course of combat operations and searching for weapon caches, the 101st came across large amounts of Ba'athist cash. They immediately turned right around and spent the money in the local economy for humanitarian efforts. Other units are now continuing the program. During 2003, all units combined seized and spent $178 million.

"1st CAV forces are currently employing 1,000 people alone in Sadr City, and this is only one of the many projects throughout the city," Brigadier General Kimmit told the press during a briefing on 30 April 2004.

Captain Rick Hinshaw served with the 101st in Mosul during the first year of the war. He's a Black Hawk pilot by trade, who personally spent $2.7 million in support of higher education. After serving with his unit in Iraq, Rick is now living at Camp Arifjan, Kuwait. "I honestly believe that we are losing the information campaign here. As soldiers fighting this war, we have an obligation to get the word out about what's really going on over here." [112]

[Rick Hinshaw]

Here's how it worked. About one week after we (the 101st) arrived in Mosul (approx. May 8th), every major subordinate command in the 101st (including mine, of course) received an order to report to Finance Headquarters, draw $10,000 U.S. cash (seized assets recovered from the old regime) and go out and spend it. There were rules and guidelines - no single purchase over the amount of $2,000. Any expenditure must benefit the Iraqi people only, and may not result in any kind of benefit to Coalition Forces whatsoever. No spending on entertainment for the Iraqis. Other than that, it was pretty much go out there and spend.

I was selected to be the project manager because of my experience handling budgets. I first went to a Civil Affairs guy who lived in the tent next to mine, and asked him if he had any good tips. He told me that the University had been severely looted, and that they could use some help with ADP products (monitors, disk drives, etc.). We went to the University, worked out the arrangements, made some connections, and delivered the products the next day. The purchase was simple - we went to a computer store across the street from the university, worked out a deal, and had them deliver the goods at the agreed time and place, at which time we paid them. We repeated this often.

After our first purchase for the university, we still had $8,000, so we stopped at a primary school and asked them how we could be of assistance. They were very happy to see us, and we communicated through our interpreter. We worked out a deal to get them school supplies, new school desks, chalkboards, etc. When our $10,000 ran out, we drew more and repeated the process. Every other major subordinate command in the 101st did the same thing we did. This continued for about 3 weeks. Once it became obvious that this operation was working, Division Headquarters decided to step things up. We were now authorized to draw $250,000 at a time (usually about one draw every two weeks), and spend up to $10,000 on a single purchase (more if we obtained the CG's approval).

MG Petraeus (the CG) then decided to split up responsibilities, to avoid duplicating our efforts. My brigade (the 159th AVN BDE) was told to focus on the University, since we had already built up a habitual relationship with them. Our umbrella of responsibility soon began to include all Higher Education through out Mosul (the University, 3 technical schools, and 1 private school). My brand-new Brigade Commander, COL William Harrison, arrived at about this time (mid-June). At COL Harrison's in brief, the CG told him that Higher Education in Mosul was our #1 priority, not flying helicopters (we had 102 Black Hawks and 34 Chinooks). COL Harrison ordered me to put together about 30 teams of officers (MAJ's, CPT's, and LT's) to increase the work effort. Each team had a specific responsibility, i.e., one team was in charge of the Medical College, another was in charge of the Library, another took on the College of Science, etc.) Each team would go out twice a week, arrange projects with their Iraqi counterpart (usually a Dean or a professor), and I would make the payments as required. We held weekly meetings where teams would submit their project requests, and I would prioritize them and ask the colonel to approve them based on the amount of money I had left to spend. When I drew more money, I'd approve more projects, and we continued on like this until we left in January of '04.

Other units within the 101st did the same thing, but within their own areas of responsibility. The Artillery BDE was in charge of rebuilding security, the Support Brigade was in charge of Lower Education (schools for kids), the 1st Infantry Brigade was in charge of rebuilding buildings and industries within the City of Mosul, etc. This is how we implemented what came to be known as the Commander's Emergency Response Program (CERP).

Of course, with each trip to the University (or occasional primary school), we were required to travel in groups of at least 9 soldiers (fully armed and fully equipped), traveling in at least 3 humvees (the trail humvees had to include a crew-served weapon, and we maintained constant 2-way radio contact with headquarters). We left our base at the airfield almost every day, and we were only attacked once. A disgruntled student threw a grenade under one of our trucks while we were leaving a parking lot at the College of Math. The blast resulted in 2 minor injuries to soldiers and minor damage to the humvee. The perpetrator escaped. We believe he was a foreign student on a Ba'ath Party scholarship that was (obviously) about to expire.

We actually used some money to compensate victims of fatalities. The Dean of Political Science, Dr. Abdul-Jabar Mustaffa, was abducted and murdered by insurgents hours after I spent $10,000 at his college. We gave his surviving widow, two twin daughters, and son a "sympathy" payment, which was authorized. His other son, an amputee, died of cancer about 2 months before the Dean's murder.

When it was all over, I had spent over $2.7 million, mostly on the University. I believe the 101st as a whole spent around $25 million (but I might be way off with that). I'm told that other Divisions throughout Iraq followed our model, since we had so much success with it. As far as I know, CERP is still ongoing.

-Rick Hinshaw

SFC Tommy Carson has sent me a dozen emails on all the things his unit, the 29th Signal Battalion is doing. Here is someone who truly believes.

[Tommy Carson]

Since the day the 29th Signal Battalion has been here, we have been involved with three different Iraqi Schools. And now we are about to open a new school of our own, built entirely with CERP funds. The school will open September 7th, and we are all looking forward to the grand opening to give these children the very best school year they have ever had!

The school is called AL SALAM and located right next to Military Village a half mile out the East Gate in BAKAR village. The school cost $77,790 dollars to build and was awarded to this community as a way of saying THANKS for the information citizens gave the U.S. about recent attacks. The school will have: 6 Class Rooms, 2 Offices, Yard, Garden, Play ground, Fence, Lights, Ceiling fans, Latrines, Septic tank, water fountains, and a Bell. This will be by far the newest school in this area and one of the very BEST!

This will also save the children a long walk through dangerous neighborhoods thus making it easier, safer and ensure they have the best school year ever!!!

From earlier school visits, I've included some photos of me passing out Tootsie Rolls.

At first they had no idea what I was passing out, so I had to open one up and put it in my mouth, then they all were anxious to get one.

The Family Readiness Group (FRG) back home at Fort Lewis, has started a project called OPERATION: Spouses Help Iraqi Children. So there is hundreds of Tootsie Roll Pops on their way, along with backpacks, shoes, clothes, school supplies, and everything else they may want, need and desire.

One child pointed to his feet with sores and blisters that have been there a long time and asked for shoes. This child had never owned a pair of shoes before. We did not have shoes at that time; we were passing out Back Packs with school supplies.

This operation the FRG's are doing have been featured on all the local TV stations and local newspapers, and businesses, families and communities are all pledging their support for this project.

The perfect backpacks are being assembled thanks to the great Northwest! Once again, everybody is chipping in and supporting the 29th on this deployment and was all so excited that we have an opportunity to make a lasting impression. As Chaplain Levine puts it, "we will be leaving a footprint in the sand for life."

It is truly exciting to know many years after we are gone, the very projects we are doing will still be in place, kids getting educated, all because the 29th Signal BN wanted to reach out and make a difference with the future of this great country, the children!

Yes, it is dangerous going outside these gates. You can kidnap or kill this old flesh, but you can NOT kidnap or kill the American Spirit! That is here to stay and will see to it a better quality of life for all Iraqis!

Even the things the great Northwest is sending represents that American Spirit, they are sending backpacks, shoes, clothes, school supplies, toys, games, sports equipment, and even the Seattle Seahawks are getting involved.

These very things represent HOPE, hope for a better tomorrow today! That is the American Spirit first hand, soldiers risking their lives to deliver the very things Americans are sending over here.

Many of the soldiers of the Battalion are excited about working with the children. SSG Roth of Bravo Company said, "I love helping the G5 pack bags and assemble things for the children, it gives me a greater sense of purpose for being over here."

CPT Rick Young, Commander of Bravo Company has background in Civil Affairs, and does a great job of keeping his soldiers informed of the variety of things we are doing to make life better for Iraqis. It is this very thing that give soldiers a greater sense of purpose for being over here, thus his company had the first three Reenlistments of this quarter. (I am also the Career Counselor for 29th Signal Battalion.)

I'm also very active with Operation Anaconda Neighborhood, which is something the G5 and 13th COSCOM have come up with to improve the local community. It shows our locals just how much we really care about them and we want to help make things better.

We go out on a regular basis to visit schools, give free medical care, improve facilities, and show them the American Spirit that we really do care and will do anything to help anybody. In return, hopefully there will be less and less attacks as they see that we do care about this country.

You see, many soldiers voluntarily go outside the gates of this compound to pass out supplies and visit with these children. Each time, lives are at stake. I say to the Iraqis, you can kill this ole flesh, you can take away this ole body, but you can NOT kidnap or kill the AMERICAN SPIRIT! That is here to stay and will see to it that future generations have equal opportunity for a better quality of life both personally and professionally! The American Spirit will see to it a better Iraq!

The very things you are sending over here are making a direct impact on these children! The mere presence of American soldiers makes these children happy. When we visit, we bring the things that you have sent to them, and they know it. So I will make sure to capture the looks on their faces when we bring them the very things that you have donated.

Operation Anaconda Neighborhood has repaired or opened up over 30 new schools and is also working with hospitals, sewage, and other places to improve our local community.

I have proposed a new idea which is popular back in America. ADOPT A HIGHWAY, cleaning roads is one of the top priorities for local Commanders, and Carson believes that getting out there and cleaning up roads is the best way to show local citizens just how much we do care, and can go a long way in making progress in this country.

So the 29th Signal BN is very active at Camp Anaconda and in the local community and is committed to leaving a permanent footprint in the sand that makes an everlasting impression of not only the American Spirit, but of the Great Northwest!

There is this electrician that I know, he is Iraqi, he does some work for us, he and his family have been through so much abuse and turmoil, and he gave me some flowers the other day and put his hand on his heart and thanked me for caring. Talk about tearing up?? He is a wonderful man and you can see the battle scars on his face, he is so thankful for Americans over here.

Less than 1% of the world will ever have a chance to do what we are doing over here, and I for one am tickled pink to be a part of the solution and not the problem! A Free Iraq and a Democracy for these people are a beautiful thing.

-Tommy Carson

From August 2003 until April of 2004, Scott Travis served in Iraq and for most of this time he worked on engineering projects, mostly rebuilding schools. His brigade, 2nd Brigade, 1st Armored Division worked in the Karadah and Karkh districts of Baghdad. Scott's Task Force used CERP funds.

[Scott Travis]

My task force (1st Battalion, 6th Infantry) commander, LTC Peter Jones, put me in charge of managing all projects for the TF in sector with the assistance of each company FSO. I worked hand-in-hand with an Iraqi Engineer (and soon to be very close friend) named Jassim Latif. He was educated in the UK in the 80s, and had worked for an Iraqi government-engineering firm prior to the war. His expertise and local knowledge of the area and the market place were invaluable. We were basically on our own in the beginning. The task force gave us the task of repairing every school in sector, and so our first task was to find all of the schools with the help of the newly formed Neighborhood Advisory Councils and the company team FSOs, who worked as company Civil Affairs Officers in each company's AO. Jassim and I would look at each school, draw up a tender for bidding by local contractors, and then Jassim would solicit bids from Iraqi businessmen in the area. He was very careful not to use the same contractor twice, and always to leave the bid evaluation process to myself and the Task Force commander for final approval.

As far as the projects are concerned, they've really been very successful. All but 2 out of a total of 56 schools in our sector have been renovated, and only because the NGO who wanted those schools has yet to begin work. All in all, from August to November, our Task Force (1st Battalion, 6th Infantry) spent just over $3 million of Ba'athist and U.S. money repairing and rebuilding the community infrastructure in our sector.

In addition to the primary and secondary schools, we've spent a lot of time improving Baghdad University and Al-Nahrain University (formerly Saddam University), which are co-located on the same campus. We installed 2 internet computer labs (1 for each University), repaired the roofs of 4 Baghdad Univ. Science College buildings (our most expensive single project at $200,000), completely gutted and rebuilt 10 chemistry and geology labs in the Baghdad Univ. Science College, replaced broken glass for 17 buildings of the Baghdad Univ. Science and Engineering Colleges, built a student health clinic at Al-Nahrain Univ., built a new, security-friendly front gate entrance for the Campus, renovated and repaired damage to the Civil Engineering Department at Baghdad Univ., renovated two dormitories and completely replaced the Baghdad Univ. Irrigation system which had been broken and out of use for 15 years.

Other projects we worked on dealt with cleaning up uncollected piles of trash and rubble throughout sector, making minor renovations and repairs at one of our orphanages, and finally clearing dumped trash from an area along the Tigris and fencing it in as a neighborhood park, complete with swings and see-saws. Again, all these projects were contracted out to local Iraqi contractors, many of which were from the neighborhoods that they worked in. The projects were paid for in American cash, and it was an experience holding $150,000 in numbered $100 bills in my hands during one of the paydays.

I've received some donated items since my September e-mail, and I want to thank everyone for sending them. My battalion chaplain is active not only with our soldiers, but also with local Iraqi families. I received some baby cloths, toys, school supplies and blankets, and half of everything I received was given to our chaplain. He distributed the donated things to families in the area of Baghdad called 'Janain'. The rest of the donated items were dropped off at one of our orphanages and at two mosques in our sector by my Engineer Advisor, Jassim.

After leave, I arrived in back in Baghdad just in time for the second round of projects to start up. Some new projects we have coming up will include the renovation of the Iraqi National Theater, more dormitories, the last two schools in sector, a children's hospital, work with two other Universities and the purchase of school supplies for all of our schools. We're also going to repair damage done to neighborhood structures in our sector that were damaged in a New Year's Eve bombing (which caught some media attention). That's definitely enough to keep us busy until we leave here in the spring.

-*Scott Travis*

Engineering (Power)

Years of neglect and no regular maintenance has severely hampered the electrical power generating capability in Iraq.

In the three northern governorates, the United Nations Development Program has rehabilitated the electricity network, which has resulted in power stability for about 2.7 million people. [113]

[Matt Gapinski]

My focus for the past two weeks has been strictly electricity. Ambassador Bremer has promised a total of 4400 Megawatts for all of Iraq by September 30th [2003]. This is a fairly significant increase from the 3200 Megawatts of power that we have been averaging over the summer. Our team is responsible for three local power plants. All are within about an hour drive of here (Camp Babylon). One of the plants (Musayyib) has the second largest capacity in all of Iraq. We have been meeting with the plant managers and their staffs of electrical engineers (two of which were headed by women), mechanical engineers, and operations managers to find out what they need help with to increase the output of their power plants. Until now, we were relying on the Iraqis to handle power generation on their own, but we should have done this awhile ago. Our team of Army reservists consists of a research chemist, an environmental engineer/project manager (yours truly), a structural engineer, a power line foreman, a college student and a grocery clerk. Chock full of electrical and power plant experience! We are augmented by what we call our secret weapon, Jozef. He is a 60-year old Polish, civilian electrical engineer who volunteered to come over here as part of the Polish contingent. He has extensive experience designing large-scale electrical systems in the U.S.

and even lived in Syosset, NY, a few towns from where I grew up. He comes with a Polish/Arabic civilian translator who is now proficient at handling all the weapons that we have.

Anyway, it is extremely irrelevant that our team, except for our secret weapon, has little to no electrical experience. The Iraqis are more than up to the task. The power plant workers are proficient at their trade. The biggest problem they have is a lack of repair parts. In some cases, for a variety of reasons (sanctions, Saddam's neglect, corruption), they have not received any repair parts in over a year. It is truly amazing when you consider the state that the plants are in. Their ingenuity is incredible. Yes, they have big problems with cooling during the summer. In order to increase the amount of cooling that occurs, they have built frames that hold packets of wood fibers. They wet the fibers, in this case with a fire hose, to aid with cooling. Pretty ingenious!

The people at the power plants are more than welcoming. We get lots of Iraqi tea and cold sodas. One plant even served us lunch. [Except for] our 4th of July cookout, it was the best food I've eaten since being here. Fresh baked pita - football-shaped pockets (still warm) stuffed with fresh vegetables (tomatoes, peppers and onions) and kabob (seasoned ground beef). It put our mess hall to shame! We have interesting conversations with the head mechanical guy at one of the plants. Iraq is a gun-oriented society (you think the NRA is bad!) so he was admiring some of our pistols and rifles. The subject came up "why would we want to hurt the Iraqis? We are here to help." He agreed and said that no one in the power plant wants to hurt us. When we asked him about the others who do, he got a little agitated and replied that he didn't know why – that they must be crazy (and uneducated)! We have lots of political discussions with him, although he does have shades of the typical Iraqi who blames everyone but themselves for their problems. Overall, working with the Iraqis at the power plants has been very rewarding. We can directly impact one of Iraq's top problems (which those of you across the Northeast experienced a few weeks ago).

The Poles are in the process of assuming control of our sector as the Marines go home. My unit is staying for now, but we are not sure what our ultimate fate will be. When the Poles see my nametag, they start talking to me in Polish, but my limited vocabulary allows me only to say hello.

There was some initial concern about communication between the Poles and the Iraqis, but one visit to the Ministry of Water Resources in Baghdad proved otherwise. The Polish officer that was with us started talking to the American advisor in Polish (it turns out their mothers were from the same hometown in Poland), then he started talking with a Czech engineer and then with the Iraqi head of the Ministry who went to school in Poland. All the while, another American officer, also of Polish descent, and I sat dumbfounded, not understanding anything that was said!

From what I read on the internet, the media (I am no fan) definitely takes a negative slant. Lots of positive things are happening. Although the Iraqis are worlds apart from us culturally, at the same time they just want to live their lives and take care of their families. I have seen minimal actual war damage. Most of the power plants, water treatment plants and other public facilities have just plain been neglected, especially over the last 12 years. Workers have done the best that they can. If they had complained under Saddam, they would have had their tongues cut out, been tortured, or thrown in jail, etc. Part of the challenge of reconstruction will be overcoming the bureaucracy. Speaking of bureaucracy, there are lots of USACE folks (from all over) in country. The Iraqis are glad that we are here and it will take some time, but things will improve for the better. Freedom is a great thing.

Greetings! I have spent the last 4 weeks in the relative comfort and safety of Kuwait, mostly at Camp Doha. Task Force 4400 was successful (although a little late), surpassing our goal of 4400 Megawatts of electricity on the 5th of October [2003]. Since then, we have been consistently above 4000 megawatts. This was a significant achievement because it represents the restoration of national electricity production to the pre-war level. The associated effort that went into it was tremendous but most likely not reported in any significant fashion by the media. I had the misfortune of being relocated back here just before the deadline while the rest of my team remained (and still remains) in Iraq. Not even afforded the opportunity to say goodbye to the hardworking and dedicated Iraqis, it was a bittersweet departure for me.

I spent the majority of my time at the second largest plant in Iraq. Because we had been able to deliver tangible results (turbine oil, valves, etc.) where all that was previously received was talk, we built a great working relationship with the plant manager, Ismail. During one of our many after working-hours discussions, he confided in me and my sergeant that he was being pressured (again) to take a job in Baghdad, a job he really didn't want. This was not freedom as he understood it. We offered some alternatives (as we understand business negotiations) for him to use to negotiate the delay of his departure from the power station until operations were more stable. In his usual manner, he used our suggestions to arrive at an even better negotiating stance.

Needless to say, he ended up leaving as the plant manager shortly after I left but has been able to fill a different position where he oversees his old plant and several others in the area. So at least the team is still working with him.

One day we got to meet his son, a student at Baghdad University. This was followed by the showing of pictures of our families back home where he made a determined effort to learn everyone's name in my family! He was a very dedicated and smart manager, always prodding us for ideas and information on how we did things back in the U.S.A. At his request, we were able to purchase safety equipment (shoes, coveralls, hardhats, eye and hearing protection, etc.) for the 500+ employees at the plant. He had worked at the plant since it was built (and rebuilt after the first Gulf War) and this was the first time that the workers had been provided any type of safety equipment. A testament to how much he cared about his workers.

One last Ismail story... Whenever Saddam was scheduled to go on TV to make a speech to the Iraqis, the plant manager would be informed that he had to generate a certain amount of electricity or else (literally). This was so that all Iraqis had electricity to watch Saddam on TV. His office has several monitors, ones that measured the output of each of the four units and one that measured the operating frequency (which served as an indicator if a unit was going to shut down). He would tell his secretary to inform him once the speech was over and to close his office door. It was a big no-no to not watch one of Saddam's speeches, but he was so nervous about watching the monitors that he couldn't even look at the TV. Even back then, he knew that it was no way to live.

Although right next door to Iraq, Kuwait is a whole different world. The facilities and accommodations at Doha rival military installations back in the states (with the exception of privacy as we live in an open-bay, barracks-style warehouse). I have been working in the Humanitarian Operations Center in Kuwait City. I am using my connections and experience in Iraq to coordinate resources that the Kuwaiti government, Non-Governmental Organizations and other countries that want to make donations to the Iraqis. Definitely less hazardous duty than in Iraq! So I spend my time e-mailing folks still in Iraq to figure out what public works-type assistance is not being met or funded by the organizations in Iraq and seeing if the Kuwaitis or anyone else can provide it. The Kuwaitis have offered generators and water treatment units, so I find out the technical specifications and limitations and then broadcast them to my contacts in Iraq to determine a match. I get to do it all while wearing civilian clothes, too.

-Matt Gapinski

Engineering (Water)

The pumping equipment in the water distribution system in Iraq is over twenty years old. This neglect has caused a shortage of potable water. Since 2003, many recent improvements have been made. Over ninety percent of the urban population is thought to have access to water, though quantities are not sufficient. Nationwide, sixty percent of the overall population has access to potable water. The goal is to raise this to one hundred percent by the end of 2005. [114]

In addition to upgrading pumping systems, eleven small, new dams have been built and 157 new water wells have been dug. [115]

[Matt Gapinski]

Although we were on heightened alert/security for paramilitary forces, suicide bombers, etc, I found the Iraqis nothing but friendly and happy that we were there. I think after Saddam, anything would be a relief. Everywhere we went, we drew huge crowds (mostly kids). They either tried to sell us cigarettes or Iraqi Dinars (currency with Saddam's picture on it) or asked for water and food. Most of the markets in town were open for business and giving food to one person would create a potential riot without having enough for all since our mission was not to deliver food. Plus their digestive systems, accustomed to their diet, would go into shock from eating our rich food. It was tough not giving the kids anything, but having gone through it before in Honduras, I know it's the best thing for them.

My mission was to assess the water treatment plants in the town. I think I took a class in grad school on water treatment some ten years ago. Anyway, our multi-service team (a Marine, a Seabee, an Air Force Camera crew, an interpreter and I) visited all the treatment plants in and around town. They were all in fairly good repair and treating water using back-up generators since the power was still out. I believe this is a testament to the proud Iraqi people (and precision-guided weapons). Most of the operators came to work without knowing whether they would get paid or not and they only wanted minor assistance in fixing the equipment that was broken.

The Southern portion of Iraq is mostly Shia (Shiite) Muslims, which is the majority of Muslims in Iraq, but they were the minority under Saddam's regime, which was Sunni Muslim. After the Shia uprising in 1991 after the first Gulf War, Saddam pretty much cut all funding to the Southern areas. Everything was pretty dilapidated. Buildings were very rudimentary construction and homes were basic brick construction. Although it was a war zone, it was probably like that long before the U.S. military arrived. All the women wore the abaya, with only a small portion of their face showing, while the men wore either western clothes or traditional dress (for lack of better terms - Arafat headdresses and/or man dress). The kids mostly wore western style clothes.

At night, we stayed at a former Iraqi Army training camp that had essentially no services. We're talking a hole in the ground for the bathroom, no running water, etc. The camp was manned by a Marine Reserve Infantry unit out of New York City (it took about 5 minutes to figure out with the accents!). We did get to sleep inside open buildings (with lots of mosquitoes) on bed frames (without a mattress, it is the same effect as a bed of nails). Throughout our travels, we did not see one picture or statue of Saddam. They were all either torn down or completely blacked out.

At one remote site, the plant operator invited our team into his house for tea with his seven sons. He also had five daughters but they were nowhere to be seen. After begging him off (since we had to visit other sights), we finally relented, figuring the water had to boiled in order to make the tea. We got the royal treatment as they laid out pillows for us even though the room was a 10' x 10' concrete block with a bare cement floor. This was just indicative of the Iraqi people - this guy offering all that he had to us strangers. Probably not how the military's reception is portrayed on the nightly news.

Returning to Camp Commando was like checking in at the Hilton. Attending the Passover Seder/service was surreal - in the dessert with Muslim Iraqi Freedom fighters who had just earned their freedom. Since the Torah/Old Testament is contained within the Koran, the Iraqis were very familiar with the Exodus. In fact, many Hebrew words were very similar to Arabic words, so there was lots of extra discussion.

I heard from some other soldiers that during the daily CENTCOM morning brief on CNN, several still photographs of our visit to one of the treatment plants were shown. I didn't get to see them myself.

-Matt Gapisnki

Engineering (Sewerage)

Another major concern is sewage removal and treatment. Today only eleven percent of Iraq has proper sewerage facilities. The goal is to increase this to thirty percent by 2005. [116]

Already there has been significant progress at the Sharkh Dijlah water treatment plant in Baghdad. The rehabilitated and expanded plant adds 225,000 cubic meters of potable water per day to the supply. This will benefit 640,000 people. [117]

411th Civil Affairs Battalion is working with local contractors to replace the worn-out pipes affecting the sewage removal in Al Thawra, the neighborhood formerly known as Saddam City. The contractor has promised to replace the lines according to American quality standards. [118]

The 358th Civil Affairs Team has completed a project to help the sewage problem in Rumaytha. They installed sewerage pipes, sump pump, pressure line and electrical backup generation system. [119]

The Third Brigade of the 1st Cavalry Regiment has begun a project on July 14, 2004 to build three sewerage pipelines in the Zaphernia neighborhood. Right now, the untreated waste is going directly into the Tigris and Diyala rivers. [120]

The 20th Engineer Battalion has rehabilitated two of fifteen lift stations in a little over two months. These lift stations pump the sewage from the streets and residences of Sadr City. This sewage infrastructure has not been updated in over twenty-five years even as the population has grown from 500,000 to 2.5 million people. The years of neglect have decreased the capacity to thirty percent of what it originally was. This meant that capability was only six percent of what was needed. [121]

Engineering (Telecommunications)

The following summary of the state of telecommunications was submitted by Dan Sudnick who was the Senior Advisor for Communications for the CPA.

[Dan Sudnick]

Shock & Awe

In those fateful nights in March 2003, Coalition military forces had targeted key facilities that were the nerve centers of Saddam's government. Twelve of Baghdad's primary telephone exchanges were reduced to piles of rubble.

From a technological viewpoint, many of the telephone exchanges in retrospect were found to have been equipped with operating museum pieces. Similar conditions existed with the telephone exchanges in Iraq's other major population centers of Mosul and al Basrah.

Before the war, only the elite of Iraq had telephones. Less than 3 of every 100 Iraqis even had access to a telephone. "Pay phones," where they existed, were rotary dial types, and were few and far in-between. Cell phones were non-existent. What the industry labels "data networks" were also non-existent.

No cell phones, no Internet, no ATM machines, no credit card banking networks, no satellite connectivity. Without telecommunications, the simplest of life's daily tasks were made difficult. Communications reverted to shouting at one's intended recipient from across a noisy street.

Internet... Then and Now

Saddam's sons, Uday and Qusay, set up the State Company for Internet Services (SCIS). Its equipment was co-located in the telephone exchanges. The SCIS was for use by an even narrower part of Saddam's elite. The network provided dial-up service only to somewhat less than 4000 customers. Rumor had it that Uday used the Internet primarily for his visiting pornographic web sites.

Immediately after the war, however, Internet cafes began springing up everywhere. With the assistance of the 101st Airborne Division based in Mosul, Coalition forces began delivering "Internet in a Box" kits for use by its troops, for morale, welfare, and recreation. The Internet in a Box provided a satellite earth station (VSAT) dish, a simple Internet router, numerous personal computers for email, and telephones using "Voice-over IP" technology. The 101st also worked side by side with the public telephone engineers and university professors to bring Internet access into the university labs and classrooms.

Budding Iraqi entrepreneurs soon began mimicking the Internet in a Box idea. Now hundreds of Internet cafes have sprung up across Iraq. Much of these same components are replicated in the cafes.

Cell Phones

Also called "mobile phones," these were non-existent. Before the war, the state-run Iraqi Telephone and Posts Company (ITPC) had begun to evaluate mobile equipment, but a perpetual state of paranoia within the Ministry of Information precluded its deployment. After all, Iraq's notorious Information Ministry routinely monitored all telephone traffic. Speakers of forbidden thoughts disappeared in the night, often never to be heard from again.

Upon occupying Baghdad, U.S. forces discovered a large, secret, distribution and cross-connect frame in back of Baghdad's Al Rashid hotel. Its sole purpose was to tap telephone calls. At the hotel itself, U.S. troops also discovered hundreds of boxes of videotapes in the hotel's basement. Since much of the Al Rashid's clientele consisted of foreign guests, all phone calls were recorded.

Putting up cell phones in the country was an imperative. Within weeks, U.S. defense agencies erected a small-scale GSM technology cell phone network. Coverage was extended to "the Green Zone" portion of Baghdad, the airport, and a few other locations in metropolitan area.

For the civil and private users of Iraq, the need to deploy cell phones nationwide becomes a new need. When compared to land line communications, its capital investment costs are minimal.

Iraq's Cell Phone Business Architecture

A highly lucrative business, and with prospects of big profits looming under normal circumstances, building and operating a telephone network in war-savaged Iraq became a race for deployment. The CPA wished to spur the foundation of the nation's emergent information economy yet keep its telecommunications industry from falling into the hands of foreign governments.

CPA divided the country into three sectors along geographic boundaries. Each sector would possess a market of approximately 5 million potential subscribers. This partitioning was to keep prospective investors from placing all of their operating eggs in the lucrative basket of the Baghdad market. In return for accepting a restrained market, each winner would be awarded an exclusive franchise and 2-year operating license within its region.

Infrastructure reuse of common facilities, such as radio towers, would, where possible, be shared. The existing monopoly operator, the Iraqi Telephone and Posts Company (ITPC) would derive incremental revenue from the lease of airspace and for interconnection into its landline network. All operators would concurrently benefit from upgrades in the fiber backbone planned by the CPA and the ITPC through Development Funds for Iraq (DFI) and U.S. supplemental budget funds. Thus, the cell phone operators could focus on building and operating their networks, re-investing their earnings in marketing and customer care, while leaving to the CPA the nationwide engineering and much larger investments required for upgraded fiber optic backbones. The upgraded fiber backbone would carry the "backhaul" traffic for the cell phone operators, that is, the part of their networks that routes calls from one part of the country to another.

Similarly, license fees were kept minimal. The protracted process of a spectrum auction was avoided; the objective was not to raise billions for the Iraqi treasury through cell phone licenses. Rather, incentivize private investors to assume the risk and make the roll-out rapid.

Both Minister Haider and the CPA conducted independent phases of due diligence on the backgrounds of individuals comprising each of the bidding entities. Safeguards were taken to ensure that individuals of the bidding entities did not have ties to the former Baathist party. Financial due diligence on each of the bidders was extensive. In addition, the tender restricted the ownership by a foreign government to a maximum of 10% of the total book value of the bidding consortium.

The Cell Phone Winners

After the source selection process concluded, including its rigorous phases of due diligence, Minister Haider announced the winners on October 7, 2003.

For the northern license, Asia Cell Telecommunications was selected. The Asia Cell consortium was comprised of investors from Watanyia, a Kuwaiti cell phone operator, and a predecessor Kurdish company of the same name, Asia Cell Telecommunications, which had been operating a small [~15,000 subscribers] cell telephone network in Sulaymania before the war under rights granted by the United Nations. The southern license was awarded to a new company by the name of Atheer Telecommunications. Its investors included MTC of Kuwait, which had extended its existing Kuwaiti-based network up the highway into Basrah. Dijla Telecommunication Company (DTC), an Iraqi company, was an equal partner in the consortium.

The central region license, the one which covers Baghdad, was awarded to an Egyptian-based company, Orascom. This company, as were all the winners, was selected by its demonstrated performance in building like-sized cell phone networks in other parts of the world. Orascom elected to name its Iraq-based operations "Iraqna", which in Arabic means, "Our Iraq". Iraqna billboards began sprouting across Baghdad like spring wildflowers.

Iraqna also sponsored the Iraqi soccer team and covered its expenses for international travel, including the 2004 Athens Olympic Games.

Cell Phone Status

As of Summer 2004, the three cell phone operators were deploying new subscriber lines at the combined rate of 15,000 per day. The number of cell phone subscribers now equals the number of landline subscribers (approximately 1.1 Million.) In addition, all three operators had installed private satellite earth stations for the routing of international calls.

The cell phone operators are now selectively upgrading their networks to the GPRS standard. With this "global packet radio standard" capability, users will be able to check e-mail, surf the Internet, and use integrated cell phone appliances such as Blackberry PDAs, camera-equipped cell phones, and the like.

The most revealing part of this story, however, is that all of these accomplishments have been achieved by private industry without a penny of U.S. taxpayers' money! The three cell phone operators, by the end of their 2-year license periods, will have collectively invested over $1 Billion in facilities, equipment, and staff to run their businesses. This accomplishment approaches, if has not indeed set, a world record for cell phone deployment.

Land Line Restoration Status

With a $45 Million emergency appropriation, the CPA began its restoration of the war-damaged land-line telephone exchanges. Led by USAID's prime contractor, Bechtel National Corporation, Baghdad's twelve telephone exchanges were quickly replaced with functionally equivalent "switches on wheels." Modern digital central office exchanges were trucked into Baghdad in self-contained trailers that were then installed on prepared sites adjacent to the destroyed facilities. Crews of Iraqis and expatriates worked side-by-side to splice cables into the new distribution frames and into the switches. By February 2004, Baghdad's switching capability exceeded its prewar levels of 540,000 lines. In addition, the new switches allowed for recognition of new blocks of telephone numbers belonging to the new cell phone carriers and their customers, and to route their traffic to and from existing ITPC landline customers.

Bechtel, and its U.S. supplier, Lucent Technologies, were able to complete the switch restorations for under $40 Million. The remaining $5 Million was applied to upgrading the badly damaged southwestern leg of the figure-8 fiber optic loop with higher-capacity telephony traffic transmission capabilities.

Although acts of sabotage were common in the immediate weeks following hostilities in early 2003, Iraq now, for all practical purposes, has a fully-functioning fiber-optic telephone network. An international satellite gateway was installed in October 2003 that handles over 770 simultaneous telephone calls. Plans are underway to interconnect Iraq's fiber network to undersea cable networks with terminus points in the Red Sea (through Jordan) and in the Persian Gulf (into the Port area of Um Qasr). These interconnections will be realized in 2005.

A Regulator for Telecommunications and Broadcast Media

A legacy of the CPA is its leaving the country and its emergent federal government with the institutions of a modern democratic government. The Administrator insisted that each Iraqi ministry possess an Office of the Inspector General (IG) to help rout out corruption and otherwise provide an internal mechanism for whistleblowers to report fraud, waste and abuse of public funds. Other CPA initiatives included founding a human rights commission, a commission on antiquities, and independent agencies to oversee the regulatory environment of key industries.

The Iraqi Communications and Media Commission (ICMC) was designed at its outset to oversee the telecommunications carriers, and to house Iraq's spectrum management organization. The ICMC will administer the three cell phone operators, the existing land line operator, and two small Kurdish-owned cell phone operators in the Northern provinces. In addition, the ICMC has assumed oversight of all terrestrial radio and TV, and satellite TV, broadcasters. (In the latter category, it is now estimated that over 2/3rds of all Iraqi homes now sprout a satellite dish for viewing satellite TV broadcasts! The commission will additionally oversee the emergent Internet industry.

Posts

At the outset of the occupation, nearly all of Iraq's 230 post offices had been looted. By April 2004, nearly all had been repaired. Supplemental funds and DFI monies used by the Ministry of Communications have gone to upgrading the postal facilities with modern physical automation tools such as bar code scanners and automated letter handling facilities. Iraq now has Zip codes.

A new international package distribution center has opened at Baghdad international airport. Common logistics facilities are shared by the Iraqi Posts along with private logistics operators (including FedEx, UPS and DHL), which have established operations at this facility. Over a million letters and packages pass through the combined facilities daily, with over 500 tons of air package traffic moving daily.

The Iraqi post offices also serve as a minor retail outlet for personal savings. As in Japan and other countries, individual savers keep their pin money safeguarded in postal savings accounts. The Iraqi government expects these savings accounts to contribute to the overall economic development of the country as it goes through its growing phases as an infant democracy.

Observations & Conclusions

Telecommunications will play an important role over the coming years in contributing to the security situation in Iraq. The US Congress provided seed monies in the amount of $90 Million for a "National Emergency Communications Network." The initial phase of this "First Responders" network has seen over 40,000 police and fire radios deployed into Baghdad for its police and emergency workers. Low cost, commercially available radios are being deployed in other cities as well. Subsequent phases of the First Responder Network program will witness the deployment of communications appliances and networks to link most of the agencies under Iraqis Ministries of Interior and Defense, including the New Iraqi Army, the Iraqi Civil Defense Corps, the Border Guards, and numerous other force protection services guards. The First Responder Network will follow industry standards and seek interoperability where practicable with Multinational Coalition Forces communications networks and equipment.

The world community is contributing to the rebuilding and growth of Iraq's telecommunications infrastructure. In addition to equipment from US manufacturers, Lucent, Motorola, and Cisco; top-flight equipment by leading European, Canadian, and Asian manufacturers is contributing to the growth of the information economy of this country of 26 million people, half of whom are under the age of 18.

Lastly, telecommunications will contribute to Iraq's eventual entrance into the global trading community. In a country where over 50% of its population depends on food imports, modern information systems that depend upon modern telecommunications networks, will ease the burden of public agencies responsible for the distribution and delivery of food stuffs. Ubiquitous access to the Internet will enable all individual citizens to witness how others on this planet live and work together. With information derived unfiltered, unedited, and from independent sources, Iraqi citizens will decide how they wish to think and to live. This will help them be free from regimes of fascism and tyranny.

-Dan Sudnick

Economy

Now that the socialist regime of Saddam Hussein is over, entrepreneurs are arriving to rebuild the country, create jobs, and return a profit for investors. Some Iraqis who had fled the country are returning out of love of their homeland and a desire to see it grow again. The U.S. Commerce Department reports that Iraqis living outside of Iraq are investing $5 million per day into ventures in Iraq. Below are more examples of Iraqi Americans going back to revitalize the country.

- James Fadul, and his brother, have invested $100,000 of their own money and have raised $16 million from other Iraqi Americans to buy up formerly state-owned business in Iraq. [123]

- Yasir Shallal, a mechanical engineer in McLean, Virginia, has spent $50,000 to form a company that will sell air conditioning units and construction materials in Iraq. [124]

- Hisham Ashkouri, an architect in Boston, has invested $450,000 of his own money and is raising $115 million to build a hotel and theater complex in Baghdad. [125]

- Subhi Khudairi, Jr., of Houston is restarting his family's paint thinner business in Iraq and has helped open a John Deere dealership in Baghdad. [126]

Besides individuals investing in Iraq many large corporations are making investments, too. Iraq is beginning to open up the economy and encourage large investors.

- The Ministry of Industry and Minerals has 150,000 people working in 239 firms under its control that include clothing, electrical, cotton and tobacco firms and factories. This Ministry is looking for outside investors in profit sharing plans. [127]

- Some Turkish and European companies are investigating the clothing sector. Some U.S. and Ukrainian companies are showing interest in the steel industry. There are some Arabs and Europeans looking into increasing capacity in a phosphate factory near the Syrian border. [128]

- The General Southern Fertilizers Company belonging to the Ministry of Industry has contracted with a Mitso, a Japanese company, for construction of an ammonia factory in the production of chemical fertilizers for agricultural use. The chemical fertilizer industry has been down since the since the beginning of the Iraqi-Iranian war. [129]

- The regional government in Sulaimaniya is actively seeking foreign investors by exempting them from taxes for five years. It is also offering other incentives such as the right to transfer profits outside the region. [130]

- Iraq has just held its first bond auction; selling $100 million dollars of government debt, letting the free market set interest rates. [131]

[Matt Gapinski]

In the end of January, I was able to work with the organizers of the Rebuild Iraq Conference held here in Kuwait City. It was sponsored by a private exhibition company out of Saudi. Fahdi, the organizer, was Lebanese. Over 1400 companies from 48 countries participated. The Humanitarian Operation Center (HOC) ran our own exhibition booth and I moderated a panel session on utilities in Iraq. Lots of companies are interested in doing business in Iraq. There is lots of money to be made there, as they pretty much need everything!

-Matt Gapinski

[Bonnie Carroll]

Saddam kept bananas as a luxury and the general population wasn't allowed to have them. So after the liberation, they were everywhere! A fruit not grown in Iraq, it was also a strong symbol of commerce flowing - green bananas were coming in and on every street corner!

-Bonnie Carroll

[Michael Parkhouse]

My office was located right next to the Strategic Communications Office. One day while attending a briefing in that office, I came across a young man who I found to be very interesting. He had come back to Iraq to help with the rebuilding process. Not only had he had come back to the land of his birth but also his older brother and his father. His father was a prominent business-man. He had a very successful import/export business along with a construction firm. His father came under suspicion after declining offers of member-ship in the Ba'ath Party. Construction projects became impossible to win because of his lack of party credentials. He was forced to find another line of work. He began a wholesale trading company. He traded in milk and other basic commodities. He imported cigarettes. He was known as the cigarette king of Iraq. He made tremendous amounts of money. His business grew by leaps and bounds.

Having an entrepreneurial spirit in Iraq has its disadvantages. The ruling family and its apparatus became very jealous. Regular payments of a "business tax" were needed to insure that your operations were given a restriction-free environment. Restriction-free environment meant that your shipments were not confiscated at the border, the trucks were not hijacked, the warehouses were not burned down, your employees were not harassed and you and your family was not jailed and beaten. Many years of tribute were paid into the extortionist's coffers.

One day a rival trader went to Uday Hussein with a proposal. Uday could take over the business himself and receive a larger portion of the profits and the rival trader would run it for him. Uday Hussein controlled the Press. So a public humiliation campaign began, accusing this man of being an enemy of the state, a supporter for the forces of Zionism, a spy for the Great Satan. Naturally the credit line at the bank dries up, no one will by your product and shipments are quarantined. Your kids lose their friends at school and the neighbors don't come around. The police show up for a friendly chat with all your family and friends. Finally your turn comes and you are guilty until proven innocent.

Several members of his family were jailed and tortured. The torture was so gruesome that even to this day some of these men still deny they were ever in jail. He supports every one of his relatives and friends who suffered for him. He is a good and honorable man. He spent many months in prison and escaped with his life. Many were not so fortunate. He made his way to the United Arab Emirates where his wife and children had fled. Eventually he made his way with his wife and sons to the United States to begin a new life. When the opportunity came to give back he gave the only thing he could give. He gave himself and his sons. He is now currently in Iraq working in the construction business trying to give the land of his birth a new life and a successful future. He is bringing the spirit of hope back to Iraq. He says the flame always burned in his heart to return and to reclaim what was lost. He sees himself as a pioneer in the land, seeking restore the hope he fled with not so many years ago.

-Michael Parkhouse

Government

How do you replace a system where a dictator had complete rule for twenty years with a democracy? People don't even know what a democracy is. Some are expecting to be led like sheep. Some are expecting free handouts. Some are seeing this as an opportunity to violently rise to the top and become a new dictator. Some see this as an opportunity to steal and amass riches. Some want a theocracy and some want a secular government. The challenge is to establish something that works, protects the rights of all and provides rule of law, security and equal opportunity for success.

Using the idea that all government is local, the first step was to start building local councils. From there, city councils and then regional governorates were established. From these leaders, they wrote a new constitution. Once security is ensured, then free nation-wide elections can take place.

Steve Smith relates his experiences in helping establish local councils. John Galt summarizes the new constitution; Zeyad, the anonymous Iraqi dentist, adds his views on elections; and Joaquin Croslin provides an overview to the New Iraqi Army.

[Steve Smith]

I'm an artillery officer assigned to an artillery battery. After the fighting officially ended, I was tasked to create a Civil Military Operations Cell. My tasks were mostly to help create local councils so the people could start to tend to their own needs. Sometimes I had to just follow which way the wind blew.

One day I was out scouting for a usable building to be used for a district council. I was looking through some unfinished building space of a satellite campus of Baghdad University when I came across a family of squatters. The wiring of the building was not up "to code as we know it." Live wires were strung and hung haphazardly. The family was not aware of the danger and had been hanging their clothes on the wires to dry. A small girl, about eight or nine years old, had just recently suffered from electrical burns, when my team and I discovered the family. They were poor and had no transportation to get to a doctor. I was able to get permission for our division's Forward Support Battalion medical team to take care of her. I then worked with the university officials to find a place for the family to live in an unused faculty housing area.

Most of the county's problems were created before the U.S. invasion. Generally people were expecting the U.S. to be able to instantly fix all their problems. People were impatient. One local nineteen-year-old told me that people are like sheep and they were looking for a leader, regardless of how cruel that leader may be.

In my sector was a large power station that produced electricity. It had four large turbines, though before the war only one worked. At one point, Siemans had the contract to get them all running. Then Uday Hussein got involved and hired a Japanese company to take over, though their parts didn't fit. Now work is back in progress to getting all four running with a new contract to Siemans.

The U.S. recognized that centralized planning was not going to be effective in quickly solving many basic needs. Working at a very local level is the best way to solve problems. It is at the local level that the new emerging leaders first take charge. There one particular new leader I was really impressed by. She was a Christian and would not back down when some of the other men refused to talk to her. A large Swiss pharmaceutical company had donated lots of needed medicines. There was no one to distribute, so this woman created a list of all the local hospitals, clinics and doctors offices and she and the brigade surgeon went to every one, distributing the donated meds. She was nominated to be on the city council, and I left before the elections so I don't know the results.

Another woman that impressed me was an engineer at the power station. Her job was to distribute power across the grid. In the old regime, Baghdad always had its power needs met and the outlying areas suffered usually as a form of punishment. This woman was working a plan to share the available electricity so the smaller towns would have power, too. She constantly had to listen to complaints from the Baghdadis about their distribution in power. One day someone just went to her house and killed her.

Eventually district councils were organized and each elected representatives to the city council. The process of building from the grass roots was working, sometimes slower than one would like, nonetheless it's coming together.

-Steve Smith

[John Galt]

Tuesday, March 02, 2004

Your News. Our News.

We have a new constitution over here. Two key facts - it was done and it was unanimous. But the devil is in the details. One key detail was a decision on a single word: "the" or "a." Is Islam "the" basis for law or "a" basis for law? "A" was chosen.

I sat with some senior people in the government, in a social setting, and they made light of the serious issue, saying that the Council recognized that there are so many different interpretations of Islam, that there is no hope of really saying "the" Islam. Sunnis and Shiites separately claim to be "the" Islam. So it was more a matter of practicality for the group. That's one way to approach the issue rather than killing each other.

Monday, March 08, 2004

Constitution

Iraq has a Constitution, unanimously signed. Iraq's Constitution has a Bill of Rights, federal structure and direct elections.

IMHO, Iraq's Constitution will have to be debated, defended and championed as long as people continue to live in the Fertile Crescent. Today's signing is a successful event and the official first day of an ongoing challenge of freedom.

I hope the Iraqis celebrate their accomplishment today. And get back to work building their country and its democracy in spite of inevitable hardships.

Tuesday, March 09, 2004

The Fundamental Principles of the Law include the following:

The system of government in Iraq will be republican, federal, democratic, and pluralistic. Federalism will be based on geography, history, and the separation of powers and not on ethnicity or sect.

The Iraqi Armed Forces will fall under the control of Iraq's civilian political leadership.

Islam will be the official religion of the State and will be considered a source of legislation. The Law will respect the Islamic identity of the majority of the Iraqi people and guarantee the freedom of religious belief and practice. Arabic and Kurdish will be the official languages of Iraq.

The people of Iraq are sovereign and free. All Iraqis are equal in their rights and without regard to gender, nationality, religion, or ethnic origin and they are equal before the law. Those unjustly deprived of their citizenship by previous Iraqi regimes will have the right to reclaim their citizenship. The government will respect the rights of the people.

The Transitional Iraqi Government will contain checks, balances, and the separation of powers. The federal government will have the exclusive right to exercise sovereign power in a number of critical areas, including the management and control of the following national security policy: foreign policy, diplomatic representation, border control, monetary policy, commerce, and natural resources.

The Transitional Executive Authority will consist of the Presidency and the Council of Ministers, including the Prime Minister.

The Presidency Council will consist of the President and two Deputy Presidents, and will be elected by the National Assembly as a group. The Presidency Council will represent the sovereignty of Iraq, may veto laws, and make appointments. All decisions of the Presidency Council will be taken unanimously.

The Presidency Council will nominate the Prime Minister and, on the recommendation of the Prime Minister, will also nominate the Council of Ministers. All ministers will need to be confirmed in a vote of confidence by the National Assembly.

The Prime Minister and the Council of Ministers will oversee the day-to-day management of the government.

The Federal Judicial Authority will be independent. A Federal Supreme Court will be created to hear judicial appeals and to ensure that all laws in Iraq are consistent with the Transitional Administrative Law. It will consist of nine members, who will be appointed by the Presidency Council upon the recommendation of an impartial Higher Juridical Council.

Federalism and local government will ensure a unified Iraq and prevent the concentration of power in the central government that enabled decades of tyranny and oppression. This will encourage the exercise of local authority in which all citizens are able to participate actively in political life.

The Kurdistan Regional Government will be recognized as an official regional government within a unified Iraq, and will continue to exercise many of the functions it currently exercises. Groups of governorates elsewhere in Iraq will be permitted to form regions, and take on additional authorities.

The governorates will have Governors and Governorate Councils, in addition to municipal, local, and city councils as appropriate.

All authorities not reserved to the Federal Government may be exercised as appropriate by the governorates and the Kurdistan Regional Government.

Elections for Governorate Councils throughout Iraq, and also for the Kurdistan National Assembly will be held at the same time as elections for the National Assembly, no later than 31 January 2005.

Iraq's security will be defended by Iraqi Armed Forces, working together with the Coalition. Consistent with Iraq's sovereign status, the Iraqi Armed Forces will play a leading role as a partner in the multinational force helping to bring security to Iraq in the transitional period. The Iraqi Transitional Government will also have the authority to negotiate a security agreement with Coalition forces.

The National Assembly will be responsible for drafting the permanent constitution.

After consulting with the Iraqi people and completing a draft, the proposed constitution will be submitted to the public in a referendum, which will occur no later than 15 October 2005. If the constitution is adopted, elections for a new government under the constitution will be held, and the new government will take office no later than 31 December 2005.

Thursday, March 11, 2004

Iraqi Governing Counfil Adopts Bill of Rights

(From CPA)

Unprecedented document for Iraq and the region:

The Transitional Administrative Law sets out the basic rights of all the people of Iraq. With the adoption of this Law, the Governing Council has taken an historic step forward toward a democratic Iraq.

Individual rights guaranteed in the Transitional Administrative Law:

"All Iraqis are equal in their rights without regard to gender, sect, opinion, belief, nationality, religion, or origin, and they are equal before the law. Discrimination against an Iraqi citizen on the basis of his gender, nationality, religion, or origin is prohibited. Everyone has the right to life, liberty, and the security of his person. No one may be deprived of his life or liberty, except in accordance with legal procedures. All are equal before the courts." (Chap 2, Article 12)

"Public and private freedoms shall be protected." (Chap 2, Article 13)

"The right of free expression shall be protected." (Chap 2, Article 13)

"Each Iraqi has the right to freedom of thought, conscience, and religious belief and practice. Coercion in such matters shall be prohibited." (Chap 2, Article 13)

"Torture in all its forms, physical or mental, shall be prohibited under all circumstances, as shall cruel, inhuman or degrading treatment...." (Chap 2, Article 15)

"Each Iraqi has the right to demonstrate and strike peaceably in accordance with the law." (Chap 2, Article 13)

"The right of free peaceable assembly and the right to join associations freely, as well as the right to form and join unions and political parties freely, in accordance with the law, shall be guaranteed." (Chap 2, Article 13)

"Every Iraqi...has the right to stand for election and cast his ballot secretly in free, open, fair, competitive, and periodic elections. No Iraqi may be discriminated against for purposes of voting in elections on the basis of gender, religion, sect, race, belief, ethnic origin, language, wealth, or literacy." (Chap 2, Article 20)

"Anyone who carries Iraqi nationality shall be deemed an Iraqi citizen. No Iraqi may have his Iraqi citizenship withdrawn or be exiled unless he is a naturalized citizen who, in his application for citizenship, as established in a court of law, made material falsifications on the basis of which citizenship was granted. Each Iraqi shall have the right to carry more than one citizenship. Any Iraqi whose Iraqi citizenship was withdrawn for political, religious, racial, or sectarian reasons has the right to reclaim his Iraqi citizenship." (Chap 2, Article 11)

"The right to a fair, speedy and open trial shall be guaranteed." (Chap 2, Article 15)

"All persons shall be guaranteed the right to a fair and public hearing by an independent and impartial tribunal, regardless of whether the proceeding is civil or criminal...."(Chap 2, Article 15)

"The accused is innocent until proven guilty pursuant to law, and he likewise has the right to engage independent and competent counsel, to remain silent in response to questions addressed to him with no compulsion to testify for any reason, to participate in preparing his defense, and to summon and examine witnesses or to ask the judge to do so. At the time a person is arrested, he must be notified of these rights." (Chap 2, Article 15)

"After being found innocent of a charge, an accused may not be tried once again on the same charge." (Chap 2, Article 15)

"Slavery and the slave trade, forced labor, and involuntary servitude, with or without pay, shall be forbidden." (Chap 2, Article 13)

"The individual has the right to security, education, healthcare and social security." (Chap 2, Article 14)

"Each Iraqi has the right to privacy." (Chap 2, Article 13)

"Police, investigators, or other governmental authorities may not violate the sanctity of private residences, whether these authorities belong to the federal or regional governments, governorates, municipalities, or local administrations, unless a judge or investigating magistrate has issued a search warrant...." (Chap 2, Article 15)

"No one may be unlawfully arrested or detained, and no one may be detained by reason of political or religious beliefs." (Chap 2, Article 15)

"The right to private property shall be protected.... No one shall be deprived of his property except by eminent domain, in circumstances and in the manner set forth in law, and on condition that he is paid just and timely compensation." (Chap 2, Article 16)

"There shall be no taxation or fee except by law." (Chap 2, Article 18)

"This Law is the Supreme Law of the land and shall be binding in all parts of Iraq without exception. No amendment to this Law may be made except by a three-fourths majority of the members of the National Assembly and the unanimous approval of the Presidency Council." (Chap 1, Article 3)

-John Galt

[Zeyad]

Thursday, June 03, 2004

Ghazi Al-Yawar

Sheikh Ghazi Ajeel Al-Yawar was announced yesterday as the first Iraqi President in post Saddam Iraq. I have to say that I have mixed feelings about Yawar. I found it a bit troubling that the head of the state is a tribal figure. Tribalism has been without doubt the most significant problem in Iraq (and the ME) for centuries, one that has been plaguing our urban societies and infecting them with a multitude of social diseases that have proven almost impossible to cure, problems that on the surface may seem to be dissipating from time to time, but which also have a high rate of recurrence. I might be judging the man harshly, since this may not necessarily apply to him personally, and I'm not denying his expertise and western education, however he will always be regarded as a symbol of our largely tribal society (maybe they were just being realistic?). Shortly after he was announced president, I noticed a few sheikhs following him around, wearing the traditional Iraqi tribal dress, which is not a good sign at all.

On the other hand, I perceive that the majority of Iraqis have accepted him as president, even welcomed the decision, of course there will always be naysayers but for the first time in months I feel there is almost a consensus among Iraqis of all backgrounds. Also Yawar is known to have good relations with Kurds, is trusted by the Shia, is respected by other Arab nations, has a clean record, and belongs to a powerful, wealthy, well-known Iraqi family that leads the Shimmar tribal confederation, one of the largest tribes in Iraq, with both Sunni and Shi'ite clans, and spanning several neighbouring countries (such as Syria, Saudi Arabia, and Turkey). That may be a unifying factor and one that Iraqis need badly at this moment of their history. After all, the presidency is almost a symbolic title.

The cabinet is impressive. We now have 5 female ministers, which is an unprecedented step in the region. Just as Iraq was the first Arab country to have a female minister in 1958, it is now also the first Arab country to grant a larger role for women in the government. I expect a much larger percentage of women in the future National Assembly or parliament. The majority of ministers are independent politically, they are mostly technocrats, and come from all Iraqi social, ethnic, religious, and sectarian backgrounds. Many old players are absent such as Chalabi's INC. Also another interesting observation is that four of the ministers are also tribal figures.

So, perhaps I'm a bit optimistic today? Maybe. But Iraqis need to be optimistic at such a critical moment. There is no use in shrugging your shoulders and saying "I don't care..." anymore. You will be left behind along with the dark forces that insist on killing more Iraqis and disrupting the new changes. I'm confident that the Arab world is now watching Iraq with eyes wide open (or wide shut). Some Iraqis are saying the new government will be just a copy of the GC. It depends. Another problem is that I can already feel that the majority of Iraqis are expecting miracles from this new and young government. Unrealistic expectations tend to create endless problems and frustrations. Just like when the GC was formed, or when the Americans first entered Baghdad and people expected that their decades-long problems would be fixed in a week.

I returned to the residence from work yesterday and headed, as usual, to the kitchen, uncovering the various pots and pans before lunch. One of the doctors hollered to me from the living room where they were all fixated on the TV. "Ghazi Ajeel is the new president," one of them announced. "Whyyyyy?" I almost wailed. "Pachachi apologised, said the other GC members didn't want him to be president," the fundie doctor said. Actually I think Pachachi made a small gamble. I believe he is working for the 2005 elections. "So who's the vice president?" I asked them. "Ibrahim Al-Ja'ffari and 'roast'." "What 'roast'?" I asked puzzled. "Oh 'roast', you know like 'roast meat'." "I don't care if he is 'roast' or 'steak', but who is he?" "He's a Kurd, from the Kurdish Democrat Party". It turned out later that his name was Rosh Shawis.

-Zeyad

Joaquin Croslin is a former military officer who accepted a position with a government contractor to teach the New Iraqi Army tactical skills.

[Joaquin Croslin]

In December 2003 I was asked to travel to Iraq to help train the New Iraqi Army (NIA) Officer Corp as a part of a Department of Defense initiative through MPRI*. My purpose was to continue the development of Iraqi junior leaders along with an established cadre who had been on site since the summer. In addition, I was tasked with developing the close quarters battle, leader situational training. It had been several years since I had left the Army so needless to say this was a daunting task.

The make-up of the NIA is volunteers who were recruited from the population with varying skill sets. Leadership roles were filled with former officers and noncommissioned officers from the old Iraqi Army. These brave men all volunteered at great duress to themselves and their families as the threat of violence still lingers from former regime members and newly arriving foreign terrorists from surrounding nations. The backgrounds of the young leaders I interacted with varied between religion and race, as Iraq is a mix of vastly different groups. This accounts for some of the hurdles to rebuilding Iraq. A trait that many of these volunteers did share was hope and determination to see Iraq reemerge as a proud, free nation.

The training we developed and conducted included all of the basic facets of combat leadership. The Iraqis seemed very excited about the program and already we have seen some successes in the field. There have been some setbacks as one should expect when rebuilding an army, but these were not insurmountable. The first fielded battalion saw several desertions and internal turmoil. The causes of this were rectified and to date, the NIA has fielded five more battalions on the road to a large professional force.

The NIA is made up of individuals from varying backgrounds. There are Shia, Sunni, Kurds, and Christians. There still exists some significant animosity between these groups (particularly between Kurds and Arabs). The bitter feelings are very real and troubling at times. During a training exercise one of the Kurd soldiers was having trouble with a task. Loud insults were exchanged between the Jundis (enlisted soldiers), and in seconds an actual fistfight broke out. Some of the soldiers began swinging their unloaded rifles like bats! Another American Cadre member and I jumped into the melee, but before we could get overly involved, an incredible thing happened. One of the Iraqi Lieutenants pushed his way into the bellicose mob and issued the following declaration (in Arabic): "Enough! There is no Arab, no Kurd, only Iraqi! The world is watching to see if we fail! Such struggles between us is failure! We must work together or Iraq will fail! We are the Army, we must set the example!" This young leader is not alone in these sentiments, I believe a free Iraq will thrive.

The NIA will continue to develop as a part of Iraq's reconstruction. As a nation we can feel proud in knowing that we are doing the right thing. This road will have many challenges but the sacrifice will benefit our safety and stability.

"Greater love has no man more than this that a man lay down his life for his friends." John 15:13

* MPRI (Military Professional Resources Inc.) is a Defense contractor with the mission of training and developing professional Armies.

-Joaquin Croslin

Chapter Nine
The Homecoming

This summer, I was listening to an old Infantry colonel. He was nearing the end of a thirty-year career. After thirty years of using his booming voice so his soldiers could hear no matter the circumstances, his voice is now no more than a coarse whisper. When he speaks, you listen, because he's been there. In the military, thirty years is a long time. He speaks fondly of that time when the exercise is over. Field Training Exercises are exhausting and the soldiers are spent. Still he says, "This is what I love about the Army. To stand next to a big fire in the dead of winter, late in the night, with a sky so big that all stars in the heavens are right there you can almost reach up a grab a few. To stand there with a canteen cup full of bad coffee and listen to the men tell their tales. They are young and full of vigor. They are still coming off a long adrenaline rush, with recent memories dominating their thoughts. They are full of 'Did you see me when?...' 'We smoke those guys' 'It was so...' There is something about just being a soldier at there on those starry nights. We count our blessings. The exercise is over and we'll be going home soon. "

Eventually the time arrives when it's time to go home. For some it is a singular event, for others it is as a member of a group. The presence still stays, the flag still stays until the work is completed. Those who do come home enjoy the homecoming. For many the time away has been up to a year or more. For most people it has been a constant work schedule. There is no real home at the end of each day. One is always there. Just the need for a rest in a safe, secure environment is needed to relieve the constant stress.

Most left loved ones. For many, those can be young spouses and small children. Twelve months out of the life of a three-year-old is an eternity for that child. Things happen than can never be re-lived. Holidays, birthdays, anniversaries, first day of school, a home run, a lost tooth, and many nights of bed-time stories will be missed. There will be an eagerness to re-unite.

Chris Gehler always fancied himself a tough guy. He had jumped into a combat zone in Panama with the 82nd Airborne Division in 1989. He deployed for Desert Shield and fought again in combat in Desert Storm. Somehow, though, coming home back to Fort Bragg, North Carolina was different this time. "The whole time in Iraq I felt like a father to my men. I was constantly worried. We had round-the-clock missions; there was always someone out there in the sky supporting an attack. One crew would come in and we'd turn the birds around with a new crew. For the first 23 days of the conflict, I never took even a cold bucket shower. I felt I just didn't have the time. I was only there four or five months. When we came home it was something else. The whole battalion came in together on one flight into Pope Air Force Base. We assembled on the Green Ramp and marched proudly into the 'chute hanger. There all the families were assembled. We had to wait and listen to some general give a speech that was much too long. Then finally, we were released and I got to hug my wife. It was very emotional. I didn't want to let go. My three kids, Madison (8), Max (5) and Zoe (3), were all wrapping their arms around my legs. Never had it felt so good to come home."

Chris's attack helicopter battalion came back without a single casualty. A month later they were back in Iraq. They were lucky their first time. Not every unit is as fortunate. Sometimes someone will come home sooner than expected.

Mrs. Birgit Smith, wife of Sergeant First Class Paul Smith was not expecting her husband to come home just yet. She has not been the only spouse to have a knock at the door by the unknown men in uniform. This is the news no one wants to ever hear. It is the possibility for all who have family.

Sergeant First Class Paul Smith, a platoon sergeant in an engineering company, was completely dedicated to his men. One day in the battle for control of the airport, he took the initiative and put his life on the line. His actions stopped a counterattack by the enemy and defended the sector of the task force, when he took charge of the .50 cal machine gun on top of an exposed M113. He fired accurate, sustained rounds at the enemy while being shot back at by a larger force. [132]

Military units have an ancient tradition of standing out in formation and taking roll. A unit may line up three times a day as the chain-of-command announces the status. The squad leader, standing at the end of the line of his squad, will salute and report, "All present." After hearing the reports from all the squad leaders, the platoon sergeant will about face and in turn report his platoon status to the first sergeant. If someone is not in formation, then he can be accounted for by being on duty for someone else or he is not present. If a soldier has died in combat, there is no status. He is not present; he is not absent. There is no one to speak for him. The squad leader and platoon sergeant remain silent as the first sergeant calls for the missing soldier.

Each time the name is called there is an eerie silence that becomes very tense as all wait, standing at attention, for a response that will never come. After three calls, a twenty-one-gun salute is rendered and taps is played.

[Gordon Cimoli]

9 December 2003

THE JOURNEY HOME

Over the past few days I have felt very excited and anxious every time I heard the roar of a landing or taking off jet. I keep thinking that I will be on one of those one day soon. I have spent the past 3 days cleaning up my area and packing my bags for the trip home. It looks like I will be able to catch a C-17 direct from here to Germany tonight.

I spent the day saying goodbye to everyone and preparing for the realism of going home! I can't really believe it.

At 6pm, Phil drove me to the passenger terminal. I went inside the tent and found that they would announce the number of seats for tonight's flight at 6:45. I waited around (and Phil waited with me too) and discovered that there were many people waiting for the flight. At 6:45, the sergeant in charge said that there were five seats available. He then prioritized people in order of Emergency Leave, Temporary Duty (TDY) then regular leave. Since I am going to an official school and had TDY orders I was able to get on the flight. Of course, the orders were bootlegged but it is true that I am going on TDY so I didn't take anything from anyone. There were 5 seats and 8 people. I was one of the 5. After the sergeant took our names, he sent us into the passenger terminal building where Phil and I sat and waited. At 9pm, Phil and I said our goodbyes and he headed back for an internet period where he would send a message to Sam and Stefanie that I was on my way.

The plane landed at 9:45pm and after unloading and refueling, we were allowed to board the plane. The inside of the plane was filled with Humvees and trailers that were securely chained to the floor. There were only 5 seats available. We were given a passenger briefing and then sat down and waited for the plane to taxi. My seat was on the outer wall of the aircraft and I was sitting between a Humvee and its trailer. Somewhere around midnight, the C-17 began to taxi.

Once at altitude, I got out of my seat and lay on the cold floor. I covered up in an Air Force blanket, my poncho liner and Gortex parka but was still cold against the floor of the C-17. Midway through the flight, I woke up to go to the bathroom. While up, the crew chief asked me if I wanted to go up and look at the cockpit. I did. I walked up there and looked around. We were over Romania, and there were only a few towns that were visible from 36,000 feet. It was dark but not pitch black. I returned to the cold floor to finish the flight.

At 2:45am, we landed in Rein Main airport. This was the same place that my family entered Germany in 2002. As I got off the plane and into the freezing weather, it seemed like everything was just the same as when I left it. As I moved into buildings and around the area, I felt as though I had never left and almost as if I were waking up from a 10-month dream of sorts.

I called Stefanie from inside the terminal to tell her I was home. She was sleeping but was happy to hear I made it. I hung up and called my mom. She was not totally hysterical but she was very pleased that I was home. Hearing the tone of her voice almost brought me to tears but I choked them back as to not make her cry or become any more emotional than she already was. It was nice to talk to her.

At 5:25am, a person from Battalion arrived to drive me back to Giebelstadt. I was wide awake as we sped along the autobahn for Giebelstadt. I was certainly getting excited to be done with this long journey.

We arrived on post at 7am, which gave me enough time to fill out some paperwork before Stefanie arrived. At 7:35, I heard the outer door to Battalion close and through the glass of a picture frame I could see her reflection. I peeked out the door and ran down the hall and picked Stefanie up with a great big hug and kiss. She looked, felt and smelled great.

The kids were at a friend's house and we enjoyed the day being alone. At 6PM, Stef went to pick them up. While she was gone, I hid inside of a large box wrapped with Christmas paper. Stef told the kids that she had been shopping all day so when she came home she told them to open the box. She said go and the kids tore in. Meanwhile, I was hidden in the box and when I felt them hit the paper I burst out of the box! All three of them were shocked (not scared) or stunned and looked at me for a second before realizing it was Daddy! They all jumped on me and gave me hugs and kisses like there was no tomorrow.

-*Gordon Cimoli*

Captain Mike Jason is the scribe for his West Point class, the Class of 1995. He wrote this for the Assembly magazine and shares it in this book.

[Mike Jason]

Classmates, it has been a tough few months for our nation, our Army, and our class. Almost two weeks to the one-year anniversary of Jimmy Adamouski's crash, we are brought together by the death of Hans Kurth. Many of us gathered from all over the globe, from as far away as Germany, Italy, and even Iraq, to Columbus, WI, for his funeral.

We met at the viewing where a large collection of photos retold the proud and noble story of a nearly perfect life. In a side room, classmates signed the "Duty, Honor, Country" print our class would present to Hans' parents. In it, GEN MacArthur warns that the Long Grey Line has never failed us. Were it to do so, a million ghosts in khaki and olive drab would rise from their white crosses thundering those three words, Duty, Honor, Country. We have no doubts that were we to fail, Hans would be standing over us, reminding us to stay the course. Greg also had KIA bracelets especially prepared and handed those out to the Kurth family and our classmates. Once of the saddest honors was in helping five-year-old John Alexander Kurth put on his.

The following morning, we gathered at Columbus High School, a mix of OD Green and dark business suits, but anyone could tell we were together. We gathered in a small room off the gym and were amazed at all the friendly faces. Nearly fifty classmates and spouses made the journey.

At the last hymn, we slowly and silently egressed out of the gym and the school. Outside we formed a cordon, two lines of classmates from the door to the hearse. As the flag-draped hero came out, those closest began the slow salute that would ripple to the last of us by the hearse. We held our salute to our fallen warrior until the door was shut. The convoy to Hillside Cemetery must have been miles long. The entire town of Columbus turned out. The streets were blocked along the route with a policeman, state trooper or fireman standing at attention at every corner. There were children holding flags, veterans saluting, and citizens watching all the way through town. In the center of town, a ladder truck held one of the largest U.S. flags I have ever seen. It rippled gloriously across the street, like a triumphant arch.

At the cemetery, there was a quiet stillness. The casualty assistance officer tried desperately to get a fly over, but no units were available. Then we looked up, and there was a flight of geese in a missing-man formation! If you missed it the first time, they squawked and came back a second time! Anyone who remembered Hans' love of the hunt knew this was no coincidence and let out a small smile. Across the sea of classmates and friends, I could see many looking up and smiling. The 21 shots rippled the quiet day and the bugle brought back the reality of such a momentous loss. As tears were unashamedly shed, Jeff Spear led us off in the "Alma Mater," surely Hans' favorite tune. Immediately, nearly 100 voices choked through the worst, yet most heartfelt, rendition of this cherished song.

Like most, I was unable to mouth the final verse. [133]

-Mike Jason

SSG Michael Hanes, United States Marine Corp, flew back with his Force Recon platoon soon after the hostilities officially ended. They flew a commercial flight from Kuwait to southern California with a re-fueling stop in Germany. Mike was impressed with the flight crew, which went out of their way to say how much they appreciated the efforts in Iraq. This gave the long ordeal meaning and put perspective on all they endured.

Landing in Germany, the mood changed as no one was allowed off the plane to stretch and walk around due to the protestors at the gate. Mike had heard the stories of the returning Vietnam veterans and was apprehensive of his arrival back in California. At least they would arrive around three or four in the morning so maybe the protestors would not choose to single out his returning flight.

As the plane taxied in the dark, the Marines climbed down the steps across the tarmac. There along the fence and at the gate was a crowd of people waving flags and holding banners with "Welcome Home" and We Love You." Back home at last – what a feeling!

On the flight back the Marines kept talking about the first thing they'd do once back home. One said all he wanted was an Egg McMuffin. MRE's for weeks on end can make one salivate about food memories. Michael, who averaged two canteen showers a month, had a different plan.

Michael stopped off at the BX and bought a green bottle of Sesame Street bubble bath. The picture of Oscar the Grouch in his trashcan reflected Michael's feelings of not ever feeling truly clean. Michael checked into a nice hotel and spent his first two hours back home in America in a hot bubble bath. Not quite the image of the tough Force Recon Marine, but Michael didn't care; he was safe and home. [134]

Geoff Burgess served in the 3rd ACR during Operation Iraqi Freedom 1. He and his unit were on the Syrian Border. Geoff served as a Headquarters Troop XO and the S4 for 1st Squadron, 3rd ACR, so his focus was logistics for a combat unit, contracts with local Iraqis. Geoff is single and arrived back in the United States with no one to welcome him.

[Geoff Burgess]

The feeling of landing on American soil was exhilarating, even though we were all tired from the extremely long flight. We landed in Colorado Springs at 1:30am or so on April 1st, and there were fellow soldiers there to meet us, despite the time, who had been sent home earlier for various reasons. We loaded busses and chatted about what we would do when we got home. A few of the guys who met us had brought cell phones, and they were being passed around the bus, the first time in a year that we could talk to a loved one without annoying static or a 2-3 second delay because of the satellite connection.

We drove the short few miles to Fort Carson, and I was struck by so many things at once. Our bus was clean and devoid of the sand that is everywhere in Iraq and Kuwait; the streets had streetlights shining brightly, something that was rare in our area of operations; there was grass everywhere!; and none of us had to worry about a roadside bomb going off, or having our weapons pointed out the window, or having to place scrap metal or additional body armor on our doors to hopefully limit the shrapnel from an RPG or bomb. As we drove onto post, we saw that there were Military Police on each corner to stop any traffic. I thought that was a little excessive given the hour, but I then saw that each of them were saluting us as we drove by. A subtle touch, very classy, and did not go unnoticed.

We arrived at a motor pool, completely devoid of our equipment (still in transit from Kuwait) and several soldiers remarked how naked the area looked without the congestion of the hundreds of vehicles usually parked there. We turned in our personal weapons, and what a glorious feeling; your weapon was at your side everyone you went, at all times, mine for 357 days, and now, finally, I could hand it to someone else. Next we were subjected to some mandatory briefings which most of us had heard before: life may have changed since we were gone so adjust slowly; where to meet the shuttle for those of us that had our cars in long term storage in Pueblo; for single soldiers, when and where to sign for their new barracks room; when to report back to work to begin the week-long redeployment processing. I recall hearing some soldiers complaining about their new roommate, obviously getting the word from someone in the know. I laughed to myself; here we were, home after a year in Iraq, having lived in 120 degree heat, sandstorms, and virtually no privacy, and these guys were unhappy about their one roommate in their clean, furnished, complete-with-shower-and-hot-water barracks room!! Some things will never change.

After everyone was complete with the briefings and some quick paperwork issues, we waited until the designated hour and drove to the Special Events Center, where friends and family were waiting. I think it was 5am, but we were wired. We lined up in formation, the doors were thrown open, country music blasted from the PA system, and we marched inside to thunderous cheering. Families were waving signs, mothers were holding children, some of which had been born during our tour, and everyone was smiling or cheering or crying. We faced the crowd, and though we were in formation, we all searched with our eyes for familiar faces. My Mom was flying in the next day, so I didn't have anyone there at that hour, but it sure felt like I did. A General spoke briefly, and we were released. My three closest friends and I shared a quick group hug (three guys who I was not friends with prior to the deployment, but with whom I formed a life-long bond while overseas), and everyone went about to find their loved ones. The last step before heading for home was finding our gear, which had been unloaded in the parking lot, and finding a ride home! I was handed a beer, and thought that it was funny that I was drinking beer at 5:30am. I had asked my roommate for a local Colorado beer, and I truly savored the taste. I went to a friend's house on post for breakfast, and then headed home.

My house had never looked better, and once again I was struck by how clean everything was. I ripped off my boots and walked around barefoot (something you just really didn't do over there), and remembered how nice carpeted floors were. Not wanting to fall asleep in order to beat the jetlag, I wandered around my house for a while, looking in drawers, looking at photos, drank water from the tap (with ice, quite a phenomena!). I went out to my car and tried to start it, nearly putting my feet through the floorboards, clutch, brake, and all (my Humvee, which I drove frequently, had pretty stiff pedals, and my Honda sure felt different). It took forever to start the car, and I realized that my battery was probably dead. So I took off in my car, able to drive by myself for the first time since the previous April, and also without three other vehicles and a minimum of two automatic weapons for security reasons. I changed the oil in the car and the battery, and then went to the mall to get a cell phone.

At the mall, I wandered again, and just looked at all of the things you could buy, something I really hardly ever did before. We had so few choices for anything overseas, and here, we just took it all for granted. I found it interesting to see American kids - the only kids I had seen for a year were Iraqi. Also, seeing women was new - we had some women that worked with us, but as I was in a combat unit, we did not have many. Also, when out on patrols, the Iraqis tended to hide their of-age women, fearing that we would see them and they would be disgraced, or that we would try to steal them away. The women we did see on the streets were clad in their traditional head-to-toe garb, so you really didn't see them. I wondered if I would know how to carry on a conversation with a female...after being around so many men for so long, your language becomes quite colorful. Limiting vulgarity would become a focus of mine for the first few weeks.

I bought my phone, a nice one since I had quite a bit of money saved up from the deployment, and got a new phone number (not realizing that a law had been passed allowing you to keep your old phone number from your previous wireless service, but I was able to get my old number back about a week later). I drove back home and started calling everyone I knew. I remember that first cell phone bill was over a hundred dollars. I must have talked for hours. It was a great day.

-Geoff Burgess

"In his youth and strength, his love and loyalty he gave – all that mortality can give. He needs no eulogy from me or any other man. He has written his own history and written it in red on his enemy's breast. But when I think of his patience under adversity, of his courage under fire, and his modesty in victory, I am filled with an emotion of admiration I cannot put into words. He belongs to history as furnishing one of the greatest examples of successful patriotism, he belongs to posterity as the instructor of future generations in the principles of liberty and freedom; he belongs to the present, to us, by his virtues and by his achievements." [135]

-General Douglas MacArthur

END NOTES

1. Captain Sean P. Kirley, "Heroes Stand out in Baghdad," (2nd Armored Cavalry Regiment, Public Affairs Office, October 3, 2003)

2. ibid

3. ibid

4. ibid

5. "Don't Let Them Pull the UN Out," *Army Reserve* magazine (Volume 49, number 3), page 36.

6. Lance Corporal Samuel Bard Valliere, "Insurgent Ambush Stage for Valiant Displays in Iraq" (United States Marine Corp, Camp Taqaddum, Iraq, June 10, 2004)

7. Greg Fontenot, David Tohn, and E. J. Degan, *On Point*, (Fort Leavenworth, Kansas: Combat Studies Institute Press, 2004)

8. Hertz, J. H. ed., *The Pentateuch and Haftorahs*, 2nd Edition, Soncino Press, London, 1981, 735-736.

9. Matthew 5:1

10. For a copy of his last sermon see http://www.ancient-history.nl/Islam/Prophet%20Mohammeds%20Last%20Sermon.htm

11. Isaiah 58:5-7.

12. Dennis Steele, "It Takes a Little Chutspah," *Army Magazine* 53, no. 11 (November 2003) 18.

13. The *Meaning of the Holy Qur'an*, 10th Edition, Surat Ma'un, Amana Publications, Beltsville, Maryland, 1999, 1704.

14. Ignaz Goldhizer, *Introduction to Islamic Theology and Law*, Princeton University Press, Princeton, New Jersey, 1981, 152.

15. Chaplain (Major) Carlos C. Huerta, "Duty-Honor-Country in Service to G-d," (United States Military Academy, West Point, NY, August 2004)

16. Kamran Gardi, (Interview with Gordon Cimoli, September 2004)

17. Anonymous 3, (Interview with author, July 2001)

18. William Bennett, *The Death of Outrage*, (The Fress Press: New York, 1998), 150.

19. Rick Atkinson. *In the Company of Soldiers*, (Henry Holt and Company: New York, 2003), 128-30.

20. Greg Fontenot, David Tohn, and E. J. Degan, *On Point*, (Combat Studies Institute Press, Fort Leavenworth, Kansas, 2004)

21. Jim Lacey, "Observations of an embedded correspondent" (*Times Magazine*, correspondent, 16 May 2003)

22. Atkinson, *In the Company of Soldiers*, 132.

23. Lacey, "Observations of an embedded correspondent,"

24. Fontenot

25. Fontenot

26. Todd S. Purdum, *A Time of Our Choosing*, (New York: Henry Holt and Company, 2003), 171.

27. Purdum, 219.

28. Fontenot

29. Human Rights Watch, "Institutions of Repression," *The Saddam Hussein Reader*, ed. Turi Munthe (New York: Thunder Mouth Press), 179.

30. Kenneth M. Pollack, *The Threatening Storm*, (New York: Random House, 2002), 10.

31. "Iraq's Mass Graves," (Department of State, Bureau of Democracy, Human Rights, and Labor, January 21, 2004) Press release.

32. Richard Engel, *A Fist in the Hornet's Nest*, (New York: Hyperion Books, 2004), p.194.

33. Engel, *A Fist in the Hornet's Nest*, p.195.

34. Jean Sasson, *Mayada: Daughter of Iraq*, (New York: Penguin Group, 2003), p.79.

35. Todd S. Purdom, *A Time of Our Choosing: America's War in Iraq*, (New York: Henry Holt and Company, 2003), p.78.

36. "The Iraq Marshlands Restoration," (United States Agency for International Development, April 2004) Special Feature

37. Kenneth Pollack, *Threatening Storm*, (New York: Random House, 2002), p.7.

38. Major Aberle, "Capture of Saddam Hussein," (4th ID, PAO, December 14, 2003)

39. Anonymous 2 (Interview with author, August 2004)

40. Vince Bzdek, "For Seven Iraqis, A Vital Part of Life is Restored" (Houston: *Washington Post*, May 24, 2004),page A1

41. Eric Berger, "7 Iraqis receive prosthetic hands," (*Houston Chronicle*, May 18, 2004)

42. ibid

43. ibid

44. ibid

45. Purdum, *A Time of Our Choosing*, 23.

46. Johanna McGeary "Inside Saddam's World," *The Saddam Hussein Reader*, ed. Turi Munthe (New York: Thunder Mouth Press), p.482.

47. Caroline Hawley, *New Hope for Mutilated Iraqis*, (BBC, June 10, 2004) http://newsvote. bbc.co.uk

48. Jean Sasson, *Mayada: Daughter of Iraq* (New York: Penguin Group, 2003), p.71.

49. ibid, p.159.

50. ibid, p.128.

51. ibid, p.108.

52. Engel, *A Fist in the Hornet's Nest*, p.197.

53. ibid, p.197.

54. Raed Ahmed, "The Public Cannot Imagine How Brutal These Guys Are," (Special to ESPN.com, December 27, 2002)

55. Sharar Haydar, "What Did We Do Wrong? Nobody Knows But Uday," as told to Tom Farrey (Special to ESPN.com, December 27, 2002)

56. David Rose, "Inside Saddam Hussein's Terror Regime," *The Saddam Hussein Reader*, ed. Turi Munthe (New York: Thunder Mouth Press, 2002), p. 474.

57. ibid, p.464.

58. David Weston, (Interview with author, September 7, 2004)

59. Zeyad, "Healing Iraq" (Blog, September 1, 2004), http://HealingIraq.blogspot.com

60. Joel Hagy, (Interview with author, September 5, 2004)

61. http://www.FallenPatriot.org

62. http://www.Fisherhouse.org

63. http://www.FreedomAlliance.org

64. http://www.OperationIraqiChildren.org

65. http://www.SpiritofAmerica.net

66. http://www.TAPS.org

67. http://www.WoundedWarriorProject.org , Wounded Warrior Project web site

68. Scott Farwell, "Working for youth, Scouts' honor," (*Dallas Morning News*, June 14, 2004)

69. http://www.thanksamillion.org

70. David Gifford (Interview with author, September 5, 2004)

71. http://www.FernHolland.com

72. Barbara Ivey, (Interview with author, July 2004)

73. Rush Limbaugh, "Frankie Mayo: Making America Work," (Transcript, web site, August 25, 2003)

74. Kendra Helmer, "Stripes Spotlight: Army reservist does it for the children," (Sinjar, Iraq, Stars and Stripes, March 1, 2004)

75. Donna Miles, "27 Years After Retirement, Doctor to Serve in Iraq," (Washington: American Forces Press Service, April 29,2004)

76. Fred Wellman, (Interview with author, July 27, 2004)

77. http://ChiefWiggles.blogspot.com, Chief Wiggles' blog

78. Captain Jason Tolbert, "Al Razi School," (2nd ACR PAO, October 2003)

79. "Iraq's Health Care System," (Coalition Provisional Authority, Baghdad, February 23, 2004) Press Release

80. Jean Sasson, *Mayada Daughter of Iraq*, (New York: Penguin Group, 2003), Appendix.

81. "Restoring Health Care," (U. S. Agency for International Development, November 2003) Sector Snapshot.

82. "Iraqi Girl in U.S. for Burn Treatment,s" (Samaritan's Purse, Galveston, Texas, June 24, 2004). Press Release.

83. "RSS Surgeons Help Iraqi Boy," (2nd ACR Public Affairs Office)

84. Sergeant Matt Epright, "1st FSSG Surgical Company Loses Its Heart to Iraqi Girl," June 13, 2004.

85. Specialist Andy Miller, "Lancer Delivers Gear to Save Babies," 122nd Mobile Public Affairs Detachment, July 15, 2004.

86. "Blind Iraqi Boy to be Treated in Japan," (Associated Press, Tokyo, June 3, 2004)

87. Private First Class Chris Jones, "US helps build Iraq Clinic," Army News Service October 24, 2003.

88. Specialist Andy Miller, "Iron Horse Brigade Aids Iraqi Boy's Recovery," (122nd Mobile Public Affairs Detachment)

89. Specialist Marie Whitney, "4-5 ADA Brings Medical care to Radwaniya," (122nd Mobile Public Affairs Detachment)

90. Caroline Hawley, "New Hope for Mutilated Iraqis," (BBC, June 10, 2004) http://news-vote.bbc.co.uk

91. "Introducing Health Care Management to the New Iraq," Army Reserve 49, no. 4, 23.

92. "2nd ACR Provides Medical Expertise to Iraqis," (2nd ACR Public Affairs Office, January 20, 2004)

93. "Rebuilding Iraq" (*Army Reserve* Magazine, volume 29, number 3), page 25.

94. Specialist Jan Critchfield, "1st Cavalry trains Iraqi doctors to save babies," (Army News Service, July 29, 2004)

95. "Elwiyah Maternity Teaching Hospital Receives Ultrasound Equipment," (First Cavalry Division, Public Affairs Office, July 2004)

96. "Health Care for Iraq's Children," (U.S. Agency for International Development, March 16, 2004) Press Release.

97. "Restoring Health Care," (U.S. Agency for International Development, November 2003) Sector Snapshot.

98. "Medicines for the Iraqi People," (Coalition Provisional Authority, Baghdad, March 29, 2004) Press Release.

99. "Polish and Phillipine Militaries Work with Iraqis to Distribute Medicine," (Coalition Provisional Authority, Baghdad, May 27, 2004) Press Release.

100. "Health Care Improvements Slated for Iraqis." (Coalition Provisional Authority, Baghdad, May 31, 2004) Press Release.

101. Fred Wellman, (Interview with author, July 27, 2004)

102. Robert S. Adams, MD, (Email to author, August 23, 2004)

103. Jean Sasson, *Mayada Daughter of Iraq* (New York: Penguin Group, 2003), Appendix.

104. "33,000 Iraqi Teachers Trained," (Coalition Provisional Authority, Baghdad, Iraq, February 17, 2004) Press release.

105. ibid

106. ibid

107. "Educational Reform in Iraq," (Coalition Provisional Authority, Baghdad, Iraq, April 3, 2004) Press release.

108. The U.S. Agency for International Development (April, 2004) Press release.

109. "World Bank Issues $40 Million Grant to Support Education in Iraq" (Coalition Provisional Authority, Baghdad, Iraq, May 24, 2004) Press release.

110. Fred Wellman, (Interview with author, July 27, 2004)

111. Ben Wallen, (Interview with author, September 7, 2004)

112. Rick Hinshaw, (Interview with author, Apr. 23 2004)

113. "Accomplishments: Electricity," (U.S. Agency for International Development) http://www.usaid.gov/iraq/accomplishments/electricity.html

114. "Accomplishments: Water and Sanitation," (U.S. Agency for International Development) http://www.usaid.gov/iraq/accomplishments/watsan.html

115. "The establishment of 5 dams in Al-Sulaymaniyah governorate and digging 157 wells for agricultural purposes,"(Iraq Directory), http://www.iraqdirectory.com/files/articles/article066.htm

116. "Accomplishments: Water and Sanitation," (U.S. Agency for International Development) http://www.usaid.gov/iraq/accomplishments/watsan.html

117. ibid

118. "Rebuilding Iraq," *Army Reserve* magazine, vol. 49, no. 3, p.13.

119. "Update on Operation Iraqi Freedom," *Army Reserve* magazine, vol. 49, no. 4, p.25.

120. Specialist Jan Critchfield, "3rd Brigade Funds Sewer Project," (122nd Mobile Public Affairs Detachment, Baghdad)

121. Captain Zachary Miller, "Helping Sadr City," (20th Engineer Battalion, Baghdad)

122. Ellen McCarthy, "Iraqis try to build nation and fortune," TODAY, *The Washington Post* (July 8, 2004)

123. ibid

124. ibid

125. ibid

126. ibid

127. Edmund Blair, "Iraq to Lease State Plants to Foreigners," *Reuters Interview* (July 12, 2004)

128. Blair, "Iraq to Lease"

129. "Japanese Company Established a Big Ammonia Factory," (Iraq Directory), www.iraq-directory.com/files/articles/article062.htm

130. "Kurdish bid to lure foreign investors," (Iraq Press, Sulaimaniya, July 9,2004)

131. Paul Wiseman, "Iraq to get new start with bond market," USA TODAY (July 8, 2004) MENAFN.com

132. Greg Fontenot, David Tohn, and E. J. Degan, *On Point*, (Combat Studies Istitute Press, Fort Leavenworth, Kansas, 2004)

133. Mike Jason, "Class Notes: 1995," *Assembly* magazine (Association of Graduates, West Point, New York, Volume LXII, number 6), 134-135. (With permission from author)

134. Michael Hanes (interview with author, August 12, 2004)

135. Jim Shufelt, editor, 72nd Volume of *Bugle Notes,* (unpublished, West Point, New York, 1980), 49-50.